# A Vision and Roadmap for
# EDUCATION STATISTICS

Larry Hedges, Melissa Chiu, Celeste Stone, Bradford Chaney, and Nancy Kirkendall, *Editors*

Panel on A Vision and Roadmap for Education Statistics

Committee on National Statistics

Division of Behavioral and Social Sciences and Education

A Consensus Study Report of

*The National Academies of*
SCIENCES • ENGINEERING • MEDICINE

THE NATIONAL ACADEMIES PRESS
*Washington, DC*
www.nap.edu

THE NATIONAL ACADEMIES PRESS    500 Fifth Street, NW    Washington, DC 20001

This activity was supported by a contract between the National Academy of Sciences and the U.S. Department of Education, under Sponsor Award No. 9199-00-21-C-0002. Support for the work of the Committee on National Statistics is provided by a consortium of federal agencies through a grant from the National Science Foundation, a National Agricultural Statistics Service cooperative agreement, and several individual contracts. Any opinions, findings, conclusions, or recommendations expressed in this publication do not necessarily reflect the views of any organization or agency that provided support for the project.

International Standard Book Number-13: 978-0-309-27350-3
International Standard Book Number-10: 0-309-27350-1
Digital Object Identifier: https://doi.org/10.17226/26392

Additional copies of this publication are available from the National Academies Press, 500 Fifth Street, NW, Keck 360, Washington, DC 20001; (800) 624-6242 or (202) 334-3313; http://www.nap.edu.

Copyright 2022 by the National Academy of Sciences. All rights reserved.

Printed in the United States of America

Suggested citation: National Academies of Sciences, Engineering, and Medicine. (2022). *A Vision and Roadmap for Education Statistics*. Washington, DC: The National Academies Press. https://doi.org/10.17226/26392.

*The National Academies of*
# SCIENCES · ENGINEERING · MEDICINE

The **National Academy of Sciences** was established in 1863 by an Act of Congress, signed by President Lincoln, as a private, nongovernmental institution to advise the nation on issues related to science and technology. Members are elected by their peers for outstanding contributions to research. Dr. Marcia McNutt is president.

The **National Academy of Engineering** was established in 1964 under the charter of the National Academy of Sciences to bring the practices of engineering to advising the nation. Members are elected by their peers for extraordinary contributions to engineering. Dr. John L. Anderson is president.

The **National Academy of Medicine** (formerly the Institute of Medicine) was established in 1970 under the charter of the National Academy of Sciences to advise the nation on medical and health issues. Members are elected by their peers for distinguished contributions to medicine and health. Dr. Victor J. Dzau is president.

The three Academies work together as the **National Academies of Sciences, Engineering, and Medicine** to provide independent, objective analysis and advice to the nation and conduct other activities to solve complex problems and inform public policy decisions. The National Academies also encourage education and research, recognize outstanding contributions to knowledge, and increase public understanding in matters of science, engineering, and medicine.

Learn more about the National Academies of Sciences, Engineering, and Medicine at **www.nationalacademies.org**.

*The National Academies of*
SCIENCES · ENGINEERING · MEDICINE

**Consensus Study Reports** published by the National Academies of Sciences, Engineering, and Medicine document the evidence-based consensus on the study's statement of task by an authoring committee of experts. Reports typically include findings, conclusions, and recommendations based on information gathered by the committee and the committee's deliberations. Each report has been subjected to a rigorous and independent peer-review process and it represents the position of the National Academies on the statement of task.

**Proceedings** published by the National Academies of Sciences, Engineering, and Medicine chronicle the presentations and discussions at a workshop, symposium, or other event convened by the National Academies. The statements and opinions contained in proceedings are those of the participants and are not endorsed by other participants, the planning committee, or the National Academies.

For information about other products and activities of the National Academies, please visit www.nationalacademies.org/about/whatwedo.

## PANEL ON A VISION AND ROADMAP FOR EDUCATION STATISTICS

LARRY V. HEDGES (*Chair*), Northwestern University
MATTHEW M. CHINGOS, Urban Institute, Washington, DC
DONALD R. EASTON-BROOKS, University of Nevada, Reno
LEILANI GARCIA, Stanislaus County Office of Education, Modesto, CA
JOSHUA HAWLEY, The Ohio State University
SAMUEL R. LUCAS, University of California, Berkeley
JOSH MCGEE, University of Arkansas, Fayetteville
AMY B. O'HARA, Georgetown University
PATRICK PERRY, California Student Aid Commission, Rancho Cordova
JUDITH D. SINGER, Harvard University
KATHRYN B. STACK, KB Stack Consulting, LLC, Great Falls, VA
S. LYNNE STOKES, Southern Methodist University
KATHERINE K. WALLMAN, U.S. Office of Management and Budget (retired)
JOHN ROBERT WARREN, University of Minnesota

MELISSA CHIU, *Study Director*
NANCY KIRKENDALL, *Senior Program Officer*
ERIC GRIMES, *Senior Program Assistant*

# COMMITTEE ON NATIONAL STATISTICS

ROBERT M. GROVES (*Chair*), Office of the Provost, Georgetown University
LAWRENCE D. BOBO, Department of Sociology, Harvard University
ANNE C. CASE, Woodrow Wilson School of Public and International Affairs, Princeton University, *Emeritus*
MICK P. COUPER, Institute for Social Research, University of Michigan
JANET M. CURRIE, Woodrow Wilson School of Public and International Affairs, Princeton University
DIANA FARRELL, JPMorgan Chase Institute, Washington, DC
ROBERT GOERGE, Chapin Hall at the University of Chicago
ERICA L. GROSHEN, School of Industrial and Labor Relations, Cornell University
HILARY HOYNES, Goldman School of Public Policy, University of California, Berkeley
DANIEL KIFER, Department of Computer Science and Engineering, The Pennsylvania State University
SHARON LOHR, School of Mathematical and Statistical Sciences, Arizona State University, *Emeritus*
JEROME P. REITER, Department of Statistical Science, Duke University
JUDITH A. SELTZER, Department of Sociology, University of California, Los Angeles, *Emeritus*
C. MATTHEW SNIPP, School of the Humanities and Sciences, Stanford University
ELIZABETH A. STUART, Department of Mental Health, Johns Hopkins Bloomberg School of Public Health
JEANNETTE WING, Data Science Institute and Computer Science Department, Columbia University

BRIAN HARRIS-KOJETIN, *Director*
MELISSA CHIU, *Deputy Director*
CONSTANCE F. CITRO, *Senior Scholar*

# Acknowledgments

This Consensus Study Report reflects the invaluable contributions of many colleagues, whom we thank for their generous time, effort, and expert guidance. On behalf of the panel, I extend our deepest appreciation to the sponsor of this work: the Institute of Education Sciences (IES) with the U.S. Department of Education. Without support from IES and staff at the National Center for Education Statistics (NCES), this study would not have come to fruition. In particular, we thank Mark Schneider, director of IES; Peggy Carr, commissioner of NCES; James (Lynn) Woodworth, former commissioner of NCES; Ross Santy, associate commissioner at NCES; and Marie Marcum, senior mathematical statistician at NCES. We also thank Gloria Vera, contracting officer's representative in IES, for administrative support of this project. The panel thanks NCES staff who attended open meetings and generously gave of their time to present material to inform the panel's deliberations. We also thank the many NCES staff who responded to numerous questions from the panel and provided comprehensive information about the Center's current programs, operations, and organizational structure.

This Consensus Study Report was reviewed in draft form by individuals chosen for their diverse perspectives and technical expertise. The purpose of this independent review is to provide candid and critical comments that will assist the National Academies of Sciences, Engineering, and Medicine in making each published report as sound as possible and to ensure that it meets the institutional standards for quality, objectivity, evidence, and responsiveness to the study charge. The review comments and draft manuscript remain confidential to protect the integrity of the deliberative process.

We thank the following individuals for their review of this report: Kathryn S. Akers, Advanced Data Analytics, System Office, Pennsylvania's State System of Higher Education; Mary E. Bohman, Acting Director's Office, Bureau of Economic Analysis; George T. Duncan, H. John Heinz III School of Public Policy and Management, Department of Statistics, emeritus, Carnegie Mellon University; Susan Dynarski, Graduate School of Education, Harvard University; Andrew D. Ho, Graduate School of Education, Harvard University; Anne Holton, College of Education and Human Development, George Mason University; Chandra L. Muller, Department of Sociology, College of Liberal Arts, University of Texas; Debra Munk, independent consultant, Vienna, Virginia; Stephen W. Raudenbush, Department of Sociology, The University of Chicago.

Although the reviewers listed above provided many constructive comments and suggestions, they were not asked to endorse the conclusions or recommendations of this report, nor did they see the final draft before its release. The review of this report was overseen by Cynthia Z. Clark, independent consultant, McLean, Virginia, and Eugenie C. Scott, former executive director, National Center for Science Education, Berkeley, California. They were responsible for making certain that an independent examination of this report was carried out in accordance with the standards of the National Academies and that all review comments were carefully considered. Responsibility for the final content rests entirely with the authoring committee and the National Academies. The panel also extends its gratitude to members of the staff of the National Academies for their significant contributions to this report. Kirsten Sampson Snyder shepherded the report through the review and production process, and Susan Debad provided useful editorial advice that streamlined the report. Eric Grimes provided administrative and logistical support for numerous panel meetings, and Joshua Lang provided document format support and countless reference checks.

Melissa Chiu, study director and deputy director of the Committee on National Statistics, with the experienced insight of Nancy Kirkendall, senior program officer, designed the study, recruited the panel, gathered resources across a wide variety of topics, and guided the study with intelligence and care. They helped the panel orient to the breadth of the study and to become familiar with some of NCES's programs and federal initiatives. Along with Celeste Stone, senior consultant, and Bradford Chaney, senior program officer, they helped the panel work its way through difficult topics and focus on the most pressing issues, by distilling and synthesizing hundreds of documents and resources, providing critical rigor, and fleshing out the panel's ideas. The panel's report rests on their diligent efforts.

To my colleagues on the panel, I appreciate your dedication and motivation to lift up NCES, a critically important resource in education data and statistics. You shared your wisdom from across a wide range of expertise areas and brought innovative ideas to the discussions. At every meeting, I learned something new or heard different perspectives that became critical nuances of this report. You gave generously of your time across numerous meetings to grapple with broad and complex issues and arrive at consensus conclusions and recommendations for advancing NCES. Thank you.

        Larry Hedges, *Chair*
        Panel on A Vision and Roadmap for Education Statistics

# Contents

| | |
|---|---|
| Synopsis | 1 |
| Summary | 5 |
| 1 Introduction | 17 |

  The National Center for Education Statistics: Context and
    Mandates, Organization, and Products and Services, 18
  Charge to the Panel, 21
  Information Gathering, 26
  Panel's Approach to the Charge, 28
  Audiences for and Organization of the Report, 31

| | |
|---|---|
| 2 Rise Up to Meet 21st-Century Education Data Ecosystem Needs | 33 |

  Meet the Mission in a Changing Social Context, 33
  Develop a Strong Strategic Plan to Make Tough Decisions, 36
  Support and Empower NCES to Set Its Own Priorities, 44
  Maximize NCES's Unique Value for Evidence Building, 46
  Adapt to the Changing World of Education: Increase Diversity
    and Awareness of Equity Issues, 51
  Expand Data-Acquisition Strategies for New Insights, 59

*xi*

| 3 | Prioritize Topics, Data Content, and Statistical Information to Maintain Relevance | 63 |

Prioritizing Topics, 63
Align Acquired Data Content with High-Priority Topics and Questions, 64

| 4 | Expand Engagement and Dissemination for Greater Mission Impact | 79 |

Create Engagement Feedback Loops to Ensure Relevance of Products and Services, 80
Expand NCES's Role Enabling Data Access to Serve and Engage Stakeholders, 90
Improve Dissemination, Focusing on Accessibility and Usefulness, 96

| 5 | Transform Internal Structure and Operations to Align with and Directly Support the Strategic Plan | 105 |

Organizational Structure, 105
Budget, 106
Reimbursable Work, 106
Staff Characteristics, 108
Staff Turnover, 109
Average Number of U.S. Dollars Managed by Each Agency Employee, 111
Use of Contractors, 111
Resources for Stakeholder Engagement, Communication, and Dissemination, 113
Intradepartmental Operations, Support, and Relations, 114
Knowledge Retention, 115
NCES's Structure and Operations—Conclusions, 115
Opportunities for Leveraging Contractors and Other Nontraditional Mechanisms for Building Agency Capacity, Retaining Knowledge, and Enhancing Resilience, 117
Evaluate Possible Organizational Structures and Features as Part of Strategic Planning, 120

| 6 | Summary of Recommendations | 123 |

Complete Listing of Recommendations and Conclusions, 124
Final Thoughts, 130

| References | 131 |

Appendixes
A  Glossary of Terms and Acronyms Used in This Report   141
B  Data Sources and Collection Approaches   157
C  Summary of Data Content Prioritization Process   185
D  Comparing Federal Principal Statistical Agencies and Units   189
E  Institute of Education Sciences and NCES Product Review
   Processes   199
F  Open Meeting Agendas and Solicited Statements   205
G  Biographical Sketches of the Panel   211

# Synopsis

The National Center for Education Statistics (NCES) is the premier statistical agency within the Department of Education (ED), responsible for collecting, analyzing, and disseminating statistics at all levels of education. In addition, NCES supports ED in a variety of ways: strengthening privacy of education data; enhancing the quality and consistency of education data at local, state, and federal levels; and supporting the states as they develop their own longitudinal data systems.

NCES faces new challenges to improve, adapt, and expand their products and to meet new demands in light of broad changes to education in the United States, which include more diverse student bodies, more students enrolled in postsecondary and adult education, and a greatly expanded role of technology in learning. Education data and policy makers' appetite for rigorous evidence have advanced rapidly as new data sources become available and the federal government pushes for more and better data through efforts such as the Foundations for Evidence-Based Policymaking Act of 2018 (commonly called the Evidence Act) and the 2021 Presidential Executive Order on Advancing Racial Equity and Support for Underserved Communities through the Federal Government (Executive Order 13985, 2021).

A panel of experts convened by the National Academies of Sciences, Engineering, and Medicine, at the request of the Institute of Education Sciences (IES), was asked to recommend a portfolio of activities and products for NCES, review developments in the acquisition and use of data, consider current and future priorities, and suggest desirable changes.

The panel approached this task by asking what a national statistical agency for education would be and do if it were newly established today, with the same level of resources. The panel reimagines NCES as a leader in education statistics, evidence building, and data governance, expanding its role as a data-access facilitator. The panel aspires for NCES to be in full control of how it meets its mission—operating strategically, anticipating environmental changes, and readily adapting to deliver high-value products and services. Finally, the panel envisions NCES as deeply engaged with stakeholders, strengthening data capacity at state and local education agencies, and as a strong partner with ED.

This report cannot take the place of strategic planning, which will require NCES to conduct an intensive self-examination and review of the educational environment. While understanding that NCES needs to decide for itself how to proceed, the panel presents its thoughts on strategic priorities, data products, services, and operations. This report provides a blueprint of key issues and ways that NCES may resolve them, including operational details and many examples to assist with implementation.

First and foremost, NCES is advised to develop a strategic plan that creates a culture of innovation, supports the collection of new types of data and new subject areas, and helps the Center make tough decisions about its data priorities and tradeoffs. This planning process will enable NCES to conduct a top-to-bottom review of its data-acquisition activities, to strengthen focus on topics most relevant to education decision makers, and to discontinue lower-value activities that are disproportionately costly and burdensome.

NCES's strategic plan should embed diversity, equity, inclusion, and accessibility (DEIA) into all aspects of the Center's work, to ensure its work is relevant and useful to an increasingly diverse set of stakeholders. It is critical that NCES's data collections, methods, and products accurately measure contemporary diverse populations and their lived experiences. To do so, NCES will need to engage with members of diverse communities and instill a culture of DEIA throughout the Center's staff, intentionally considering DEIA issues throughout the data life cycle, from data collection through analysis and publication.

Second, the panel suggests that NCES work to maximize its unique value for evidence building and work with ED and IES to expand its role in providing statistical leadership to ED and the U.S. government. The secretary of education, director of IES, and NCES commissioner should review and update departmental policies, divisions of responsibility, and processes to enable the NCES commissioner to most effectively carry out the responsibilities of the statistical official delineated in the Evidence Act and to support evidence-building needs across ED. NCES can also increase collaborations with other federal statistical agencies and build partnerships with external researchers and analysts.

Third, the panel suggests that NCES explore and develop new sources of data, including administrative and web-based data, to complement its survey-based and assessment data, lessening the burden on survey respondents and possibly increasing timeliness. Collaboration with other federal statistical agencies and IES is advised, to assist the process of testing and adopting new methods for harnessing alternative data.

Fourth, the panel advises NCES to expand its engagement and dissemination efforts to increase the Center's impact. Strategies could include creating engagement feedback loops, expanding NCES's role enabling data access, and improving dissemination with a focus on accessibility and usefulness. Increasing NCES's impact will require a better understanding of the diverse needs of stakeholders and will necessitate strategic decisions about which audiences to serve. While NCES's Statewide Longitudinal Data Systems Grant Program is a strength, the panel encourages NCES to do even more to support state and local education agencies.

Finally, to successfully implement its strategic plan, NCES will need to transform its internal structure and operations. It may be desirable to shift from a structure based on data source type to one that promotes blending data sources and other innovations, insightful evidence building by education topic, and staff teamwork and cross-fertilization. NCES should address its current overreliance on contractors, including through staffing arrangements in which contractors collaborate with staff to build internal capacity.

# Summary

In 2021, the director of the Institute of Education Sciences (IES) at the Department of Education (ED) asked the National Academies of Sciences, Engineering, and Medicine to provide a vision for the National Center for Education Statistics (NCES), excluding its Assessments Division, for the next 7 years. The vision would include a modernized portfolio of statistical products and services to increase NCES's impact. The National Academies were asked to review developments in collecting and using data, consider recent trends and future priorities, and suggest changes to NCES's programs, operations, staffing, and use of contractors, with a focus on NCES's statistical programs and not its assessment programs.

In response to this request, the Committee on National Statistics convened an interdisciplinary panel of experts. The panel approached this task by asking what a national statistical agency for education would be and do if it were newly established today, as a means of reimagining how NCES could meet its mission effectively with the same level of resources.

## RISE UP TO MEET 21ST-CENTURY EDUCATION DATA ECOSYSTEM NEEDS

Education in the United States is changing rapidly as student bodies become more diverse, more students enroll in postsecondary education, and technology plays a greater role in learning. Education data and policymakers' appetite for rigorous evidence have advanced rapidly as new data sources come online and the federal government pushes for more and better data, through efforts including the Foundations for Evidence-Based

Policymaking Act of 2018 (commonly called the Evidence Act)[1] and the 2021 Presidential Executive Order on Advancing Racial Equity and Support for Underserved Communities through the Federal Government (Executive Order 13985, January 20, 2021).

The panel reimagines NCES as a leader in education statistics, evidence building, and data governance, expanding its role as a data-access facilitator. The panel aspires for NCES to be in full control of how it meets its mission—operating strategically, anticipating environmental changes, and readily adapting to deliver high-value products and services. Finally, the panel envisions NCES as deeply engaged with stakeholders, strengthening data capacity at state and local education agencies, and as a strong partner to ED.

This report cannot take the place of strategic planning, which will require NCES to perform an intensive self-examination and review of the education environment, collaborating with stakeholders and consultants. While understanding that NCES needs to decide for itself how to proceed, the panel presents its thoughts on strategic priorities, data products, services, and operations. This report provides a blueprint of key issues and ways that NCES may seek to resolve them, including operational details and many examples to assist with implementation.

The full report includes 5 conclusions and 15 recommendations. These recommendations require planning, will, and discipline to achieve within NCES's constraints. The panel suggests that NCES begin by investing in strategic planning, infusing diversity, equity, inclusion, and accessibility (DEIA) considerations throughout its organization and work, exploring alternative datasets, and effectively fulfilling its role as ED's statistical official. Some recommendations require collaboration with other individuals and agencies. Progress on the fundamental recommendations alone would substantially advance NCES as a leader in the education data ecosystem. NCES is already actively involved in certain recommended actions and can build on them. The Center can also invest some internal resources to activate external resources as a force multiplier, by aligning those external resources to its strategic plan. While there is much work to do, if NCES seriously acts on these recommendations, the Center can take the helm as a meaningful leader in the nation's education data ecosystem.

Themes and recommendations are summarized in the sections that follow.

---

[1] Pub. L. 115-435. Available: https://www.congress.gov/bill/115th-congress/house-bill/4174.

## FUNDAMENTAL RECOMMENDATIONS CRITICAL FOR ORGANIZATIONAL TRANSFORMATION

The following sections present the fundamental recommendations that are most critical to advancing NCES as a leader in the education data ecosystem. The full report provides details, conclusions, ideas, and suggestions in Chapter 2.

**Theme: Develop a Strong Strategic Plan to Make Tough Decisions**

RECOMMENDATION 2-1: To direct its future, NCES should develop and implement a bold strategic plan that incentivizes innovation and creative partnerships and that will produce relevant, timely, and reliable statistical products to assist education decision makers at every level of government. NCES should develop and begin implementation of the plan within 1 year of the release of this report.

Strategic planning allows an organization to focus on high-value products and services for maximum effectiveness and mission impact. Not only has the social environment for education statistics changed, NCES's mission itself has expanded in scope. To meet its mission effectively, any government agency needs to understand its identity and core values, so that it can establish priorities that guide decision making and operations. Strategic planning helps agencies to proactively clarify the tradeoffs and greater goals that must be navigated during decision making.

Such forethought is even more critical for a small agency like NCES, with limited resources, many stakeholders, a proportionally large administrative burden, and unfunded mandates. Strategic planning will allow NCES to determine its identity, values, priorities, and tradeoffs, to understand where it can add the most value, and to determine how it can best move forward in the 21st century. Once NCES institutionalizes its strategic intentions and implements its priorities with discipline, the Center will be proactive and nimble rather than being so "responsive to immediate demands"[2] that its long-term progress and overall effectiveness are impaired. Investing time in strategic planning is an essential step towards NCES directing its own future.

NCES's strategic plan needs to be comprehensive—describing priorities, gaps, and goals, and delineating ways to leverage new tools and technologies to build forward-looking operations and the necessary infrastructure to achieve stated goals. The panel suggests that the plan also indicate the level of effort needed to manifest goals and objectives, possibly in stages as

---

[2] NCES response to question from the panel, p. 56.

programs and initiatives evolve. Areas to be addressed in the strategic plan are covered in the remainder of this summary.

### Theme: Support and Empower NCES to Set Its Own Priorities

RECOMMENDATION 2-2: The secretary of education, director of the Institute of Education Sciences, and NCES commissioner should collaborate to ensure that NCES is independent in developing, producing, and disseminating statistics.

While NCES is responsible for its own strategic planning and priorities, to achieve the Center's vision, the secretary of education, other offices in ED, and the director of IES need to fully support NCES. It is essential for IES and ED to empower NCES to manifest its vision and strategic priorities. Together, ED, IES, and NCES are advised to revisit and update internal policies and procedures, to ensure that NCES operates under well-established principles and practices for federal statistical agencies (NASEM, 2021b). NCES should have the authority to make decisions on the scope, content, and frequency of its data and statistics; select and promote professional staff based on skills and knowledge; and "be able to meet with members of Congress, congressional staff, and the public to discuss the agency's statistics, resources, and staffing levels" (NASEM, 2021b, Practice 2, p. 54). NCES should also have highly qualified staff to make decisions on data content based on scientific and professional considerations, and to gather input on data needs from stakeholders and ED officials (NASEM, 2021b, Practices 3, 4, 5, 9). The panel encourages ED, IES, and NCES to collaborate to ensure NCES operates with its full authority as a federal statistical agency and effectively serves its stakeholders in IES and across ED.

### Theme: Incentivize Innovation, Experimentation, and Continuous Learning

The panel recommends that NCES's strategic plan incentivize innovation, experimentation, and continuous learning throughout all facets of the Center. The strategic plan should consider practices that support a culture of innovation (see NASEM, 2021b). For example, not only is it advisable for NCES to hire staff with cutting-edge skills, but the Center should invest in the ongoing development and professional advancement of its existing staff (NASEM, 2021b, Practice 4). Retaining institutional knowledge is critical for the efficient and effective long-term operation of any agency. NCES can also develop an active research program that includes substantive analyses and evaluates new methods, operations, and alternative data sources for fitness for use (NASEM, 2021b, Practice 5). Finally, to accelerate the shift to a culture of innovation, the panel advises NCES to forge strong partnerships with other components of IES, innovative agencies, the Center's contractors, and other external experts to identify best practices and pilot new, potentially transformational approaches (NASEM, 2021b, Practice 7).

### Theme: Maximize NCES's Unique Value for Evidence Building

**RECOMMENDATION 2-3:** The secretary of education, director of the Institute of Education Sciences, and NCES commissioner should immediately take actions to enable the NCES commissioner to most effectively fulfill the responsibilities of the statistical official delineated in the Foundations for Evidence-Based Policymaking Act of 2018 and to support evidence-building needs across the Department of Education.

The Evidence Act effectively expands NCES's mission by giving statistical agencies new data-acquisition authority, duties to facilitate data access, and new roles and relationships in evidence building. The Evidence Act establishes NCES's commissioner as the chief statistical official (SO) of ED, to work closely with the chief data officer (CDO), the chief evaluation officer (EO), and others, to advance ED's development and use of scientifically rigorous evidence. Evidence-based decision making is the purview of the entire ED, and NCES is congressionally mandated to serve a specific role. Implementation of the Evidence Act is relatively nascent[3] and this moment presents an opportunity for the secretary of education, the director of IES, and the commissioner of NCES to establish a central role for NCES as a meaningful partner in ED's evidence-building activities. Together, the three entities are advised to determine how to best maximize the unique value NCES brings as a producer of credible and relevant evidence, a recognized leader in data standards, and a data-access facilitator. The secretary, director, and commissioner should update all related policies, divisions of responsibilities, processes, and practices, to empower the NCES commissioner to effectively perform the SO duties. The SO brings an important connection between the CDO and the EO, by turning data into high-quality information fit to be used to inform policy and decision making.

The IES director, NCES commissioner, and commissioners of other IES centers should collaboratively determine how to leverage NCES's unique value. The Evidence Act presents evidence goals to be fulfilled and encourages departments to use new techniques, share and analyze data, and form new partnerships. NCES and IES alone can fulfill this need for ED. The panel urges NCES and other centers within IES to come together to build strong

---

[3] At the time of writing, OMB had not issued guidance for the implementation of Titles II and III or the Evidence Act.

partnerships, grasp these enormous opportunities, and lead ED's evidence building and research. These ideas are presented in detail in Chapters 2 and 4.

### Theme: Adapt to the Changing World of Education by Increasing Diversity and Awareness of Equity Issues

**RECOMMENDATION 2-4:** NCES should proactively embed diversity, equity, inclusion, and accessibility in all areas of its work and organization, to adapt and serve contemporary communities of the changing world of education.

NCES's mission includes being relevant and useful to key stakeholders. Thus, the Center's data and statistics should address contemporary issues, such as changes in student populations and school environments (e.g., online learning). DEIA efforts are critical to ensuring that NCES's work is relevant and useful to an increasingly diverse set of stakeholders and society. As a significant producer of education statistics, NCES's data collections, methods, and products should accurately measure contemporary diverse populations and their lived experiences. To maintain relevance, NCES will need to intentionally consider DEIA issues throughout the data life cycle, from data collection through analysis and publication, including by engaging with members of diverse communities and instilling a culture of DEIA throughout the Center's staff.

### Theme: Expand Data-Acquisition Strategies for New Insights

**RECOMMENDATION 2-5:** To improve its efficiency, timeliness, and relevance, NCES should continually explore alternative data sources for potential use in data and statistical products, conduct studies on the quality of these sources and their fitness for use, and expand responsible access to data from multiple sources and linkage tools. Testing and adoption of new data-science methods for harnessing alternative data should be done in collaboration with other federal statistical agencies, as well as with other components of the Institute of Education Sciences that are actively exploring ways to strengthen the impact of these techniques.

**RECOMMENDATION 2-6:** For primary collections, NCES should modernize standard language on consent and planned usage, to permit secure secondary uses that enable high-quality follow-up studies, such as through privacy-protected linkages with other data sources.

In recent years, many federal and state agencies have used administrative data for statistical purposes, including as evidence building for decision making and evaluation of government programs. At the same time, there has been an explosion of alternative data sources, including commercial data; social media and network data; and internet documents, webpages, and videos that can be harvested or "scraped" (see Appendix B). These potential data sources present enormous opportunities for NCES to advance evidence building.

The panel strongly urges data-source exploration and expansion to be part of NCES's strategic plan. NCES will need to study the quality and fitness for purpose of alternative data sources, as well as the potential benefits and costs of integrating alternative data sources into existing operations and products. The investment is critical to NCES's culture of evidence-based decision making and the Center's ability to keep up with stakeholders' needs for credible, objective, and timely education data and statistics.

In anticipation of data linkage, NCES should reconsider the consent language and planned usage of all primary collections, to support ongoing uses for statistical activities. The language could ask respondents to allow linkages to other data, could ask for recontact for future requests, or could establish other levels of permission, depending on the respondent population. NCES is advised to look to other federal statistical agencies for best practices when drafting statements regarding privacy of survey respondents' data and its potential uses. NCES is also encouraged to engage with potential respondents when designing appropriate consent language.

## ADDITIONAL RECOMMENDATIONS

The following sections elaborate on additional areas to be addressed by NCES's strategic plan. The full report provides details, conclusions, ideas, and suggestions in Chapters 3, 4, and 5.

### Theme: Prioritize Topics, Data Content, and Statistical Information to Increase Relevance

**RECOMMENDATION 3-1:** NCES should conduct a top-to-bottom review of its data-acquisition activities, to prioritize topics most relevant to understanding contemporary education, and to discontinue activities that are disproportionately costly and burdensome relative to their value.

**RECOMMENDATION 3-2:** NCES should revisit priorities mandated by Congress and, where appropriate, make recommendations for changes.

Some of NCES's data collections (such as the Fast Response Survey System and the School Survey on Crime and Safety) are no longer active due to a lack of adequate staffing, and NCES can expect to make additional hard choices due to limited resources. Thus, it is critical that NCES strategically prioritize its data collections and acquisitions based on its strategic plan. The panel illustrates a process that NCES might follow (see Appendix C) and discusses key topics expected to be covered in the Center's strategic plan.

NCES recognizes that addressing topics of equity and equal access is a top priority. NCES has strong data collections in place for these topics, which collect basic demographic data and data on student outcomes. Data collection is weaker with regard to measuring the educational process. NCES primarily collects data on the traditional education infrastructure and will need to expand measurement of actions outside of that infrastructure, such as early childhood education, adult education, and career and technical training. Greater attention is needed on the access to and use of technology, including, but not limited to, online learning. NCES may be able to expand the extent and usefulness of its data through increasing its linkages with other agencies at all levels. NCES faces multiple federal mandates for data collection and is recommended to work with Congress to determine whether the need for some of these mandates has changed, and to explore whether alternative data-collection approaches might help address its mandates.

## Theme: Expand Engagement and Dissemination for Greater Mission Impact

NCES is the nation's premier statistical agency concerning education. Thus, the Center should be a primary source of data for Congress, the White House, federal agencies, state and local policy makers, students and their families, education practitioners, researchers, the civil rights–monitoring community, the news media, advisory boards, and professional associations. The following suggested engagement and dissemination activities will help NCES to achieve this goal.

### Create Engagement Feedback Loops to Ensure Relevance of Products and Services

**RECOMMENDATION 4-1:** NCES should deepen and broaden its engagement with current and potential data users, to gather continuing feedback about their needs and ways that NCES can meet those needs more effectively. This feedback will help NCES shape its efforts to develop and disseminate standards, provide technical assistance, and strengthen its user community.

RECOMMENDATION 4-2: NCES should actively collaborate with other data-holding federal agencies and organizations to develop useful products and processes, including those that utilize data from alternative sources, to provide timely, policy-relevant insights.

RECOMMENDATION 4-3: NCES should explore and establish creative models for a nimble, ongoing consulting body, supplemented by a pool of ad hoc consultants, to help NCES innovate and be accountable for progress on strategic goals.

NCES has many stakeholders, and it is a challenge to adequately understand all stakeholder needs. Broad engagement is important to identify and monitor the current and emerging issues that drive product and service effectiveness and improvement. Federal and nonfederal organizations that hold and steward data are also critical stakeholders for NCES.

NCES is connected with the federal statistical agencies through the Interagency Council on Statistical Policy, and the Center could leverage those relationships more fully to advance education statistics and insights. Many agencies and organizations are aggressively pursuing partnerships to link data for evidence building. NCES, too, can enhance the value of its data through linkage projects, research, and dissemination. NCES can and should expand its network to support creative evidence building and increase its mission impact.

NCES should engage a nimble and flexible consulting body, not subject to Federal Advisory Committee Act regulations, to provide strategic advice, innovative ideas, and accountability. This body should have full knowledge of NCES's work and organization and should provide backing when the Center makes difficult decisions. For topics that require particular expertise, NCES should engage a set of ad hoc consultants to complement the ongoing consulting body.

### Expand NCES's Role Enabling Data Access to Serve and Engage Stakeholders

RECOMMENDATION 4-4: NCES should strengthen state capacity to link data across systems, adopt shared data standards, and provide actionable information to state and local education agencies to help improve student learning outcomes. NCES can leverage its Statewide Longitudinal Data Systems Grant Program to achieve this goal.

RECOMMENDATION 4-5: NCES, in collaboration with the Institute of Education Sciences, should establish a joint statistical research program that includes matching internal staff with highly qualified external researchers, statisticians, and data scientists to develop new data analyses, tools, and publications.

NCES can maximize its mission impact with minimal investment by expanding its role in data governance, by helping to create the processes and metrics that aid the use of information. NCES already performs aspects of data governance and manages restricted data-use licenses. NCES can expand this governance role by assisting states and organizations with data linkage. NCES can streamline data linkage, prepare and curate data, develop templates, and simplify processes. NCES could provide guidance to state and local data providers regarding best practices for establishing and configuring data infrastructure.

The panel finds that NCES is underutilizing its ability to engage states in achieving its goals. NCES can increase its mission impact by aligning the resources of other organizations to the Center's strategic goals. For example, in implementing its strategic plan, NCES could consider leveraging the goals and outcomes of the Statewide Longitudinal Data Systems Grant Program (NCES, 2021m). The panel recommends that NCES then promote and circulate these intentions to the states and award proposals to advance these goals.

NCES can support its expanded role in data governance and evidence building by leveraging its existing data-licensing program while also directing data analysis. ED will make faster progress in its evidence-building efforts by both broadening the community of researchers and policy makers that can access data for analysis and by signaling important topics, such as those for which NCES especially wants data. For mutual benefit, we recommend NCES establish a joint statistical research program for external researchers and fellows. NCES would also benefit from expanding and modernizing its data-licensing program, to further increase responsible data access for evidence building.

### Improve Dissemination, Focusing on Accessibility and Usefulness

RECOMMENDATION 4-6: NCES should release data and data products that are useful, actionable, and timely for local and state education agencies and other stakeholders. To increase timeliness, NCES, in collaboration with the Institute of Education Sciences, should review and revise its internal and external quality assurance processes.

The content of NCES's data products and tools is important for building a broad user base. Individual stakeholders have distinct needs for content, quality of information, and timeliness. To be more helpful to state and local school districts with few resources for data analysis, NCES should deliver products that help local education agencies improve their schools and their students' outcomes. NCES's Public School District Finance Peer Search (NCES, 2021i) is an approach the panel recommends extending to other topics. NCES could add analytic features, tools, or templates that provide statistical testing for samples.[4] For practitioner-oriented products, NCES could partner with the National Center for Education Evaluation and Regional Assistance, to connect users to relevant research in the What Works Clearinghouse (IES, 2021c). Such collaboration could cross-promote products and boost both centers.

Regarding timeliness, NCES is encouraged to engage with stakeholders about their needs and then determine what is feasible, while exploring acceptable quality tradeoffs to decrease lag time. NCES, in collaboration with IES, is also advised to conduct a top-to-bottom review of both NCES and IES Standards Review Office[5] quality assurance processes, to revise review criteria for products requiring improved timeliness, with a goal of being transparent about quality tradeoffs.

### Theme: Transform Internal Structure and Operations to Align with and Directly Support the Strategic Plan

**RECOMMENDATION 5-1:** NCES should utilize contractors and creative staffing arrangements to work collaboratively with staff to build internal capacity. To enhance resilience, NCES should also explore greater use of flexible contract types, stronger incentives for contractors to adopt cost-effective innovations, and performance-based requirements.

Within NCES, the statistics units experienced a net loss of 25 full-time equivalent (FTE) employees (30%) between fiscal years (FYs) 2003–2021, though the assessment units had a net gain of 2 FTEs (7%).[6] Parts of NCES are understaffed, resulting in the discontinuation of some surveys and the inability to advance new initiatives. NCES relies heavily on contractors to conduct its day-to-day activities. This trend has increased steadily since FY 2003. Today, on average, NCES staff manage 3.7 contracts[7] which amounted to $2.8M per year in FY 2020 (U.S. OMB, 2020)—NCES has

---

[4] See, for example, U.S. Census Bureau's Statistical Testing Tool. Available: https://www.census.gov/programs-surveys/acs/guidance/statistical-testing-tool.html [March 2022].

[5] The Education Sciences Reform Act of 2002 (20 U.S. Code § 9501 et seq.) requires IES to have a peer review process. See: https://ies.ed.gov/director/sro/ and https://ies.ed.gov/director/sro/ppt/Scientific_Peer_Review.pptx [March 2022].

[6] IES document provided to the panel, "IES & NCES Historical FTE Data and IES Appropriations Historical"; NCES response to question from the panel, pp. 7–10.

[7] NCES response to question from the panel, p. 15.

the highest budget-to-staff ratio among the federal statistical agencies.[8] Wide use of contracts and contractors has been effective in extending and supplementing NCES's staff when staffing allocations from ED were unavailable. However, a contracting approach can be more costly and can, over time, deteriorate NCES's institutional knowledge. NCES should consider ways to leverage contractors and other external partners to build and maintain institutional knowledge and in-house innovation. NCES should also partner with contractors to create and revise templates for all steps of the data pipeline—from data-use agreements to presentation graphics style—to embed innovations across the Center and its contractors. NCES's organization by data source encourages stovepiping and can be a barrier to the innovation, blended data, and cross-fertilization that will be central to the Center's future success. As NCES expands its audience and adapts its value proposition, its organizational structure needs to evolve to fulfill the Center's new strategic goals.

The panel finds that NCES is in danger of losing institutional knowledge and innovation capabilities because of decreasing staff size, increasing reliance on contractors, and the Center's current organizational structure. While many organization-related recommendations will be dependent on the specifics of the Center's strategic plan, some important activities need to take place as part of the strategic-planning process. While writing a strategic plan, NCES is advised to carefully and thoroughly evaluate options for various organizational structures and features, while considering the agency-specific advocacy necessary to make fundamental changes.

---

[8]This is the average number of dollars calculated as direct funding in FY 2020 divided by the number of FTE permanent staff. It is used to express the average number of dollars managed by each agency staff member. NCES has a budget-to-staff ratio of approximately $2.75M per FTE—more than seven times the median ratio for the 13 principal federal statistical agencies—according to American Statistical Association–compiled data for the 13 federal statistical agencies (Pierson, 2021).

# 1

# Introduction

Education, long an important aspect of social and economic life, has changed substantially in recent decades. The student population has grown in diversity and needs, with more students from economically disadvantaged groups seeking higher education but struggling with the economics. The teaching workforce has changed too—not just demographically, but due to an expected wave of retirements and spot shortages in certain fields. Adults are obtaining education for a broader variety of reasons, with many taking advantage of nondegree industry credentials. Grodsky et al. (2021) offer an analysis of trends and impacts of adult education based on a 2015 follow-on study to the 1982 High School and Beyond Survey. Formal education has shifted dramatically in the direction of online learning, particularly during the COVID-19 pandemic. To provide one example, from April to September 2020, the percentage of households reporting homeschooling of school-age children increased from 5.4 to 11.1 percent (Eggleston and Fields, 2021).

Simultaneously, the digital era has created an explosion of data and statistics that are readily available to the public. Policy makers are increasingly reliant on data, as momentum for evidence-based decision making increases. To support these diversifying and expanding demands, the nation needs an education statistics agency that leads the production and distribution of high-quality data that are useful, timely, and responsive to the needs of many stakeholders. With this report, the panel on A Vision and Roadmap for Education Statistics presents a bold new vision of a federal education statistics agency for the 21st century.

## THE NATIONAL CENTER FOR EDUCATION STATISTICS: CONTEXT AND MANDATES, ORGANIZATION, AND PRODUCTS AND SERVICES

"Founded in 1867, NCES is the second oldest and third largest in budget among the Office of Management and Budget's 13 principal federal statistical agencies." NCES "provides objective, reliable, and trustworthy statistics about the condition of education through administrative data collections, statistical surveys, longitudinal studies, and assessments" (American Statistical Association et al., 2021, p. 1) (see Box 1-1).

### Context and Mandates

Thirteen principal statistical agencies, including NCES, and 96 smaller statistical programs and units comprise the federal statistical system. The chief statistician within the U.S. Office of Management and Budget (OMB) helps to encourage collaboration and cooperation among statistical agencies through the Interagency Council on Statistical Policy (ICSP) (consisting of the heads of the principal statistical agencies and the chief statistical officials from all other cabinet departments), and the Federal Committee on Statistical Methodology (FCSM) (consisting of staff from statistical agencies appointed for their technical expertise). The NCES commissioner represents

---

**BOX 1-1**
**The Mission of the National Center for Education Statistics**

"The mission of the Statistics Center shall be—

(1) to collect and analyze education information and statistics in a manner that meets the highest methodological standards;
(2) to report education information and statistics in a timely manner; and
(3) to collect, analyze, and report education information and statistics in a manner that—
   (A) is objective, secular, neutral, and nonideological and is free of partisan political influence and racial, cultural, gender, or regional bias; and
   (B) is relevant and useful to practitioners, researchers, policymakers, and the public."

SOURCE: The Education Sciences Reform Act (of 2002). H.R. 3801, Section 151(b). Available: https://www.govinfo.gov/content/pkg/BILLS-107hr3801enr/pdf/BILLS-107hr3801enr.pdf [March 2022].

the Department of Education (ED) on the ICSP, and selected NCES technical staff serve as appointed members of FCSM. NCES also represents ED on the OMB-chaired Federal Geographic Data Committee.[1]

In 2020, NCES was the third largest statistical agency in terms of budget, but the ninth largest in terms of staff. "The majority of the 13 Principal Statistical Agencies (PSA) have a line item in the President's Budget showing the total annual funding request. However, for some PSAs [such as NCES] the funding request is made at the level of their parent organization, who subsequently allocates funds" (U.S. OMB, 2020, p. 8).

The functions most commonly associated with statistical agencies, also referred to as evidence-building activities, are the "collection, compilation, processing, analysis, and dissemination of data and information, to create general purpose, policy- and program-specific (including program evaluation and public health surveillance), or research-oriented statistics and datasets." (U.S. OMB, 2020, p. 4.) Each statistical agency has a unique set of functions, which are accomplished using multiple approaches.

The official list of typical statistical functions above does not include research. However, research is critical to the PSAs for keeping official functions up to date; for taking advantage of new technologies, new data sources, and new methodologies; and for identifying and solving emerging data gaps (NASEM, 2021b, Practice 5). Typically, the ICSP and FCSM convene working groups consisting of staff members from the PSAs, to address challenging new research issues and to determine promising approaches. NCES staff participate in many of these, including (but not limited to) the Federal Interagency Work Group on Race and Ethnicity Measurement Research, Innovating Data Collection Working Group (formerly called the Adaptive Survey Design Interest Group), the Measuring Sexual Orientation and Gender Identity (SOGI) Research Group, the Federal Partners in Bullying Prevention Working Group, and the COVID-19 Data Strategy and Execution Working Group.

The predecessor of NCES was established in 1867 "for the purpose of collecting such statistics and facts as shall show the condition and progress of education."[2] By the time of the 1994 reauthorization, NCES was a well-established independent statistical agency within the ED's Office of Educational Research and Improvement (OERI). The Education Sciences Reform Act of 2002 (ESRA)[3] replaced OERI with the Institute of Education Sciences (IES). NCES became one of the four centers within IES; the others

---

[1] For more information, see https://www.fgdc.gov/ [March 2022].
[2] 20 U.S. Code § 9001(a), Repealed. https://uscode.house.gov/view.xhtml?req=granuleid:USC-2000-title20-section9001&num=0&edition=2000 [March 2022].
[3] https://www.govinfo.gov/content/pkg/BILLS-107hr3801enr/pdf/BILLS-107hr3801enr.pdf [March 2022].

are the National Center for Education Evaluation and Regional Assistance, the National Center for Education Research, and the National Center for Special Education Research.

ESRA nibbled away at NCES's independence. For example, section 114(f)(5) of ESRA specifies that the director of IES shall "establish necessary procedures for technical and scientific peer review of the activities of the institute, consistent with 116(b)(3)," which states the National Board for Education Sciences "will review and approve procedures for technical and scientific peer review of the activities of the institute"[4] (see Chapter 4 for a discussion of the IES and NCES review process). Additionally, some of NCES's administrative functions, such as budgeting, personnel, and contract control, were centralized within IES (see Chapter 5 for discussion of personnel issues such as hiring and contracting). ESRA also replaced NCES's Advisory Council on Education Statistics with IES's National Board for Education Sciences (see Chapter 4 for a discussion of advisory and consulting groups; see Elchert and Pierson (2020) for additional discussion of the decline in NCES authority and autonomy). However, ESRA's reorganization of research-focused IES could benefit NCES. NCES would be well suited to play an integrative role within IES, in the spirit of a new social science that emphasizes replication, generalization, and data linkage—including linkage between IES experimental data and national survey data, and upgrading the collection of correlational and predictive data. NCES can be envisioned as a research agency in its own right, facilitating collaboration with IES research centers and the academic community, and identifying emerging new data needs while maintaining policy neutrality. These efforts would also enable NCES to be nimbler in the adoption of new approaches and technologies.

## Organization

The current organization of NCES is depicted in Figure 5-1. A commissioner heads the Center, and there are three divisions, all of which collect or compile data. Each division represents a different type of data source: Sample Surveys, Administrative Data, and Assessments. The Statistical Standards and Data Confidentiality Staff and the Annual Reports and Information Staff are smaller groups that perform crosscutting functions.

NCES currently employs about 90 full-time equivalent (FTE) employees, with 58 organized in the statistics units and 32 mainly organized

---

[4] https://www.govinfo.gov/content/pkg/BILLS-107hr3801enr/pdf/BILLS-107hr3801enr.pdf [March 2022]. ESRA § 116 (20 U.S. Code § 9516) established the National Board for Education Sciences as a board of directors for IES.

# INTRODUCTION

in assessments units (Table D-2, Figure D-1).[5] NCES's current staffing level represents a decline of 23 people (20%) overall and 25 people (30%) for the statistics units from fiscal years (FY) 2003–2021. Compared to the peak in FY 2010, the loss is greater, at 34 FTEs (27%) for NCES as a whole and 28 FTEs (33%) for statistics units. NCES's annual turnover rate since FY 2018 has ranged from 9 to 11 percent (Table D-3) and is an indicator of the risk for further staff (and knowledge) loss.

Even as NCES's staffing declined, the scope of the Center's work increased substantially. For example, the Common Education Data Standards and the Statewide Longitudinal Data Systems (SLDS) Grant Program did not exist in 2003. The National Assessment of Educational Progress (NAEP) and the Integrated Postsecondary Education Data System have undergone substantial expansion since 2003, and EDFacts was a large addition to NCES's work in 2013. Chapter 5 and Appendix D discuss how NCES utilizes its internal employee resources (funded indirectly from ED's Salaries and Expenses appropriation) versus its contractors (funded by program appropriations) to manage its scope of work.

## Products and Services

"NCES collects, analyzes, and disseminates education statistics at all levels, from preschool through postsecondary and adult education, including statistics on international education" (U.S. OMB, 2020, p. 40) (see Box 1-2 and Table B-1). In addition, NCES supports ED in a variety of ways: strengthening privacy of education data; enhancing the quality and consistency of education data at local, state, and federal levels; and supporting SLDS (see Box 1-3).

## CHARGE TO THE PANEL

In 2021, to keep pace with the changes in education and the emergence of new data sources and technology, the director of IES asked the National Academies of Sciences, Engineering, and Medicine to recommend a vision

---

[5]The statistics count includes the Administrative Data Division, Sample Surveys Division and its predecessors, Statistical Standards and Data Confidentiality Staff, Annual Reports and Information Staff, and the Office of the Commissioner FTEs working on statistics. The assessments count includes the Assessments Division plus one FTE from across multiple employees located in the Office of the Commissioner, who work on assessments for some of their time. The organization of staff into statistics and assessment units does not align with program appropriations (Figure D-2) because staff are paid indirectly through an allocation of the ED's Salaries and Expenses appropriation. The organization of FTEs does not fully reflect the functional roles of the staff. For example, staff located in a statistics office may also support assessment work.

> **BOX 1-2**
> **NCES Information Products and Collections**
>
> *Important information products* include:
>
> - The Nation's Report Card (congressionally mandated);
> - Condition of Education Report (congressionally mandated); and
> - Digest of Education Statistics.
>
> *Longitudinal surveys* typically include interviews with students, parents, and teachers, as well as administrative data and transcript study results that code and summarize transcript information in a consistent way. With this portfolio, which includes some follow-on studies, NCES has gone beyond providing descriptive data to policy makers and provided the research community with invaluable data for studying myriad questions about education and its improvement. Examples of longitudinal surveys include:
>
> - Early Childhood Longitudinal Survey, Birth Cohort (2001) and Early Childhood Longitudinal Survey, Kindergarten Cohort (1998, 2010, and 2022).
> - Middle Grades Longitudinal Survey (2017).
> - The high school series: National Longitudinal Survey (1972), High School and Beyond (1982), National Education Longitudinal Survey (1988), Education Longitudinal Survey (2002), High School Longitudinal Survey (2009), and High School and Beyond (2022).
>
> *Cross-sectional surveys* include the National Household Education Survey, with its variety of modules targeting different populations, and collaborative efforts such as the education module on the Bureau of Labor Statistics' Current Population Survey and the School Crime Supplement to the Bureau of Justice Statistics' National Crime Victimization Survey. They also include the National Postsecondary Student Aid Survey (NPSAS), the School Pulse Panel, the National Teacher and Principal Survey, and the Private School Survey. Particularly innovative studies include NPSAS and the School Pulse Panel. NPSAS is a combination of a sample survey with an administrative records collection for a national probability sample of students. In addition to collecting data directly from students and the postsecondary

institutions they attend, NPSAS incorporates data from the Federal Student Aid Central Processing System, the National Student Loan Data System, and commercial databases such as the National Student Clearinghouse, ACT, Inc., and College Board. The School Pulse Panel began in 2021 as a panel survey to monitor the impact of the COVID-19 pandemic on students and staff in U.S. public schools, with monthly results. (NCES Sample Surveys Division)

*Administrative records collections* inform key NCES products, such as the Common Core of Data (CCD) and the Integrated Postsecondary Education Data System. The integrated CCD was first implemented in the 1986–87 school year. CCD is an administrative records collection that produces summary data describing all public schools in the United States. It represents one of the earliest statistical products to rely on administrative data. (NCES Administrative Data Division)

*Assessment surveys* (probability sample surveys combined with assessments), include the National Assessment of Educational Progress (NAEP), Trends in International Science and Mathematics Study, and the Program for International Student Assessment, as well as other international assessments. These activities allow for both national and international comparisons of education outcomes. NAEP was the first combination of a probability sample survey with an item response theory model, and the program has continued to evolve and innovate. (NCES Assessments Division)

*Other data products* include the "Education Demographic and Geographic Estimates program, which designs and develops information resources to help understand the social and spatial context of education in the U.S. It uses data from the U.S. Census Bureau's American Community Survey to create custom indicators of social, economic, and housing conditions for school-age children and their parents. It also uses spatial data collected by NCES and the Census Bureau to create geographic locale indicators, school point locations, school district boundaries, and other types of data to support spatial analysis."[a] EDGE is an example of using existing data in innovative and exciting ways to support data analysis.

---

[a] https://nces.ed.gov/programs/edge/About#a [March 2022].

**BOX 1-3
NCES Services**

*Activities that support ED* include:

- EDFacts collection of administrative data from states and local education agencies. NCES provides collection expertise and technical assistance to U.S. Department of Education (ED) program offices managing formula grant programs. (NCES Administrative Data Division)
- Support for ED's Office for Civil Rights in managing and improving the Civil Rights Data Collection. (NCES Administrative Data Division)
- The ED School Climate Surveys are a suite of survey instruments developed by NCES to be fielded by schools, districts, and states. The system provides automated support and is available to local users through the ED's National Center for Safe Supportive Learning Environments. NCES has also developed psychometric benchmarks to enable meaningful comparisons between student subgroups and between schools. (NCES Sample Surveys Division)
- College Scorecard, for which NCES was a key collaborator in establishing a process for merging student-level data held by ED's Student Aid Office with annual Internal Revenue Service income data (managed by the Social Security Administration) to produce aggregate earnings data, by school, for students that received federal student loans and grants. The College Scorecard is currently overseen by ED's chief data officer in the Office of Planning, Evaluation, and Policy Development.

*Assistance for the Statewide Longitudinal Data Systems (SLDS)*, including:

- The SLDS Grant Program, which provides grants to states to improve their longitudinal data systems and to use them in creative ways. (NCES Administrative Records Division)
- The National Forum on Education Statistics, which facilitates the exchange of ideas among states (NCES Statistical Standards and Data Confidentiality Staff)

*Initiatives that strengthen the protection of privacy* of education data:

- The Institute of Education Sciences' (IES's) Disclosure Review Board within NCES's Statistical Standards Program approves procedures for protecting data to be publicly released and reviews disclosure risk analyses within IES, to ensure that released data do not disclose the identity of any indi-

vidual respondent. (NCES Statistical Standards and Data Confidentiality Staff)
- Support for ED's Disclosure Review Board, managed by the Student Privacy Policy Office in the Office of Planning, Evaluation, and Policy Development. (NCES Statistical Standards and Data Confidentiality Staff and Administrative Data Division)
- The Privacy Technical Assistance Center, funded from the SLDS Grant Program appropriation, provides on-site technical assistance to states regarding privacy issues. (Initially developed by NCES, now managed by the Student Privacy Policy Office)
- NCES data products are made available to researchers through restricted-use data licenses and (most recently) through the Coleridge Initiative. (NCES Statistical Standards and Data Confidentiality Staff)

*Programs and classifications that enhance the quality and consistency* of education data at local, state, and federal levels:

- Statistical Standards Program to help to assure the quality of education data. (NCES Statistical Standards and Data Confidentiality Staff)
- "The CEDS [Common Education Data Standards] project is a U.S. national collaboration to develop voluntary, common data standards for a key set of education data elements to streamline the exchange, comparison, and understanding of data within and across P-20W (early learning through postsecondary and workforce) institutions and sectors."[a] (NCES Administrative Data Division)
- The Classification of Secondary School Courses and School Codes for the Exchange of Data facilitates schools' and districts' maintenance of secondary-level transcript data over time and transfer of those data among districts and states (NCES Statistical Standards and Data Confidentiality Staff).
- "The Classification of Instructional Programs (CIP) provides a taxonomic scheme that supports the accurate tracking and reporting of postsecondary fields of study and program completions activity."[b] It includes a crosswalk developed jointly by NCES and the Bureau of Labor Statistics of CIP program codes to the Standard Occupational Classification system. (NCES Administrative Data Division)

---

[a]https://adlnet.gov/research/working-groups/ [March 2022].
[b]https://nces.ed.gov/ipeds/cipcode/Default.aspx?y=56 [March 2022].

for NCES to achieve in the next 7 years. The National Academies were asked to consider recent trends and future priorities; to suggest changes to NCES's portfolio of activities and products, operations, staffing, and use of contractors; and to focus on NCES's statistical programs and not the assessment programs conducted by the NCES Assessments Division (i.e., the NAEP).[6]

In response to this request, the Committee on National Statistics appointed an interdisciplinary panel of experts to conduct the study. The panel included experts in education research, policy, and federal, state, and local government programs; as well as experts in statistics, data science, survey methods, data governance and infrastructure, and federal statistical policy. The panel drew heavily on the knowledge and experience of its members to develop a strategic approach that NCES could adopt to remain current and relevant in the face of societal changes.

To increase NCES's mission impact, the panel was first asked to review trends and developments in the use of survey data, administrative data, and other potential data sources; and to consider NCES's priorities, operations, staffing, size, and use of contractors. The panel was then to use this information to develop recommendations and key milestones to advance NCES to a future, high-impact state. This report prioritizes areas and activities for NCES to pursue, with recommendations for changes and expansions to NCES's statistical program areas, data collections, data governance, products, and distribution of resources (i.e., budget implications).

The full Statement of Task is shown in Box 1-4.

## INFORMATION GATHERING

To meet the scope of this charge, the panel gathered information broadly, holding eight public sessions to collect information from 23 speakers with stakeholder perspectives, from federal and state government, nonprofit and policy organizations, and academia. During this study, the panel solicited speakers and expert testimony across a wide range of topics. Education topics included higher education, adult literacy, elementary and secondary education, and early childhood education; the curriculum and instruction for mathematics, sciences, and language arts; child development and students with disabilities; career transitions; and student equity and civil rights issues in education. Speakers presented on trends and developments in

---

[6] IES concurrently commissioned two other studies from the National Academies. One addresses key strategic issues related to the NAEP program, including opportunities to contain costs and increase the use of technology. The second addresses the future of education research at IES, including critical problems for which new research is needed; new methods or approaches for conducting research; and new types of research training investments.

> **BOX 1-4**
> **Statement of Task**
>
> The National Academies of Sciences, Engineering, and Medicine will appoint an ad hoc panel to recommend the future portfolio of activities and products for the National Center for Education Statistics (NCES). As part of its fact finding, the panel will:
>
> 1. Review trends and developments in the use of survey data, administrative data, as well as other potential data sources;
> 2. Consider current and future priorities, operations, and staffing, including how contractors are used; and
> 3. Based on those developments, suggest any desirable changes in the NCES statistical program areas, data collections, data governance, and products.
>
> The panel will produce a final report that prioritizes areas and activities for NCES to pursue, as well as a vision for what NCES should aspire to be and how it should operate, including staffing, size, use of contractors, and implications for its budget. The report will also include recommendations for ways to increase the impact of educational statistics produced by NCES, and identify key milestones for NCES to work towards modernizing education statistics.

their use of survey data, administrative data, and other data sources. Some speakers informed a potential portfolio of activities by discussing their data infrastructure, governance, collections, and collaborations for data sharing, linkage, and insightful analytics. Others informed a potential portfolio of products, by sharing their high-priority analytic questions in education, data needs, and potential ways for NCES to add value.

NCES staff made multiple presentations to the panel to explain the Center's mission and organization, operations, staff, use of contractors, and budget, in addition to its survey and administrative data programs, stakeholder engagement and technical assistance, data governance, current programmatic priorities, and recent innovations and initiatives. The panel did not address NCES's assessment programs, which are discussed in a separate, concurrent National Academies report.

To learn more about NCES's role in ED's implementation of the Foundations for Evidence-Based Policymaking Act of 2018 (commonly referred to as the Evidence Act),[7] the panel heard from ED's chief statistical official (i.e., the NCES commissioner) and the chief evaluation officer, and received a statement from the chief data officer.

---

[7]Pub. L. 115-435. Available: https://www.congress.gov/bill/115th-congress/house-bill/4174.

Given the scope of the charge, the panel also reviewed over 300 documents and dozens of webpages. Documents included information about NCES's organization, budget, and performance, as well as processes, programs, and stakeholders. In addition, the panel asked NCES a series of questions over a period of several months, which the Center answered in writing.[8] The panel also considered advisory reports from the National Institute of Statistical Sciences, a workshop from the National Academy of Education, and editorials from the American Statistical Association. For signals on strategic direction and priorities, the panel considered NCES's authorizing laws and other mandates, executive orders and presidential memoranda, implementation guidance from OMB, ED's strategic plans since 2007, ED's Data Strategy (U.S. ED, 2020), and the Committee on National Statistics' (CNSTAT's) *Principles and Practices for a Federal Statistical Agency* (NASEM, 2021b).

The panel reviewed information on models of data infrastructure, forward-thinking SLDS, new data approaches to studying education, and general data modernization and methodology reports, including from CNSTAT. The panel also reviewed trend data on education topics, such as the demographic composition of students and the teaching workforce, students' disability status, subjects taught, online learning, and school context. The panel sought information about other federal agencies, particularly the PSAs, to serve as NCES's peers for comparison, examples, and best practices. Documents included the OMB publications on statistical programs from 2003 to 2020, as well as searches on PSAs' websites for products, programs, and processes. Finally, the panel deliberated over all evidence during 18 closed meetings.

## PANEL'S APPROACH TO THE CHARGE

The panel approached this task by asking what a national statistical agency for education would be and do if it were newly established today, with the same level of resources. This led to a full reimagining of how NCES could meet the growing demands for policy-relevant, education-related statistical analyses and data, focusing on equity and the importance of improving approaches to address the needs of changing demographics. The panel reenvisioned NCES's stakeholder engagement with key federal, state, and local decision makers and the compelling ideas and priorities that

---

[8]The questions and answers from NCES and IES are available on request from the project's Public Access File, along with the other unpublished documents provided by NCES and IES, speaker presentations, and testimony submitted to the panel. Many of the citations in the report are to NCES responses to specific questions from the panel. For access, contact the National Academies of Sciences, Engineering, and Medicine's Public Access Records Office, https://www8.nationalacademies.org/pa/information.aspx.

engagement could bring to the surface. Engagement could include establishing liaisons in each state to advance data infrastructure and products, encouraging the adoption of Common Education Data Standards, and providing the Center with feedback.

Importantly, NCES can harness opportunities created by rapidly changing technologies and policy developments. New technologies and data sources are readily available and continue to proliferate. Many agencies and organizations have strategically integrated multiple data sources to gain new insights into evolving needs.

The panel found many exciting examples of data-source integration. Federal agencies, including Statistics of Income (SOI), the Economic Research Service, and the National Center for Health Statistics have partnered with other federal agencies, state offices, and organizations to produce new knowledge. The Post-Secondary Employment Outcomes Program, a partnership between the U.S. Census Bureau and higher education systems in 17 states, is one example (U.S. Census Bureau, 2021d). Leading states, such as Massachusetts and Ohio, have partnered state offices across social domains (e.g., education, labor, and health and human services), leveraging their SLDS to understand student outcomes. Other states are partnering with each other for data exchange, such as the Western Interstate Commission for Higher Education and the Midwest Collaborative through the Coleridge Initiative.

Data linkages like these result in cutting-edge insights that integrate research and statistical analyses. A leading example is the work of Raj Chetty and colleagues, studying long-term income and earnings outcomes by blending SOI data with the Department of Housing and Urban Development's (HUD's) Moving to Opportunity randomized controlled trial data (Chetty et al., 2016). This study substantially increased the value of both SOI's and HUD's data, resulting in new information about HUD's housing voucher program that is pertinent to decision makers. A second example is the Multi-State Postsecondary Dashboard from the Coleridge Initiative (2022), designed by the states of Kentucky, Ohio, Tennessee, and Indiana, to show earnings and employment regionally, building on both state-specific unemployment insurance and higher education files (Midwest Collaborative, 2020).

This explosion of available data sources coincides with increased demand for actionable data to inform decisions at all levels. The Evidence Act solidified and validated the momentum building towards evidence-driven decision making. The 2021 Presidential Memorandum on Restoring Trust in Government Through Scientific Integrity and Evidence-Based Policymaking (Biden, 2021) has further bolstered the movement, as has the Executive Order on Advancing Racial Equity and Support for Underserved Communities through the Federal Government (Executive Order

13985, 2021), which explicitly emphasizes the need for disaggregated data for studying equity. This movement is not limited to federal agencies. State education agencies, local school districts, private schools, and institutions of higher education are focused on data describing student outcomes, equity, and effective methods, in addition to understanding how their policies affect outcomes. As consumers of education, students and their families are also increasingly seeking data, particularly regarding higher education and adult education. It is with this backdrop of dramatic social changes that the panel reimagines NCES as leading education statistics.

To address these trends in education and statistics, the 5 conclusions and 15 recommendations in this study report provide:

- A vision for what NCES should aspire to be, including roles and responsibilities;
- Methods for NCES to attain that vision, including key milestones;
- A process with goals and specific ideas for creating a future prioritized portfolio of products, including modernization of NCES's statistical program areas, primary data collections, and data-source acquisitions;
- A future portfolio of activities, including modernization of NCES's role in data governance and data facilitation;
- A process with goals and suggestions for how NCES can organize and operate, including staffing, size, use of contractors, and implications for its budget; and
- Specific ways to increase the impact of NCES's educational statistics.

The panel provides process recommendations for some aspects of the charge. While the panel developed and completed a process for evaluating data-content priorities (see Appendix C), the panel has insufficient information to recommend which specific data content should be prioritized or deprioritized. Making such a determination requires a rigorous process with full information on NCES's resources, the level of effort needed to produce content, the numbers of users and types of uses for each product or collection, and the long-term goals for building new operational infrastructure or leveraging existing data-collection processes. The panel provides a goal for prioritizing data content, a process for evaluating the priority level of various education topics, and specific content ideas, generated from the results of the panel's prioritization of topics based on limited information (see Chapter 3 and Appendix C).

The panel provides a potential process for modifying NCES's organization and staffing, with additional specific recommendations on use of contractors. The panel lacks the depth of information to make more specific recommendations on organizational structure, staffing level, and budget implications. The panel recommends that drivers for organizational and operational changes come from NCES's strategic goals and objectives. Similarly, the panel provides key milestone dates, but the timing of achieving other recommendations depends on the priorities in NCES's strategic and implementation plans. While NCES could begin work simultaneously on all but the organizational recommendations (see Chapter 5), the specific milestones and metrics cannot be determined before NCES's own prioritization of activities and products. Chapter 6 provides significant goalposts and relative milestones for making progress towards the recommendations.

## AUDIENCES FOR AND ORGANIZATION OF THE REPORT

This report is of interest to multiple audiences across the nation's education data stakeholders. First, the panel hopes that NCES leaders and personnel find this report helpful, inspiring, and motivating. Second, the panel wishes that IES and key stakeholders in ED take to heart recommendations for strong partnerships with NCES, to advance education evidence building and implementation of the Evidence Act. Third, this report may be of interest to data-holding agencies and organizations in the public and private sectors that may want to invest in and engage with NCES in data exchange for mutual benefit. Fourth, education researchers are key users of NCES data and partners in advancing the science of education. Fifth, policy makers and practitioners in state and local education agencies may use this report to learn about NCES's resources and to engage with the Center on potential products and services that would be useful and actionable. Sixth, this report is intended to be accessible to the public—both consumers of education programs and the general taxpaying public. To the extent that NCES is publicly funded, it is obligated to serve the interests of the American people. Finally, this report could serve as a useful template for other federal statistical agencies and units that want to broaden their impact, enhance their engagement, support evidence building, modernize their data sources, or otherwise act strategically. We hope this report serves all these audiences.

Chapter 2 discusses the vision and key recommendations necessary for NCES to meet its mission amid social, technological, and policy shifts and the immense opportunities they present; this chapter addresses the panel's vision for the future of NCES and reviews trends in the use of various data sources. Chapter 3 discusses data collection and acquisition in terms of topical priorities, such as equity in access and outcomes. It suggests ways for NCES to redirect efforts and resources towards high-value topics, to create a future portfolio of prioritized products and data collections for the Center's statistical programs. Chapter 4 presents recommendations for engaging with stakeholders and disseminating data and statistical products.

Examples and ideas are discussed, not only for obtaining feedback on the relevance and impact of products, but also for leveraging external resources, such as partnerships and grant-making power, to extend NCES's ability to serve the education data ecosystem. This chapter also addresses NCES's priorities for a future portfolio of activities, including data governance and data linkage to increase the value of NCES's data collections and acquisitions. Chapter 5 presents recommendations for NCES's operation as an agency, its organization, and how to use its contracting resources; this chapter addresses future operational priorities, including staffing, size, use of contractors, and budget implications. Chapter 6 summarizes the recommendations, all of which address ways to increase the impact of educational statistics produced by NCES. Key goalposts and relative milestones are provided.

Seven appendices contribute detailed information for the interested reader. Appendix A provides a glossary of terms and acronyms used in this report. Appendix B defines and describes a variety of relevant data sources. Appendix C describes the process and criteria for rating the importance or national value of assorted topics in education, as well as NCES's capacity to collect or acquire data on each topic. Appendix D provides a comparison of the federal statistical agencies on dimensions such as the number of FTEs and contractors, budget, and budget-to-FTE ratio. Appendix E provides information and metrics on IES and NCES product-review processes. Appendix F acknowledges speakers and people who submitted statements or other testimony. Appendix G provides biographical sketches of the panel.

# 2

# Rise Up to Meet 21st-Century Education Data Ecosystem Needs

The panel reimagines NCES as a leader in education statistics, evidence building, and data governance. The panel aspires for NCES to be in full control of how it meets its mission—operating strategically, anticipating environmental changes, and readily adapting to continue delivering high-value products and services. Finally, the panel envisions NCES as deeply engaged with stakeholders and a strong partner supporting evidence building within the Department of Education (ED).

## MEET THE MISSION IN A CHANGING SOCIAL CONTEXT

Three dramatic demographic and social changes have affected NCES's impact as a statistical agency. First, over the last few decades, the student population has grown more diverse in terms of race and ethnicity, sex and gender identity, disability status, and age. In parallel, the field of education has become more aware of the diversity of student needs and experiences, as well as the impact of institutions, instruction, and other factors on student outcomes and equity. The workforce and military are also experiencing rapidly changing training needs, as adults increasingly engage in continuing education or retraining. This has prompted practitioners, policy makers, and researchers to ask new questions, as advancing the field and understanding contemporary and emerging education issues require new types of information.

Second, recent decades have seen an explosion of data sources. Data production is no longer the sole province of a few large organizations. For example, more organizations and businesses are harnessing data collected while doing business (e.g., administrative data, commercial data). States have developed administrative data systems with the support of NCES, in part through the Statewide Longitudinal Data Systems (SLDS) Grant Program. Other data sources are produced on the internet or electronically and, with new technologies and methods, can be transformed into analyzable data (e.g., "scraped" data and natural language processing of text documents). These data sources have provided unique insights, such as the use of data from charter school websites to study school choice and educational stratification (Haber, 2021). However, NCES has done little to grasp the opportunities created by this rapidly changing data and technology environment.

Third, contemporary policy makers, practitioners, and other stakeholders hunger for relevant and timely evidence to inform understanding and decision making. The momentum of recent years has been codified in the Foundations for Evidence-Based Policymaking Act of 2018 (commonly referred to as the Evidence Act), which establishes the commissioner of NCES as the chief statistical official of ED, who is expected to work closely with the chief evaluation officer and chief data officer to build evidence. Thus, NCES has many stakeholders, including Congress, the President, ED, and other federal agencies, along with state and local education agencies, school districts, policy makers, nonprofit organizations, academic researchers, and, of course, students and their families. While NCES may serve some stakeholders, such as academic researchers, adequately, the Center does not understand or serve all audiences equally well. This lack of broad stakeholder engagement intensifies the effects of the other two changes in the social context: the needs of the education system and the availability of non-NCES data sources to inform issues.

NCES's relevance has declined simultaneously with these broad social changes. NCES has been seeking ways to stand out among all available data providers and to improve stakeholder engagement, with the long-term goal of making the Center's "website and its data summaries the first stop for questions about the U.S. education system for audiences of all backgrounds and experiences" (NISS, 2021a, p. 6). Multiple presenters gave testimony on cutting-edge data innovations and education evidence-building projects that do not involve NCES, but where the Center could serve a constructive role (Appendix F). Further, NCES's data products are often out of date upon release. For instance, data products released in late 2021 include 2-year-old provisional data on fiscal year 2019 revenues and expenditures for public school districts (NCES, 2021k), and a "First Look" product showing 3-year-old data on school year 2017–18 student financial aid (NCES, 2021a). Despite its declining relevance, over the last few decades NCES has advanced the field of education statistics with innovative data-collection approaches and rigorous statistical standards.

In studying the current situation, the panel's core findings drive all its recommendations:

- NCES lacks an agency-level strategic plan or other systematic way to prioritize high-value products and services.
- NCES has not kept up with the changing and expanding needs of its stakeholders.
- NCES is neither leading nor seizing opportunities presented by the recent explosion of administrative data and other data sources that could provide new analytic insights.
- NCES is often left out of important discussions within ED and has a weak voice in important national conversations about education data, statistics, and evidence building.

These findings are broadly similar to those of previous review panels (NISS, 2016; NASEM, 1986). This similarity indicates that NCES needs transformative rather than marginal change to make true progress on ongoing issues. The conditions are better than ever to take action. The director of the Institute of Education Sciences (IES) requested this study, demonstrating an interest and commitment to support a new vision for NCES. The Evidence Act is a recent mandate that highlights and supports the role of statistical agencies in developing and facilitating access to data for evidence building. Particularly in the last 5 years, decision makers at every level of government have exhibited an increasing demand for useful data and statistics to help inform decisions. In fact, most states have created a chief data officer role to support this new emphasis on using data. With the availability of alternative data sources, NCES can stand out as a leader, particularly on data standards and quality. Although the conditions are ripe, transformative change always requires substantial, thoughtfully directed investment. The panel recommends that:

- NCES develop a strong strategic plan to make difficult tradeoff decisions (Recommendation 2-1);
- ED and IES support and empower NCES to set its own priorities (Recommendation 2-2);
- ED, IES, and NCES maximize the Center's unique value for evidence building (Recommendation 2-3);
- NCES adapt to the changing world of education by increasing diversity and awareness of equity issues (Recommendation 2-4); and
- NCES expand data-acquisition strategies for new insights (Recommendations 2-5, 2-6).

These fundamental recommendations are discussed in further detail below (and additional recommendations are discussed in Chapters 3, 4, and 5). The panel recognizes that NCES is currently addressing some aspects of these recommendations and asks that NCES push further, to fully embody each recommendation. Since recent reports (e.g., NISS, 2016) may not have provided enough information to be actionable, the panel provides operational details to assist with implementation. The panel offers ideas and examples to illustrate implementation details, especially for projects conducted by other federal statistical agencies. The panel discusses its thoughts on strategic priorities, data products, services, and operations, yet understands that NCES needs to decide which options to adopt. Achieving these recommendations within NCES's constraints will require planning, will, and discipline. If NCES achieves these fundamental recommendations, the panel is confident that the Center will make substantial progress towards the vision we offer and could take the helm as a meaningful leader in the nation's education data ecosystem.

## DEVELOP A STRONG STRATEGIC PLAN TO MAKE TOUGH DECISIONS

To meet its mission effectively, any government agency needs to understand its identity and core values, so that it can establish priorities to guide decision making and operations. By clarifying tradeoffs and greater goals, strategic planning helps agencies be proactive when making difficult decisions. The north stars of strategic foresight and planning are especially necessary for navigating today's evolving environment, particularly when an agency's mission changes. Not only has the social environment for education statistics changed, but NCES's mission has also expanded in scope.

NCES's core mission is to collect, analyze, and report education information and statistics that are high quality, objective, timely, and useful to key stakeholders, including "practitioners, researchers, policymakers, and the public."[1] As a federal statistical agency, NCES has further roles and responsibilities to protect its data. Importantly, in January 2019, the Evidence Act substantially increased the roles and responsibilities of statistical agencies for evidence-building activities both within and outside the federal government, including assigning them a special role within their executive branch departments.[2] Despite this expanded mission, NCES does

---

[1] 20 U.S. Code § 9541(b). Available: https://www.law.cornell.edu/uscode/text/20/9541 [March 2022].

[2] 44 U.S. Code §§ 3581–3583 and 5 U.S. Code §§ 311–314. Available: https://www.law.cornell.edu/uscode/text/44/chapter-35/subchapter-III/part-D [March 2022], and https://www.law.cornell.edu/uscode/text/5/part-I/chapter-3/subchapter-II [March 2022].

not have an agency-level strategic plan to address this change in scope. In fact, to the panel's knowledge, NCES has not had a strategic plan in recent decades.[3]

The panel does not imply that NCES is uninterested in innovation or in achieving greater mission impact. In fact, NCES is constantly innovating to increase its relevance and impact. NCES has been highly engaged with ED's program offices and Office of the Chief Data Officer.[4] In 2021, NCES fielded its timely School Pulse Panel, to understand the effects of the COVID-19 pandemic on education (NCES, 2021l). Further, NCES has engaged the National Institute of Statistical Sciences on dozens of advisory reports to improve specific programs, processes, or products (NISS, 2021b). However, these studies do not always connect to each other, resulting in a piecemeal approach to agency improvement.

NCES lacks an articulated prioritization plan for its products, services, and related improvements that is governed by a set of principles guiding the deployment of resources to achieve a vision. While the National Assessment of Educational Progress has conducted strategic planning, in recent decades NCES has lacked a routinized, holistic strategic-planning process covering the entire Center—its organization, operations, and programs.[5] The lack of such a strategy makes it challenging to understand how new or old initiatives contribute to the Center's mission and which products and activities to prioritize or discontinue. Thus, the panel's strongest recommendation presents NCES with a method for making operational and tactical decisions resulting in an effective organization that can adapt to changing needs in education and changes in data used for evidence-based decision making.

> **RECOMMENDATION 2-1:** To direct its future, NCES should develop and implement a bold strategic plan that incentivizes innovation and creative partnerships and that will produce relevant, timely, and reliable statistical products to assist education decision makers at every level of government. NCES should develop and begin implementation of the plan within 1 year of the release of this report.

Disciplined strategic planning will help NCES focus on high-value products and services so that it can achieve maximum effectiveness and mission impact. The panel recognizes the challenges of deprioritizing products and services, especially since every product has at least one stakeholder. NCES cannot be all things to all stakeholders and instead should focus on areas in which it can add the most value. Planning requires investment and

---

[3] NCES response to question from the panel, p. 56.
[4] NCES response to question from the panel, pp. 50–51.
[5] NCES response to question from the panel, pp. 56–57.

implementation but can result in the efficient and effective use of limited resources. Other reports have also advised NCES to develop "strategic prioritization" (NISS, 2016, p. 11) or "a conceptual framework for organizing its program and for setting priorities in light of available resources" (NASEM, 1986, p. 27). Given that this recommendation has been repeated across decades, the panel cannot overstate the importance of NCES investing time to develop its own strategic plan for raising the Center's overall effectiveness. With NCES's new leadership, the Center has an exciting opportunity to control its future and discover new ways to create mission impact.

Such forethought is even more critical for a small agency with limited resources, many stakeholders, a disproportionately large administrative burden, and unfunded mandates. The Bureau of Transportation Statistics is an example of a small federal statistical agency with an up-to-date, short strategic plan (Bureau of Transportation Statistics, 2022; see Box 5-1) (see Appendix D for an overview of federal statistical agencies and their comparability to NCES). NCES can do the same.

Strategic planning is not a compliance exercise. To paraphrase President Eisenhower, plans may be worthless, but planning is essential. NCES can take this opportunity to self-assess, determine its identity, values, and goals, and decide how to move forward in the 21st century. The panel advises NCES to include many of the recommendations in this report. However, even if NCES disagrees with these recommendations, the key point is that NCES should perform strategic planning for the Center's own sake. Once NCES institutionalizes its strategic intentions throughout the staff and implements its priorities with discipline, the Center will be proactive and nimble rather than being so "responsive to immediate demands"[6] that its long-term progress and overall effectiveness are diminished.

Visioning, strategic planning, and implementation are time-consuming investments. It is difficult to set aside time for these processes amidst urgent production needs. Given that NCES is a small agency with vast contract resources, the panel suggests that NCES engage a consultant to assist with the most intensive strategic plan-related activities, such as holding leadership, staff, management (i.e., ED and IES), and stakeholder interviews; facilitating conversations; reviewing internal documents and data; and reviewing guidance on law, federal policies, and ED strategic plans. The consultant could integrate the information into a proposed plan and contribute ideas gleaned from experiences with other agencies. Engaging a consultant could substantially reduce staff time needed for strategic planning.

Whether or not a consultant is utilized, NCES would benefit from conversations about what the Center is, its strengths and weaknesses, what

---

[6]NCES response to question from the panel, p. 56.

it wants to be, what its opportunities are, and how it wants to bring the most value to the education data ecosystem (e.g., state and local education agencies). The panel has a strong vision for NCES, but NCES will need to either adopt that vision or determine its own vision. Then NCES will need to examine the structures and resources that exist to support the vision, like the SLDS, and consider how to apply such forward-thinking models elsewhere. The panel recommends that NCES also utilize internal information to examine and understand the challenges that prevent it from fully achieving its vision. Given the marginal observable improvements in response to past review reports, the panel advises NCES to thoroughly investigate its operations and organizational structure, to find and fix the systemic and infrastructure issues. Finding a strategic path to overcome these obstacles can only occur through difficult and frank conversations, which can also increase employee engagement and empower employees to improve the organization.

After NCES determines its vision and the strategic plan begins to congeal, the NCES commissioner should engage IES and ED leadership to ensure buy-in and alignment of the strategic goals of ED and IES and to advocate for sufficient resources. The National Board for Education Sciences[7] could provide external backing for NCES's strategic priorities. Ensuring support from above is critical to the success of NCES's strategic plan.

The strategic plan would benefit from an accompanying implementation plan that is executed with discipline. The implementation plan could include specific areas of prioritization and deprioritization, time lines, a plan for stakeholder engagement, steps for developing and studying new data sources, and an agency-level analytic agenda. The panel recommends that NCES invest effort and time into infusing the strategic and implementation plans throughout the Center. Organizational transformation requires repeated messaging, along with openness to feedback from all levels of staff. The panel suggests that NCES's leadership team take the time to endorse the plan and engage the entire staff, to gain buy-in on its implementation. For the strategic plan to succeed, NCES staff at all levels must be aligned to that plan and use it to guide all decisions.

The strategic plan should be a comprehensive package describing priorities, gaps, and goals and explaining how new tools and technologies can be leveraged to build forward-looking operations and infrastructure to achieve those goals. It would also be useful for the plan to indicate the level of effort needed to manifest goals and objectives. Some programs and initiatives may need to be divided into stages. The panel recommends that NCES's strategic plan address each of the seven areas considered in

---

[7] See 20 U.S. Code § 9516(b) – National Board for Education Sciences, Duties. Available: https://www.law.cornell.edu/uscode/text/20/9516 [March 2022].

the sections that follow, where the first four are especially critical to the Center's transformation.

### Incentivize Innovation, Experimentation, and Continuous Learning

The panel advises that NCES's strategic plan incentivize innovation, experimentation, and continuous learning throughout all facets of the Center. Innovation frequently results from challenges, and NCES often faces challenges that are largely beyond the Center's control, such as changing presidential priorities. Experimentation (i.e., trying something new) is a key component of adaptability and resilience in the face of challenges. Moreover, continual improvement and innovation is a fundamental principle of federal statistical agencies (NASEM, 2021b). The panel suggests that NCES's strategic plan address ways that the Center can encourage and incentivize an organizational culture of innovation and experimentation.

Throughout the strategic-planning process and beyond, NCES leadership and staff will need to actively, consciously, and explicitly inhabit the culture-of-innovation mindset to draft an actionable, thoughtful strategic plan. Without this mindset, NCES will be unable to thoroughly examine challenges, set priorities, or imagine new, effective solutions.

The strategic plan would benefit from practices that support a culture of innovation. For instance, a program or competition to improve processes, methods, and cost-effectiveness could encourage staff to improve their functions within the Center (NASEM, 2021b, Practice 3). In the panel's opinion, not only should NCES hire staff with cutting-edge skills, but it should invest in the ongoing development, retention, and professional advancement of its staff, through activities such as presenting at professional conferences and engaging with research fellows (NASEM, 2021b, Practice 4). NCES's seasoned and dedicated staff[8] deserve to use and extend their knowledge and skills beyond just managing contracts. Moreover, retaining institutional knowledge is important for the long-term, efficient, and effective operation of any federal agency.[9] NCES can develop an active research program that includes substantive analyses, as well as studies evaluating new methods, operations, and the fitness of alternative data sources (NASEM, 2021b, Practice 5). Finally, to accelerate the shift to a culture of innovation, the panel advises that NCES build its staff capabilities while forging strong partnerships with other components of IES, especially the new data sciences

---

[8] About 83 percent of NCES's staff have advanced degrees. Nearly half of the staff have earned doctorates (PhD or EdD) and another 34 percent have master's degrees or are doctoral candidates (i.e., "all but dissertation"). NCES response to question from the panel, p. 46.

[9] For the private-sector benefits of retaining in-house professional services, see Ding et al., (2020).

> **BOX 2-1**
> **Encouraging and Incentivizing a Culture**
> **of Experimentation and Innovation**
>
> Experimentation is necessary for innovation. Here are some ideas for organizational experimentation, rooted in best practices at other federal statistical agencies:
>
> - Challenge the staff, partners, and stakeholders to win an *experimentation or operational efficiency award*.[a] Communicate the award through both traditional and new channels.
> - Hire or contract an internal *communications specialist*, dedicated solely to NCES, for at least a year. Charge the communications specialist with adding new communication channels to learn from and communicate effectively with incoming cohorts of respondents, staff, and decision makers. Revisit the arrangement yearly and adjust accordingly.
> - Use an existing model of making experimental products available to the public.[b]
>
> ---
>
> [a]See example: Callen, J. (2016). The U.S. Census Bureau: Driving cost savings and operational efficiency by leveraging employee creativity and innovation. Guest blog post, July 13. U. S. Department of Commerce. https://2014-2017.commerce.gov/news/blog/2016/07/us-census-bureau-driving-cost-savings-and-operational-efficiency-leveraging.html [March 2022].
> [b]U.S. Census Bureau. (2021g). What are Experimental Data Products? Washington, DC: U.S. Census Bureau. Available: https://www.census.gov/data/experimental-data-products.html [March 2022].

unit in the Office of the Director,[10] innovative agencies, and other external experts, to identify best practices and pilot new, potentially transformative approaches (NASEM, 2021b, Practice 7). Additional ideas are provided in Box 2-1.

### Expand NCES's Presence in Education Evidence Building

The Evidence Act has expanded NCES's mission in the absence of additional funding. In the panel's opinion, NCES's strategic plan should address how it wants to meet this expanded role and its relationship with other offices in the IES and ED, including its goals for data acquisition, sharing, provisioning data access for evidence-building purposes, and evidence

---

[10]NCES document provided to the panel, "Relevant excerpts from the approved December 2021 IES reorganization justification."

building itself. A recommendation and specific ideas for NCES, IES, and ED to advance evidence building are discussed later in this chapter.

### Increase Diversity and Equity Awareness to Maintain Relevant Data Content

The panel recommends that NCES's strategic plan address how the Center can proactively consider diversity, equity, inclusion, and accessibility (DEIA) (see Appendix A), to better reflect the experiences of the increasingly diverse student population and other contemporary education trends in its data designs, processing, and analyses. The plan should consider ways to embed DEIA awareness into other aspects of NCES's work, including stakeholder engagement, hiring, retention, and work culture. A recommendation and specific ideas for leveraging DEIA awareness into stakeholder-relevant products and activities are discussed later in this chapter.

### Explore Data Sources to Support Analytic Insights

The panel recommends that NCES's strategic plan incorporate pathways and priorities for exploring new data sources, particularly administrative data, for use in statistical products and services. NCES's Administrative Data Division is already exploring data sources including the Social Security Administration's Master Earnings File and the Internal Revenue Service's Education Tax Credit and Income Data, among others.[11] The strategic plan would benefit from prioritizing datasets and partnerships to pursue and including some intermediate goals, objectives, and milestones. Recommendations for exploring, evaluating, and incorporating alternative data sources into NCES's statistical programs are discussed later in this chapter.

### Prioritize Data Content, Services, and Activities

The panel recommends that NCES's strategic plan describe its priorities, to establish the guiding principles and criteria for keeping, changing, and removing data content, services, or activities (NASEM, 2021b, Practice 6). Currently, NCES appears to add stakeholder content in the absence of overarching strategic principles. Sometimes a product can supersede the mission of an agency, particularly if it is the status quo, has been collected for years, and has an invested user base. While this "autopilot" mode may be good for efficiency, it is not necessarily good for maintaining the Center's effectiveness. NCES is encouraged to review every collection and product routinely (e.g., every few years), to check that the content still fits

---

[11]NCES response to question from the panel, pp. 28–29.

the Center's strategic goals, remains relevant to the social context, and continues to provide valid measures of the changing population.

NCES would benefit from eliminating content that is outdated, no longer useful, or that has lost value. If outdated content is federally mandated, NCES is encouraged to request Congress to change the statute. A recommendation and detailed suggestions on content priorities and guiding principles for prioritization are presented in Chapter 3 and Appendix C.

### Expand Creative Partnerships and Engagement with Stakeholders

In the panel's opinion, NCES's strategic plan should include goals, objectives, and milestones for establishing creative partnerships and increasing engagement with stakeholders. Areas for NCES to consider include creating engagement feedback loops; expanding its role enabling data access, particularly for state and local education agencies; and improving dissemination, focusing on accessibility and usefulness. Chapter 4 discusses several recommendations and suggests pathways to expand NCES's creative partnerships and engagement.

### Align Operations and the Organization to Support NCES's Mission and Vision

In the panel's opinion, NCES's strategic plan should address aligning its organization and operations to meet or make progress towards its new vision and strategic goals. Unlike the other areas addressed by the strategic plan, which NCES can begin to work on during the planning process, the organizational aspects are driven by the content of the plan and need to be considered later in strategic planning and during implementation planning. Achieving the vision and mission requires resources, effective operations, and a plan for maximizing use of resources. Determining the level of effort needed to meet specific strategic goals is a difficult process and NCES will need to make hard decisions, given the net loss of 33 percent of its statistical staff along with flatlined program appropriations since FY 2010, which have resulted in a loss of contract buying power when adjusted for cost inflation (see Figures D-1 and D-2). Based on these recent trends, the panel assumes no increase in resources for NCES's statistical programs.

NCES can conduct its strategic planning to achieve its vision and strategic goals using the Center's existing level of resources. The strategic plan should address how NCES attracts, develops, and retains staff with the skills needed to achieve the Center's vision (Chapter 2, above). The strategic plan can address objectives to leverage external resources as a force multiplier (see Chapters 4 and 5) and can indicate where internal resources may be needed to leverage external resources. The Panel suggests that, during planning, NCES consider the type of organizational structure (perhaps combined with a specific program-management model) that would best support progress towards its vision, given the Center's existing resources. Chapter 5 discusses recommendations and ideas for transforming NCES's current organizational alignment, staffing, and use of contractors and other resources to support the strategic plan.

If NCES is disciplined in its approach to strategic planning, prioritization, and implementation, its workload will decrease as lower-value activities, collections, and products are eliminated. Identifying new data sources or technologies that gain efficiencies and ending low-value and costly collections and contracts will free up program appropriations that NCES can strategically redirect to high-value uses.[12] However, all else equal, NCES's vision could be achieved more quickly with a higher number of strategically deployed full-time equivalent employees (FTEs), as well as more program funding (see Box 2-2).

## SUPPORT AND EMPOWER NCES TO SET ITS OWN PRIORITIES

While NCES is primarily responsible for its own strategic planning and priorities, IES and its subunits and other offices in ED need to fully support and collaborate with NCES for the Center to achieve its vision. Currently, NCES "does not have complete control over its priorities" and "has limited discretionary flexibility when setting priorities for its activities."[13,14] This is due, in part, to the many constraints NCES operates under, along with its dependence on IES and ED for support services and resources. IES's director and commissioners will need to determine the appropriate distribution of resources between NCES and other centers. In such discussions, NCES needs to be clear on its goals and its progress towards them, the value added from achieving the goals, and its resource needs. IES may also need to advocate for NCES to the secretary of education and to Congress. Overall, for NCES to successfully manifest its visioning, strategic planning, and implementation, ED and IES need to fully support their NCES colleagues.

---

[12]All staff are paid indirectly through an allocation of the ED's Salaries and Expenses appropriation. The organization of staff into statistics and assessment functions does not align with program appropriations, which funds contracts. NCES response to question from the panel, pp. 3–10.

[13]NCES response to question from the panel, p. 55.

[14]"Each Commissioner, except the Commissioner for Education Statistics, shall carry out such Commissioner's duties under this title under the supervision and subject to the approval of the Director [of IES]." 20 U.S. Code § 9517(d). Available: https://www.govinfo.gov/content/pkg/USCODE-2015-title20/pdf/USCODE-2015-title20-chap76-subchapI.pdf [March 2022].

> **BOX 2-2**
> **Using the Strategic Plan to Increase Resources**
>
> Overall, a successful strategic plan will ensure that NCES can build the in-house knowledge to best use its FTEs, thus supporting justifications for future FTE increases. Further, as NCES makes progress on its strategic goals, its value to the nation will hopefully become so clear that Congress and others will increase the Center's staffing levels to scale successful programs and implement effective business models in other areas.
>
> **Example 1: Strategic Communications with Congress and the Secretary**
> The Energy Information Administration (EIA) is a moderately sized statistical agency in the Department of Energy, whose position is comparable to that of IES within ED. In the mid-2000s, EIA hired a senior communication advisor in the administrator's office to help with communications with the Department of Energy and Congress. The employee had strong expertise in energy economics and policy, had worked as a congressional staffer, and understood how to engage Congress. EIA's then-administrator thought this helped EIA substantially in terms of increasing its budget for programs and staffing.
>
> **Example 2: Opportunities for Recognition**
> Professional awards can provide external recognition of the value of NCES's work, which can be used to justify increases in resources. Such awards have the further benefit of increasing staff morale. Some relevant awards include the Roger Herriot Award for Innovation in Federal Statistics, from the Washington Statistical Society, for dedication to the issues of measurement, efficiency of data collection, and use of statistical data for policy analysis;[a] the Links Lecture Award, from the American Statistical Association, for the advancement of official statistics in the areas of data linkage, privacy, researcher access, and reproducibility of results;[b] and other awards recognizing achievements in statistics, given by the American Statistical Association.[c] A small group of people within NCES who actively consider and prepare nomination packages for deserving Center staff could help increase visibility and improve staff morale.
>
> ---
>
> [a]Washington Statistical Society: Roger Herriott Award. Available: http://washstat.org/awards/herriot.html [March 2022].
> [b]American Statistical Association: Links Lecture Award. Available: https://www.amstat.org/ASA/Your-Career/Awards/Links-Lecture-Award.aspx [March 2022].
> [c]American Statistical Association: Awards and Scholarships. Available: https://www.amstat.org/ASA/Your-Career/Awards-and-Scholarships.aspx [March 2022].

RECOMMENDATION 2-2: The secretary of education, director of the Institute of Education Sciences, and NCES commissioner should collaborate to ensure that NCES is independent in developing, producing, and disseminating statistics.

Together, ED, IES, and NCES are should revisit and update internal policies and procedures to ensure that NCES can operate under the well-established principle and directives stating that federal statistical agencies must be independent from undue external influence in developing, producing, and disseminating statistics (NASEM, 2021b, Principle 4; U.S. OMB, 2008, 2014b). The Office of Management and Budget's Statistical Policy Directive No. 1 outlines the fundamental responsibilities of federal statistical agencies to conduct "objective, credible statistics" (U.S. OMB, 2014b, p. 71610). Statistical Policy Directive No. 4 provides requirements on the release and dissemination of statistical products, by requiring federal statistical agencies to "adhere to data quality standards through *equitable, policy-neutral*, and timely release of information to the public [emphasis added]" (U.S. OMB, 2008, p. 12624).

The National Academies of Sciences, Engineering, and Medicine (NASEM, 2021b) describe multiple practices that support this principle of independence. It is particularly important for NCES to have the authority to make decisions on the scope, content, and frequency of its data and statistics; to select and promote professional staff based on skills and knowledge; and to "be able to meet with members of Congress, congressional staff, and the public to discuss the agency's statistics, resources, and staffing levels" (NASEM, 2021b, Practice 2, p. 54). NCES should also have highly qualified staff[15] to make decisions on data content based on scientific and professional considerations, and to gather input on data needs from stakeholders and ED policy and program officials (NASEM, 2021b, Practices 3, 4, 5, 9). The panel encourages ED, IES, and NCES to act as partners to ensure NCES operates with its full authority as a federal statistical agency, which includes serving its stakeholders in IES and across ED.

## MAXIMIZE NCES'S UNIQUE VALUE FOR EVIDENCE BUILDING

It is an exciting time for evidence-based decision making, particularly in the federal government. The momentum towards data- and evidence-driven decision making was substantially boosted by the Evidence Act, enacted in January 2019, and was further enhanced by Presidential Memoranda and Executive Orders issued in 2021 (e.g., Biden, 2021; Executive Order 13994, 2021; Executive Order 14000, 2021). Laws and other mandates advance the development of, access to, and statistical use of data and evidence for strategic and operational decision making by governments at any level,

---

[15] Qualifications needed include expertise in data analysis and science (defined broadly), sampling statistics, assessment development, survey methodology, and statistics. NCES response to question from the panel, p. 18.

researchers, and others.[16] The Evidence Act and related mandates place statistical agencies at the heart of evidence-based decision making. Through these mandates, NCES has great opportunities to make an enormous impact on evidence building and to establish new avenues for retaining stakeholder relevance.

The Evidence Act, particularly in Title III, effectively expands NCES's mission by giving statistical agencies new authorities, duties, roles, and relationships for evidence building. The Evidence Act directs all departments to make government data open by default and to share administrative and other data with statistical agencies, upon request, for developing evidence.[17] The statistical agencies are, in turn, directed to expand secure access to data (i.e., restricted, acquired, linked, etc.) for evidence building, while protecting privacy.[18] As leaders of the Interagency Council on Statistical Policy, the statistical agencies supported OMB in developing a Standard Application Process (SAP), by which federal "agencies, the Congressional Budget Office, state, local, and Tribal governments, researchers, and other individuals, as appropriate, may apply to access the data assets… for purposes of developing evidence."[19] The SAP highlights the mandate of statistical agencies to work with each other and with external stakeholders as data-access facilitators and governors.

The Evidence Act further establishes the NCES commissioner as the chief statistical official (SO) of ED, directed to work closely with other senior executive officers to advance ED's development and use of scientifically rigorous evidence. Thus, the Evidence Act further bolsters the relationship between NCES and two of its most important stakeholders: IES and ED. The SO is mandated to work in partnership with the chief data officer (CDO), the chief evaluation officer (EO), and other chief executive officers to further evidence-based decision making based on high-quality data, statistics, and other evidence to inform ED's "learning agenda," or strategic agenda of analytic questions.

Because of the importance of federal statistical agencies in the movement towards data-driven decisions, the panel feels that NCES and the SO

---

[16] 44 U.S. Code § 3583 – Application to access data assets for developing evidence. Available: https://www.law.cornell.edu/uscode/text/44/3583 [March 2022].

[17] 44 U.S. Code § 3581 – Presumption of accessibility for statistical agencies and units. Available: https://www.law.cornell.edu/uscode/text/44/3581 [March 2022].

[18] 44 U.S. Code § 3582 – Expanding secure access to CIPSEA data assets. Available: https://www.law.cornell.edu/uscode/text/44/3582 [March 2022].

[19] 44 U.S. Code § 3583. Available: https://www.law.cornell.edu/uscode/text/44/3583 [March 2022]. See also U.S. OMB (2022) and "Standard Application Process (SAP) Policy." Available: https://www.federalregister.gov/documents/2022/01/14/2022-00620/the-interagency-council-on-statistical-policys-recommendation-for-a-standard-application-process-sap and https://www.regulations.gov/document/OMB-2022-0001-0001 [March 2022].

can and should be central in ED's implementation of these mandates. NCES provides technical assistance to many offices within ED, by:

- Managing ED's ED*Facts* collection;
- Collecting the Civil Rights Data Collection for the Office for Civil Rights;
- Supporting the Office of Postsecondary Education and the Office of Career, Technical, and Adult Education with data updates or collections;
- Supporting effective implementation of the College Scorecard with ED's Office of the Chief Data Officer in the Office of Planning, Evaluation and Policy Development, to ensure stronger alignment between the Scorecard and NCES tools that use Integrated Postsecondary Education Data System data;
- Serving on ED's Data Governance Board Steering Committee; and
- Supporting ED in creating an ED Disclosure Review Board.[20]

Given the new mandates, however, NCES's support of ED offices goes well beyond technical assistance. NCES has significant new roles and responsibilities and, in the panel's opinion, should be more proactive in leading ED on acquiring and managing data for evidence building in a privacy-protected manner. For instance, ED's Data Strategy mentions IES only once, to note that IES provides "localized" access to restricted data (an NCES function), then dismisses the role of IES since a departmentwide solution is needed (U.S. ED, 2020, p. 15). Regarding the current division of labor for evidence building, ED's EO notes that, when obtaining data for evidence building, he would expect the SO to facilitate access to data at a statistical agency, but would turn to the CDO to obtain data in general.[21] ED's EO notes that the first serious test of the Evidence Act's presumption of accessibility of data for evidence building will arise when a roadblock is encountered when seeking external data, and how that challenge is overcome. This suggests that ED has not fully considered how to leverage NCES's new mandates to acquire data and facilitate data access for evidence building.

In recent years, NCES has rarely interacted directly with the secretary of education's office and, further, most contact pertains to the National Assessment of Educational Progress, not the statistical programs. In the past, direct, in-person communication with the secretary and the ED chief

---

[20]NCES response to question from the panel, p. 14.

[21]Matthew Soldner, "Comments for the National Academies' Panel on a Vision and Roadmap for Education Statistics," presentation to the National Academies of Sciences, Engineering, and Medicine, August 2, 2021.

of staff occurred fairly often and was especially true during the release of high-profile reports such as the Nation's Report Card. The NCES commissioner and associate commissioner conducted embargoed briefings for the secretary and senior ED staff in the secretary's conference room or office.[22] Given the strong momentum behind evidence-based decision making, coupled with NCES's newly mandated role, now is the time for NCES to reassert itself.

> RECOMMENDATION 2-3: The secretary of education, director of the Institute of Education Sciences, and NCES commissioner should immediately take actions to enable the NCES commissioner to most effectively fulfill the responsibilities of the statistical official delineated in the Foundations for Evidence-Based Policymaking Act of 2018 and to support evidence-building needs across the Department of Education.

Evidence-based decision making is the purview of the entire ED, and NCES is mandated to serve a particular role. Implementation of the Evidence Act is relatively nascent[23] and this moment presents an opportunity for the secretary of education, the director of IES, and the commissioner of NCES to establish a vision and value proposition for NCES's role in ED's evidence-building activities. Together, the three entities are encouraged to determine how to best maximize the unique value NCES brings as a producer of credible and relevant evidence, a recognized leader in data standards, and a data-access facilitator.

The secretary, director, and commissioner should update all related policies, divisions of responsibilities, processes, and practices to empower the NCES commissioner and leadership team to most effectively carry out the SO's duties. Further, NCES needs to both affirm its authority as central to ED data and evidence conversations and back up that authority by making meaningful contributions in partnership. In the past, NCES has successfully positioned itself as an essential voice in ED conversations informing education policy.[24] NCES is fully capable of returning to this stature if its entire leadership team aligns with a visionary strategy for engagement on evidence building.

NCES can ensure its standing by contributing its expertise as an important information source as decisions are being made. Combined, the Evidence Act and the Information Quality Act (U.S. OMB, 2019b, 2004, 2019a) direct government agencies to make decisions based on high-quality

---

[22] NCES response to question from the panel, p. 51.
[23] At the time of writing, OMB had not issued guidance for the implementation of Titles II and III of the Evidence Act.
[24] NCES response to question from the panel, p. 51.

evidence. To enable this, the SO needs to collaborate with the CDO and EO in ED-wide data governance, overseeing the use of data in ED's evidence building, developing learning agendas, and identifying data needed to inform learning-agenda questions. NCES adds value to the partnership in many areas, including semantic data-standards expertise, privacy-protection practices, rigorous methods for developing data and evidence, determinations of data relevance and fitness for use or purpose, the authority to ask for and receive government data, and the duty and expertise to provide data access to a broad range of stakeholders for evidence-building purposes. The CDO emphasizes ED's data, data governance, inventories, formats, and open data. The EO has purview over the analytic educational and operational questions needed to advance understanding in a strategic way (U.S. OMB, 2019b). The SO connects the CDO and the EO by turning data into high-quality information fit to inform policy and decision making.

The Evidence Act presents evidence goals to be fulfilled and encourages departments to use new techniques, share and analyze appropriate data, and form new partnerships. NCES and IES can fulfill this need, which can be filled by no one else in ED. The panel urges the centers within IES, which currently appear siloed, to come together to build stronger partnerships, grasp these enormous opportunities, and lead ED's evidence building and research.

The National Center for Education Research awards grants for education research (IES, 2021a). The National Center for Education Evaluation and Regional Assistance, whose commissioner is ED's EO, leads ED's learning agenda (strategy) and related evidence building and evaluation. NCES collects data, acquires[25] secondary data, provides access to restricted data, evaluates fitness for use, and has rigorous quality standards for its statistics and analyses. By working together strategically, the centers could explore the important ideas and current questions in education, determine how to rigorously test research hypotheses, and decide how to operationalize new learnings in education data and statistics, with each center contributing its unique expertise. Further, the centers could collaboratively decide the priority datasets NCES should acquire and link (e.g., long-term outcomes on experimental data), determine which data could be made public, and provide restricted data access to external researchers as a force multiplier for answering learning-agenda questions (see Chapter 4).

Similarly, NCES and the other IES centers could collaborate with the CDO to determine data needs, data standards, open-data formats, and product-release timing that would be of high value to ED and its stakeholders. NCES needs to constantly fuel evidence building by identifying

---

[25]In this report, data collection means primary data collection, whereas data acquisition includes acquiring secondary data in addition to primary data.

opportunities to use various data sources, establishing standards and techniques for increasing data quality, ensuring data are fit for purpose, and protecting privacy. NCES's leadership is essential for the effectiveness of ED's Data Governance Board and ED Data Strategy (led by ED's CDO), as well as ED's Disclosure Review Board (led by ED's chief privacy officer or senior agency official for privacy). The Evidence Act has immense potential for advancing education data and analytics. This innovative era presents great opportunity for NCES to increase its relevance and expand its impact. The Evidence Act is best implemented with full and equal partnerships between the SO, EO, CDO, and other key officials in ED. It will take vision, strategic planning, and collaboration between NCES, IES, and ED to fully leverage the evidence-building power of the SO role.

## ADAPT TO THE CHANGING WORLD OF EDUCATION: INCREASE DIVERSITY AND AWARENESS OF EQUITY ISSUES

NCES's mission includes relevance and usefulness to key stakeholders, which means that the Center's data and statistics must address contemporary issues in education. In recent decades, the nation has become more diverse in terms of race/ethnicity, sex, gender identity, students with disabilities, and sexual orientation. For instance, children (ages 5–17) shifted from 75 percent white and 9 percent Hispanic in 1980 to 50 percent white and 26 percent Hispanic in 2020 (Figure 2-1) (NCES, 2021e, Table 101.20). The diversity in public school systems is more pronounced, projected to be 44 percent white and 28 percent Hispanic by 2029 (NCES, 2021e, Table 203.50). Broadly similar trends are seen in higher education, with increasing racial and ethnic diversity and more women than men attending university or higher (NCES, 2021e, Table 306.10).

Disability status is another important trend among students. The number of students ages 3–21 who received services under the Individuals with Disabilities Education Act nearly doubled, from 3.7 million in the 1976–77 school year to 7.3 million in the 2019–20 school year (NCES, 2021e, Table 204.30). The types of disabilities children face have also changed. In 1976–77, the top three conditions were speech or language impairment, intellectual disability, and specific learning disability, accounting for 83 percent of all disabilities (Figure 2-2). By 2019–20, the conditions diversified as more became known and diagnosed. For example, autism now makes up 11 percent of student disabilities. As these conditions, and how they affect learning, become better understood, the data on these students, their needs, and their teachers will also need to adapt.

Other education trends are broader. For instance, more students are attending college and beyond than in the past, nearly doubling from 11 million in 1976 to 20 million in 2019, with a peak of 21 million in 2010

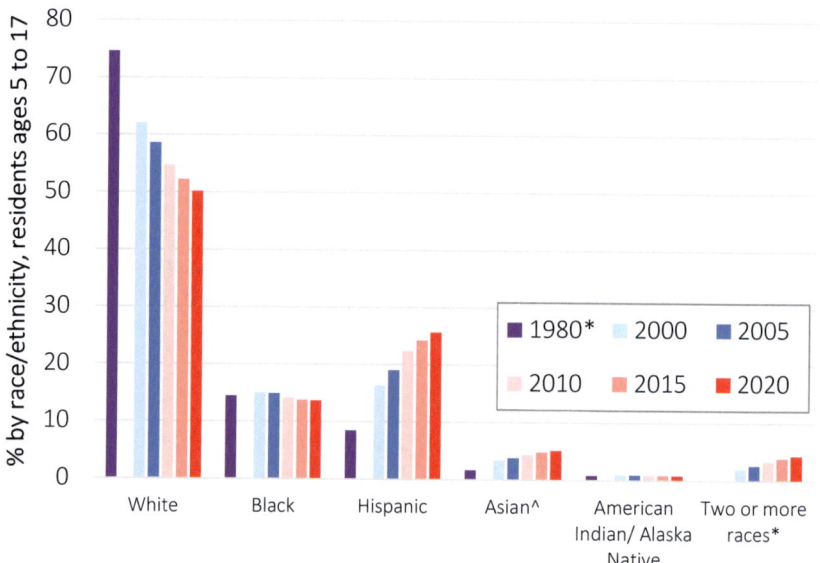

**FIGURE 2-1** School-age populations grew more racially and ethnically diverse from 1980 to 2020.
SOURCE: NCES, 2021e, Table 101.20 Estimates of resident population, by race/ethnicity and age group: selected years, 1980–2020.
NOTES: *Data on persons of two or more races were collected beginning in 2000. Direct comparability of the data (other than Hispanic) for years prior to 2000 with the data for 2000 and later years is limited by the extent to which people reporting more than one race in later years were reported in specific race groups in earlier years.
^For 1980, Pacific Islanders were included under Asian. For years 2000 and later, Pacific Islanders comprised 0.2 percent of the population and are not shown.
Resident population includes civilian population and armed forces personnel residing within the United States; it excludes armed forces personnel residing overseas. Race categories exclude persons of Hispanic ethnicity. Detail may not sum to totals because of rounding. Some data have been revised from previously published figures. Population estimates as of July 1 of the indicated reference year.

(NCES, 2021e, Table 306.10). More students from economically and racially disadvantaged groups are aspiring to higher education, but have lower enrollment and college completion rates than their peers (Backes et al., 2015; NCES, 2021e, Tables 306.10, 326.10, 326.15; NCES, 2022a). The number of adults obtaining education has increased as well, and this pattern is closely tied to equity issues (Grodsky et al., 2021). The numbers of institution types, sites, and modes of instruction have increased, with home schooling, internet elementary and secondary schools, online

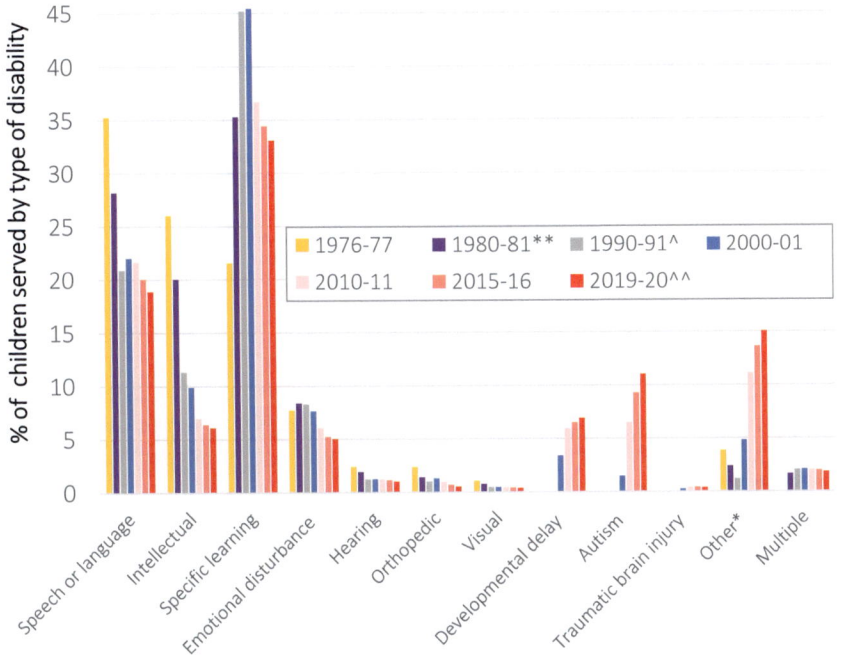

**FIGURE 2-2** The conditions of students with disabilities grew more diverse from 1976 to 2019.
SOURCE: NCES, 2021e, Table 204.30. Children 3 to 21 years old served under Individuals with Disabilities Education Act (IDEA), Part B, by type of disability: Selected years, 1976–77 through 2019–20.
NOTES: *Other health impairments include limited strength, vitality, or alertness due to chronic or acute health problems such as heart condition, tuberculosis, rheumatic fever, nephritis, asthma, sickle cell anemia, hemophilia, epilepsy, lead poisoning, leukemia, or diabetes.
**For 1980–81, data are not shown for deaf-blindness. This category comprises 0.1 percent in 1980–81 and rounds to zero percent for all years afterwards.
^For 1990–91, preschool children are not included in the counts by disability condition but are separately counted at 8.3 percent (not shown). For other years, preschool children are included in the counts by disability condition.
^^Data in 2019–20 include 2015–16 data for 3–21-year-olds in Wisconsin because 2019–20 data were not available for children served in Wisconsin. Data by disability type for Iowa are imputed based on the reported 2018–19 percentage distribution by disability type applied to the 2019–20 total number of children served in Iowa.

*continued*

**FIGURE 2-2** *Continued*

Prior to October 1994, children and youth with disabilities were served under Chapter 1 of the Elementary and Secondary Education Act (ESEA) as well as under the Individuals with Disabilities Education Act, Part B. Data reported in this table for years prior to 1994–95 include children ages 0–21 served under Chapter 1 of ESEA. Data are for the 50 states and the District of Columbia only. Increases since 1987–88 are due in part to new legislation enacted in fall 1986, which added a mandate for public school special education services for 3- to 5-year-old children with disabilities. Detail may not sum to totals because of rounding.

---

colleges, and training provided by noncolleges now existing alongside public, private, and charter schools, many of which also offer online learning. Program and curriculum content have changed, as have instructional styles. Schools, teachers, policy makers, and others want to understand how these trends factor into student outcomes, and data are needed for this purpose.

There are many more dimensions of population diversity that have become nationally significant in recent decades (e.g., rural and urban status, sexual orientation and gender identity, immigrant students, Native American students). The aspects of education that are policy relevant will continue to change. Data are needed to understand these changes and NCES currently measures some of these dimensions. However, data collections designed in the past are no longer adequate to understand today's diverse students and educational contexts, so understanding the current education situation requires an adjusted approach to data collection and products. We have seen no evidence that the rate of change in the social context is lessening. Thus, it is likely that the education context will continue to evolve, requiring NCES to continue to revisit its approach to remain effective. The challenge here, for any statistical agency, is that providing relevant and useful information on current education conditions requires addressing deeply embedded equity issues throughout the data life cycle, such as underlying assumptions in questionnaire design or imputation algorithms. Addressing such issues will require the sustained involvement of relevant communities, to decide which questions need to be informed by data collections, which data to collect, how to collect those data, how to organize and present data, and how to make meaning from data. While this process obviously requires engagement with the stakeholders that represent the diversity in American education, the process is likely to be facilitated by staff and contractors who also represent that diversity (Executive Order 14035, 2021). Thus, we suggest that NCES address diversity in the composition of internal and contractor staff, assess the inclusiveness of the Center's internal cultures, and ensure data products accurately reflect contemporary communities as society evolves.

**RECOMMENDATION 2-4: NCES should proactively embed diversity, equity, inclusion, and accessibility in all areas of its work and organization, to adapt and serve contemporary communities of the changing world of education.**

The panel takes a strong view that becoming adaptable and staying relevant to stakeholders relies on NCES addressing DEIA issues (see Appendix A). A key principle for federal statistical agencies is to provide "objective, accurate, and timely information that is relevant to important public policy issues" (NASEM, 2021b, p. 27). To maintain relevance, statistical agencies should:

- Regularly evaluate their data collections to ensure relevance (NASEM, 2021b, Practice 6);
- Have staff analyze the agencies' own data (NASEM, 2021b, Practice 5); and
- Work with data users and other stakeholders to keep abreast of evolving data needs (NASEM, 2021b, Practice 9).

DEIA issues and disparities have long been relevant topics in education policy, with the groups of interest changing over time. Grappling with DEIA issues is critical for NCES's relevance and ability to adhere to these practices by:

- Ensuring validity of survey instruments and measurements, not only for measures of demographic characteristics, segregation indices, or other direct measures of population diversity and equity, but also for any concept or measure that may be interpreted differently over time and context by respondents with varying lived experiences (Box 2-3);
- Ensuring that data processing and analyses accurately reflect the diverse perspectives and lived experiences of today's students and education workforce rather than reiterating historical and systemic assumptions, emphases, and absences in the data; and
- Deepening engagement with a broadly diverse group of stakeholders to understand their needs for data content, data products, and statistical information, to include equity (Box 2-3).

NCES has made notable efforts in some aspects of DEIA. For instance, the Center produces data and analyses on groups that have been historically disadvantaged, such as reports disaggregating by race and ethnicity (NCES, 2018, 2020, 2021j). Not only is this type of information an important aspect of measuring diversity and equity, but all federal agencies

> **BOX 2-3**
> **Why Does DEIA Thinking Matter for**
> **Data Design and Collection?**
>
> To create studies and survey questions that accurately reflect people's experiences and understanding of the world, issues of diversity, equity, inclusion, and accessibility must be considered.
>
> **Example 1: Measuring the Concept of The Family**
> Which relatives matter for a child's education? The nuclear family model dominant in certain cultures asserts that a child's mother and father are the most important influencers. What about cultures that connect children to more extended kin? What do researchers and survey methodologists miss by unreflectively assuming the nuclear family model when collecting and reporting data on families and children?
>
> **Example 2: Mutual Benefits**
> A diverse set of scientists produced the COVID-19 vaccine, and outreach to diverse communities would benefit from the help of scientists from historically marginalized groups in promoting the safety and efficacy of the vaccine. Similarly, involving a diverse set of scientists in data design and collection may help the legitimacy of these efforts and increase the public's acceptance of many NCES products. Increasing diversity in these ways could improve response rates while also supporting communities.

have also been directed to disaggregate data by groups that have been "historically underserved, marginalized, and adversely affected by persistent poverty and inequality" to advance equity (Executive Order 13985, 2021, p. 7009). However, the panel believes that proactively embedding DEIA considerations involves much more than disaggregating analyses by groups, such as race and ethnicity or disability status. To adequately measure and address DEIA issues in its data, NCES needs to embed DEIA considerations throughout the Center's workforce, not only via staffing decisions, but by creating a culture of proactive thinking about DEIA issues throughout its data designs, data acquisitions, standards, analyses, stakeholder engagement, relationship building, partnerships, and contracts.

The panel recommends infusing DEIA thinking throughout the data life cycle, starting with data design (e.g., standards setting, questionnaire design, construction of measures and indicators) to ensure validity and measure diverse populations as we now understand them. Creating new categories to measure important, socially recognized characteristics and issues, such as NCES's new collections on student acceptance groups based on gender identity and sexual orientation, is a critical part of addressing changing populations, but it is still insufficient (Hansen, 2019). At a minimum, NCES should revisit questionnaire language to ensure it is bias-free (American Psychological Association, 2021). To go deeper, accurate measurement of demographic characteristics and life outcomes is founded on understanding people, lived experiences, and social issues. Survey instruments and questions reflect those who write them and need to be reevaluated and revised if they are no longer appropriate for understanding today's students (NASEM, 2021b, Practice 6). NCES can better understand students by thinking more deeply about and being exposed to the ever-evolving diversity of lived experiences and how those experiences relate to student outcomes in education and other areas of life. Such understanding is a critical first step in the data life cycle and will help NCES to stay relevant as the social context evolves. From this improved understanding follows the need to continually ensure validity and accuracy of data and statistical activities in a changing world.

In the panel's judgment, NCES should adjust its approach to questionnaire and study design to understand diverse student perspectives and to decide which information is relevant to that understanding (Box 2-3). Importantly, NCES needs to involve members of these diverse communities in the initial stages of data design, using qualitative methods such as focus groups and cognitive interviewing. This process begins with members learning how they see themselves, how their lived experiences may lead to interpretations of data collections that are different than those assumed or intended by researchers, and which life outcomes (e.g., earnings, health, social connectedness) are meaningful to them. Survey methodologists may not be intentionally biased, yet they often reflect unique lived experiences; even survey methodologists from diverse backgrounds may not fully understand all dimensions of diversity. Thus, it is crucial to learn from diverse communities to understand and measure concepts and social issues in ways that resonate with them. Survey questions and instruments need to be redesigned and cognitively tested to ensure the validity of the measures.[26]

NCES should further examine, from an ethical standpoint, the dynamic between researchers and survey participants—especially participants in historically disadvantaged communities—to consider how the data-collection interaction can be beneficial to respondents and their communities. For example, every time a teacher completes a survey, an opportunity is created for NCES to support that teacher and demonstrate the Center's commitment to advancing equity. When designing data collection operations,

---

[26] For examples of testing measurement of sexual orientation and gender identity, see NASEM (2022) and Ellis et al. (2018). For race and ethnicity concept measurement, see studies at https://www.census.gov/about/our-research/race-ethnicity.html [March 2022]. For an example of testing concepts other than dimensions of diversity, see de la Cruz (2011) and Jensen (2013).

NCES is encouraged to seek out members of diverse communities to help survey operations experts understand how to approach various populations and provide benefits to survey respondents (NASEM, 2018; NISS, 2020). This approach of reciprocity often improves survey response rates as well (Box 2-3). Engaging members of the public at this stage of design requires expertise in qualitative methods. NCES can collaborate with other centers in IES or can contract out this work, but permanent NCES staff need to be closely involved to assure that knowledge is retained and to develop a culture of DEIA awareness that can be applied to other areas of NCES's work.

Instilling DEIA thinking into analytics includes not only responsible interpretation of statistics and analyses, but also consideration of data processing and other structural features underlying the analysis. For instance, imputation methods during data processing or recodes for an analysis can result in statistically biased estimates. Care should be taken to use ethical and empathetic methods for imputing data, particularly for studies on equity for historically disadvantaged groups (Brown et al., 2021). Machine learning and predictive algorithms typically reinforce outcomes based on assumptions, emphases, and absences from historical social systems. Critical assessment of analytic questions is also important—rephrasing a research question can help a study to be more equitable and inclusive. For example, asking "Are school systems ready to educate local 5-year-olds?" instead of "Are 5-year-old children ready to attend school?" shifts the burden of readiness from individuals and families to schools.[27] In terms of product content and presentation, the panel believes that NCES should ensure analysts use inclusive language in all products, and that the use of colors and icons, and the ordering of information in data visualizations, supports inclusivity.[28] The panel suggests that NCES also think deeply about DEIA considerations in terms of data-dissemination formats (particularly for people with disabilities), as well as the general usability of all its products, tools, and services. The panel presents specific ideas and suggestions for data content, engagement, and dissemination in Chapters 3 and 4.

NCES can also benefit from infusing DEIA throughout the organization: its staffing decisions, its culture, and its partners. By engaging with diverse stakeholders (e.g., schools with diverse student populations) and relationship building (e.g., advisory forums, scholars of color), NCES can better propel change in the education data ecosystem. From its stakeholders, NCES can learn what types of data it should be collecting and can gain an understanding of stakeholders' needs for data, data products, and

---

[27] Gabriela Katz, "StriveTogether Cradle to Career Network," presentation to the National Academies of Sciences, Engineering, and Medicine, August 6, 2021.

[28] See examples: https://content-guide.18f.gov/our-style/inclusive-language/, https://nasaa-arts.org/nasaa_research/inclusive-language-guide/, and Schwabish and Feng (2021) [March 2022].

statistical information. This will help NCES to deliver useful and relevant products to its stakeholders. In granting licenses for data access, NCES can solicit projects from scholars of color. This would both support DEIA values and expose NCES staff to new insights and perspectives on diverse populations.

NCES should instill a culture of DEIA throughout its staff, rather than burdening only staff from diverse backgrounds. NCES leadership should demonstrate DEIA values by taking actions, such as those suggested above, to grapple with DEIA issues. NCES leadership should consider diversity in hiring and staffing decisions, and the Center is encouraged to develop an inclusive work environment to attract and retain staff from diverse communities. NCES can also put DEIA on individuals' performance plans, particularly those of managers, to support an environment that provides a sense of belonging to all staff. Supportive actions can include seeking opportunities to ally with staff, calling on those who are having difficulty speaking up,[29] and promoting a DEIA perspective in all aspects of NCES's work. A work environment that proactively seeks to understand diversity and equity issues supports a better understanding of study populations, higher productivity (Carr et al., 2019), and greater in-house innovation (Rock and Grant, 2016; Rock et al., 2016). These benefits reinforce the importance of staff obtaining and retaining knowledge from engaging with diverse communities during data design. Further, since many of NCES's data collections are conducted by contractors, it is essential that DEIA issues are integrated into its contracts. Finally, to maximize impact, NCES can leverage its SLDS grants to encourage thoughtfulness around DEIA issues at the state and local levels.

Embedding DEIA considerations throughout its work, relationships, and organization will help NCES to anticipate evolving needs. NCES is currently performing some of this work, however, the panel recommends that the Center critically consider all aspects of its programs, to determine how to infuse DEIA thinking and actions that will advance NCES as an equitable government agency. Following its strategic plan, NCES can then determine when and how to change its products and services to maintain the Center's usefulness and relevance.

## EXPAND DATA-ACQUISITION STRATEGIES FOR NEW INSIGHTS

The education data ecosystem envisioned by the panel will incorporate data from three categories: probability sample surveys (traditionally used by many federal statistical agencies, including NCES), administrative

---

[29]For examples, see: https://adurolife.com/blog/employee-well-being/how-to-create-a-sense-of-belonging-in-the-workplace/ [March 2022].

records data (which have always been important to NCES and are growing in importance within the government data ecosystem[30]), and new and emerging data sources. The number of new data sources is huge, diverse, and growing, and includes commercial data available for purchase from private vendors (e.g., household panel data, scanner data from businesses); transactional data (e.g., credit card purchases, job openings); social media and networking data; archival data and video recordings (e.g., NCES's Trends in International Mathematics and Science Study data); and internet documents, webpages, and videos that can be harvested, "scraped," or processed with natural language processing to create an analytic database.

Each of the three data categories has pros and cons. Sample surveys provide representative population estimates with quantifiable accuracy and can deliver a rich variety of information. However, they are expensive, and it is becoming more difficult to gain the cooperation of respondents. Administrative records data often have little incremental cost, since they were previously collected for another purpose, and they may contain complete records from a selected population of interest, for example, participants in a specific program. However, administrative data can have systematic biases in coverage. Available data may not contain the precise measurements of interest or may not be fit for use (having been collected for another purpose), may have variable quality, and may be difficult to access. Often, statistical agencies must invest in data cleaning and standardization, which adds to the cost. New and emerging data sources are highly diverse. Many potential sources have the advantages of timeliness, granularity, ease of access, and low cost. Disadvantages include lack of representation, lack of quantifiable accuracy and, in some cases, a lack of mature methodological analysis tools (see Appendix B for details on data sources).

Statistical agencies have been experimenting with the use of administrative records and alternative data sources and have found that, when taken together and carefully integrated, the three sources—surveys, administrative records, and new and emerging sources—can significantly enhance information content, timeliness, and granularity of information systems. Likewise, new data sources may enrich education research by providing data that are unavailable via surveys or administrative data. These emerging data sources present enormous opportunities for NCES to advance evidence building.

**RECOMMENDATION 2-5: To improve its efficiency, timeliness, and relevance, NCES should continually explore alternative data sources**

---

[30]There has been a strong push in recent years for federal agencies to use administrative data for statistical purposes, including building evidence for decision making and evaluation of government programs, as evidenced by OMB guidance (U.S. OMB, 2014a) and the passage of the Evidence Act.

for potential use in data and statistical products, conduct studies on the quality of these sources and their fitness for use, and expand responsible access to data from multiple sources and linkage tools. Testing and adoption of new data-science methods for harnessing alternative data should be done in collaboration with other federal statistical agencies, as well as with other components of the Institute of Education Sciences that are actively exploring ways to strengthen the impact of these techniques.

The panel strongly advises that data source exploration and expansion be a part of NCES's strategic plan. The panel understands that it takes time to study the quality and usefulness of alternative data sources. It takes additional planning and time to understand the potential benefits and costs, integrate alternative data sources into existing operations and products, conduct bridge studies (such as those successfully performed by the National Assessment of Educational Progress program) to evaluate shifting measures and ensure continuity, and assess the privacy implications. Ideally, acquiring more data sources will grow NCES's community of users, as demand for responsible access to blended data increases. NCES should use parts of its strategic plan (e.g., those covering data content priorities and engagement) to guide a phased plan to prioritize development of specific data sources and use of their content.

Many other federal, state, and local agencies, along with other organizations, are taking advantage of data linkage and blending to conduct innovative analytics and to create experimental products that may eventually become operational. With strategic alignment and engagement, NCES can do the same. NCES can also create tools to combine its data more easily with users' data sources. For example, NCES already produces public school catchment geographic areas and could enhance their use by incorporating new data and geographic linkage keys. Chapter 4 provides detailed recommendations and suggestions. NCES can conduct ongoing data development to operate more efficiently, cost-effectively, and with higher impact.

> **RECOMMENDATION 2-6:** For primary collections, NCES should modernize standard language on consent and planned usage, to permit secure secondary uses that enable high-quality follow-up studies, such as through privacy-protected linkages with other data sources.

In anticipation of data linkage, NCES should reconsider the consent language and planned usage for all primary collections, to support ongoing uses for statistical activities. An extreme example is the National Education Longitudinal Study of 1988, in which participants were expressly promised they would not receive additional follow-up contacts from NCES.[31] This prohibits NCES from recontacting respondents to request consent for uses other than the originally stated purposes. Modernized consent language could ask respondents to allow secondary uses and linkages, could ask for recontact for future requests, or could establish other levels of permission, depending on the respondent population. The panel suggests that NCES look to federal statistical agencies for best practices when drafting statements regarding privacy of survey respondents' data and its potential uses. NCES is also encouraged to work with potential respondents to learn how to design appropriate consent language.

For data linkage, the panel recommends that NCES ask ED's Office of General Counsel for a modernized interpretation of what is possible within existing laws regarding personally identifiable information (PII) and the holding of a national-level population dataset.[32] For instance, NCES could ask whether it can hold a state or other subnational administrative dataset, with or without PII, or a national sample of administrative data from the states. The panel urges NCES to anticipate demand for data linkage by directing its contractors, who collect and hold PII from NCES's primary collections, to deposit PII linkage keys with partner federal statistical agencies such as the U.S. Census Bureau. Examples of federal partnerships are discussed in Chapter 4.

---

[31] NCES response to question from the panel, p. 33.
[32] For details, see 20 U.S. Code § 9572 – Prohibitions, and 20 U.S. Code § 1015c – Database of student information prohibited. Available: https://www.law.cornell.edu/uscode/text/20/9572 and https://www.law.cornell.edu/uscode/text/20/1015c [March 2022].

# 3

# Prioritize Topics, Data Content, and Statistical Information to Maintain Relevance

This chapter describes a process that NCES can pursue to review its current and future priorities and to determine desirable changes in its data collections and products, illustrated through examples. The panel believes that making such choices now would be premature, and that these choices are best made by NCES as part of its strategic-planning process. The strategic plan and its implementation plan should also allow for changes over time to accommodate changing priorities or to meet immediate special needs. Information availability also changes over time, and the optimal approach for collecting data today may differ from the optimal approach 5 years from now.

This chapter also elaborates on the important high-value topics in education, discussing the data-content needs and areas in which NCES can advance those topics. While survey research has been NCES's standard approach to data collection, some of these needs might best be met through administrative data and linkages to other data sources. Using such resources could limit respondent burden, possibly improve data quality, and maximize NCES's effectiveness in this time of limited financial resources.

## PRIORITIZING TOPICS

To determine topics to be given the highest priority, the panel first gathered information from stakeholders (see Appendix F and Chapter 1). The panel created a list of over 100 pertinent education topics and rated all topics based on predetermined criteria, by first and most critically examining the importance or value of the topic, and then examining the level of effort, or whether NCES could make progress on the topic (see Appendix C).

Topics were assigned a yes/no determination for all criteria. No attempt was made to assert equal value for the 19 criteria; however, the number of criteria satisfied can serve as a rough measure of the importance and/or feasibility of the topic. About half (48%) of the topics satisfied 8 or more of the 10 criteria with regard to importance, reflecting a broadly based need for many types of data. Many of the topics were interrelated; for example, there were multiple topics related to measuring equity.

The prioritization process was created to address NCES's limited resources, which may necessitate hard choices going forward. A high rating in the panel's prioritizing process reflects a broad consensus that a topic is important and satisfies multiple needs. However, NCES will need to consider its entire package of data products, which may lead to different conclusions than generated by the individual rankings. For example, NCES may discover duplication in its data products, even those of high importance, or a topic may appear low in importance but satisfy a key need. Decisions to keep or drop a data product should be made by NCES, ideally assisted by a consulting group, and based on NCES's strategic plan.

The panel evaluated topics in terms of enduring priority—that is, topics that have been important and will continue to be important for the next 7 years. Thus, the presence of a COVID-19 learning gap received a relatively low rating (meeting 3 of the 10 criteria on importance) compared with more encompassing topics like equity, access, and technology. This does not mean that NCES should not collect information on timely topics like COVID-19. In fact, the panel views the NCES School Pulse Panel on COVID-19 as an excellent example of innovation and flexibility that needs to be more widely incorporated. NCES's strategic plan should systematize decision making and prioritization of work while incorporating enough flexibility to adapt to sudden changes in strategic priorities, such as those posed by the COVID-19 pandemic.

## ALIGN ACQUIRED DATA CONTENT WITH HIGH-PRIORITY TOPICS AND QUESTIONS

NCES performs, and has performed, a wide variety of data collections, ranging from relatively small surveys on highly specific topics (e.g., through the now discontinued Fast Response Survey System [FRSS] and the current School Pulse Panel) to large systems such as the National Assessment of Education Progress (NAEP), which includes surveys of principals, teachers, and students, along with assessments of student knowledge and skills, and which has expanded to support state-level estimates.

Some of NCES's surveys have recently been discontinued due to the lack of staffing (e.g., FRSS and the School Survey on Crime and Safety [SSOCS]). NCES will continue to face hard choices about which data collections to keep and which to drop, and these choices need to be based on the strategic plan.

> RECOMMENDATION 3-1: NCES should conduct a top-to-bottom review of its data-acquisition activities, to prioritize topics most relevant to understanding contemporary education, and to discontinue activities that are disproportionately costly and burdensome relative to their value.

### Prioritize Equity and Access Issues

The related concepts of equity, access to education, and opportunity to learn stand out in importance. Issues relating to equity are major news topics, important to federal, state, and local policy makers, and a major research focus. Inequality precludes full use of our nation's human resources and negatively affects societal cohesion. Measures related to equity stood out among the 112 topic areas reviewed by the panel, with multiple measures satisfying all 10 criteria of importance: socioeconomic status, urban/rural/suburban location, race/ethnicity data, gender, English proficiency, mobility, disability, and "professional and academic areas in which Blacks are underrepresented."[1]

This section delves into issues relating to equity to illustrate how NCES might broadly review its measures to better align them with its priorities. This exercise also illustrates how reorganization within NCES could be beneficial; as we note elsewhere, NCES's current structure is compartmentalized based on the primary data source or focus of individual surveys. We discuss organizational structure later in this report, and different structures have distinct strengths and weaknesses. Still, creating a comprehensive structure to review topics such as equity might help to facilitate increased collaboration across the surveys to, for example, share experiences in utilizing new data sources or addressing particular research topics. There is a need for a comprehensive examination of how the Center's surveys address each topic area, helping to ensure that all surveys are compliant (or that noncompliance is intentional). By contrast, an organizational structure focused on the primary data source of individual surveys may leave important topics unaddressed or inconsistently handled.

Studies of equity require multiple types of measures: demographic measures, to identify groups that are of interest; process or implementation

---

[1] This topic is defined in law and does not mean that other underrepresented groups are unimportant. See 20 U.S. Code, Part B – Strengthening Historically Black Colleges and Universities, § 1061 Definitions. Available: https://www.law.cornell.edu/uscode/text/20/1061 [March 2022].

measures, to determine whether groups are treated differently; and outcome measures, to examine whether groups experience different outcomes.[2] NCES's current strengths lie in measuring demographics and outcomes.

- Demographic data: It is routine for NCES surveys to contain basic demographic characteristics such as race/ethnicity and sex, and sometimes to include disability status and socioeconomic characteristics such as education levels and household income or poverty status.[3] Further, the Common Core of Data (CCD) and Integrated Postsecondary Education Data System (IPEDS) measure demographic distributions within schools, districts, and higher education institutions. NCES might consider expanding its data collections to include other dimensions of inequality addressed by federal laws, which include national origin, sexual orientation, and gender identity. However, such data are considered more personal and intrusive, and may be harder to collect. Reactions to such unequal treatment may be easier to collect without requiring the assignment of labels to individuals.
- Outcome data: NCES also has multiple outcome measures, including assessments of students' knowledge and skills (measured in NAEP and several longitudinal surveys), student retention, and degree attainment.[4] Note that measures of outcomes are broader

---

[2] Another way of categorizing equity measures is as outcomes versus access, as in NASEM (2019a). This report uses slightly different categories because: (1) often there is value in having basic demographic information without a specific research question in mind, especially in public-use data files that are meant to support multiple research uses; and (2) some types of educational processes, such as imposing disciplinary actions, do not fit well as either outcomes or access. Access might be measured either through basic demographic measures (e.g., whether schools differ in their race/ethnicity compositions) or process (e.g., whether schools use tracking).

[3] Income or poverty status is one of the most difficult characteristics to measure because such information is considered highly personal and confidential. Some surveys collect income levels using broad categories, making the request less intrusive. Often, eligibility for free or reduced-price lunches or school Title I status are used as surrogate measures of poverty levels, but participation in the free lunch program is lower for secondary-school students, making the measure less reliable at that level. At the postsecondary level, participation in Pell Grants is often used as an indicator of financial need, but students who are eligible may choose not to apply, and students' levels of financial need may vary across colleges. The National Postsecondary Student Aid Study collects the most complete financial information, with finances as a primary focus. The National Education Longitudinal Study of 1988 and earlier studies also collected a household items index. Household items also can be used as a measure of cultural capital, which is another potentially important factor in education. The Education Longitudinal Study of 2002 asked for total family income using 13 categories.

[4] NCES assessments are not discussed in detail here because they are being addressed in a separate study. However, they are relevant for creating a picture of the kinds of data needed and currently collected.

than just final outcomes, and include disparities in academic readiness, self-regulation and attention skills, engagement in school, and performance in coursework (NASEM, 2019a). NCES also supports the Statewide Longitudinal Data Systems (SLDS) Grant Program through grants and performs annual surveys to monitor SLDS's progress. SLDS contains both demographic and outcome data. The Program for the International Assessment of Adult Competencies (PIAAC)[5] is both a source of data on the success of the education system with regard to literacy and a measure of need, particularly with regard to immigrant populations. Measuring outcomes is often difficult without longitudinal follow-up, and following up with students, especially after they leave college, can be difficult. A snapshot of one time point will lack data on later outcomes, such as graduation and job attainment.

- Implementation data: Measuring whether the education process is applied equitably is a significant weak point, but some data are available. Implementation data are often interrelated with issues of access, such as whether there are disparities in access to effective teaching, enrollment in rigorous coursework, and high-quality academic supports. Data from CCD and IPEDS can be used to examine whether students are unequally distributed across schools and colleges in terms of their demographic characteristics. Transcript data can be used to determine whether specific groups of students tend to follow different courses of study. The Parent and Family Involvement Survey collects data on parent involvement and school choice. NCES developed the Department of Education (ED) School Climate Surveys as survey instruments that schools, districts, and states can use to monitor school climate. Though the data do not belong to NCES, they could possibly be systematized to produce process information. Process data are difficult to collect because the process of interest may vary from one study to another and may consist of intangibles that are difficult to measure or are not routinely measured. There may also be questions about the accuracy of reporting, particularly for data viewed as either damaging or self-serving. Still, some types of data on school or district policies are relevant, such as whether a school uses tracking to separate high-achieving and low-achieving students. NCES has inconsistently collected data on tracking (e.g., in the 2017–2018 but not the 2020–2021 National Teacher and Principal Survey).

---

[5] After a prepublication version of the report was provided to NCES, the program name was corrected throughout the document to reflect the Center's current vehicle for collecting information on literacy.

One way to expand data collection in this area is to collect subjective data. For example, do students (or staff) perceive that they are treated unequally based on their groups? How do students decide which courses to take or which careers to pursue? Other types of process data may be available from school or district data. Data on disciplinary actions (such as suspensions and expulsions) might be considered process data or outcome data, depending on research goals. NCES also reports on, but does not collect, data from the Campus Safety and Security Survey, conducted by the Office of Postsecondary Education within ED. These are aggregate data at the institution or campus level and might be considered partial measures of the campus environment.

The types of equity data needed depend on the application. Data sources such as CCD, SLDS, and IPEDS are valuable due to their comprehensive coverage. They can be used to determine the distribution of various demographic groups in schools and colleges, to create statistical or purposive samples for surveys or other research designs, or they can be merged with other types of data to add key equity data. Relating equity data to specific topics of interest, such as student achievement or literacy, is another application. NCES has several surveys of this type, including NAEP, Education Longitudinal Study, PIAAC, and SSOCS, though other surveys could be appropriate depending on the analytic goal. Finally, one might consider creating a data source specifically focused on equity. Such a source might explore attitudes towards equity (including both self-perception and attitudes towards others) and experiences relating to equity within the educational environment.

Data can also be classified as objective, record-based data; other objective data; or subjective data. Some researchers prefer one data type over another, but each type has advantages and disadvantages.

- Objective, record-based data include attendance records, health records, course transcript data, and other administrative data. Record-based data may not be in electronic format, and even when they are, the data may be divided among multiple databases and with varying formats, even within a single school or district. There is a common perception that electronic data can be readily processed, but considerable work may be required to format and prepare data before they are ready for analysis, and records may not contain all the data that are needed (e.g., because the person maintaining the data may have different uses for it than a researcher does). One role for NCES could be to promote standardization of both which data are stored and how record data are maintained, so that data may be more easily shared and processed.

- Other types of objective data are not record based. These might include school policies such as those regarding disciplinary actions. Some of these data might be available electronically, perhaps as posts on a school website, but not stored in databases or in a format that can be readily analyzed statistically. The technological tools for web scraping and data mining are progressing rapidly and may ultimately provide a useful means for collecting and analyzing web-based data. However, it may be less expensive and more reliable to collect such data through a survey using statistical sampling.
- Subjective data are often dismissed as less reliable but may be the only source of certain data. There are also situations in which subjective data are directly useful. For example, many incidents of unequal treatment will never be reported on official databases, and self-reports can augment data available on databases. Further, even if self-reports are incomplete or reflect misperceptions on the part of the person reporting unequal treatment, the perception may itself be a matter of interest.

SLDS is a tremendous resource supported and monitored by NCES, though the Center is not involved in data collection or maintenance. The Common Education Data Standards program is critical in setting standards for state data systems and could be a vehicle through which NCES could lead on equity-related efforts, by helping states collect more disaggregated data on race/ethnicity, gender identity, and other data on populations of interest. Additional types of data could be used to address equity issues. U.S. states and local governments have the primary responsibility for elementary and secondary education, so they, not the federal government, are often the best source of program data. However, the Elementary and Secondary Education Act (especially Title I) and the Individuals with Disabilities Education Act involve the federal government in elementary and secondary education, and the Higher Education Act (especially Titles III and IV) involves the federal government in postsecondary education, so federal program data could be a rich resource. NCES might also contribute by setting standards for school/district/college databases, in terms of contents and definitions. Even if the standards are voluntary, producers and purchasers of database software might view the standards as an important target which, over time, will increase the shareability of data.

## Collecting Data on All Levels of Education

Data covering all levels of education (early childhood, elementary and secondary, higher education, and adult education) are necessary for a complete picture of the educational process, and for understanding how various parts are interrelated.[6] Generally, NCES has been strongest when measuring traditional education and at traditional ages, but a longer and more comprehensive time frame is needed. A student's difficulty at one educational level may result in continuing or greater difficulties at higher levels and may lead to the need for greater compensatory strategies in later years. For example, postsecondary education is increasingly involved in remedial or developmental education. To fully measure the impact of education, it is also helpful to measure posteducation outcomes such as employment and income.

The panel finds that topics in early childhood education are particularly important, such as access to early childhood education and state and local agencies' early childhood school readiness activities. In 2001, NCES conducted the Early Childhood Longitudinal Study (ECLS) with a birth cohort, but more recent ECLS cohorts have started with kindergarten, leaving a data gap for younger children.[7] NCES also studies early childhood through the National Household Education Survey (NHES). Research on early childhood is challenging because much of early childhood falls outside of the standard education infrastructure, and is thus less amenable to standard research approaches. Young children may be at home, with friends or relatives, or in daycare centers. Besides household surveys such as NHES, NCES might consider studies of the regulatory and certification structures set up to monitor and improve daycare, and may wish to create linkages to data from public-assistance programs, since economically disadvantaged children are a major focus of interest. (Creating linkages is discussed in greater detail later in this chapter.)

Career and technical education (CTE) is an often-ignored area that is increasingly important as the U.S. addresses workforce issues. NCES measures CTE that occurs within high schools and traditional postsecondary education but lacks robust data on the growing number of noncredit and certificate programs for adult learners that are operated by community colleges and private providers. With CTE, NCES may also need to broaden the types of data it collects; for example, retention and attainment of a degree or certificate may be less important than measuring participants' success in obtaining jobs or upgrading occupational skills. Sometimes a single course or sequence of courses may be all that is needed.

Related to, but broader than, CTE is adult education, including adult literacy, and NCES's efforts in this area need strengthening. IPEDS does not collect data on noncredit courses in higher education, and much of adult education falls outside of the traditional education infrastructure. PIAAC

---

[6]Gabriela Katz, "StriveTogether Cradle to Career Network," presentation to the National Academies of Sciences, Engineering, and Medicine, August 6, 2021.

[7]See: https://nces.ed.gov/ecls/ [March 2022].

and the NHES are NCES's primary vehicles for examining the education status of the adult population. Much information is needed, including the number of non-Workforce Innovation and Opportunity Act programs, where programs are located, what services are provided, how instruction is delivered (i.e., online, in classrooms, or a hybrid), and what outcomes are attained, as well as adult-learning demographics, practitioner demographics, and funding methods.[8] Additionally, more data are needed on adult learners, such as their motivations, resilience, self-regulation, sensory difficulties, mental illnesses, cognitive challenges, and chronic health issues. Additional information is needed about adult learning programs, describing existing resources, instructors' backgrounds, instructors' employment status (e.g., full-time, part-time, volunteer), and the professional development instructors receive. Education statistics need to be crafted to capture the fact that the student population is older than it was in the past, and that adults comprise a larger fraction of all levels of schooling beyond high school.

Certain populations are of special interest, including the homeless, the incarcerated and those on parole, and English-language learners who are not literate in their native languages. Some such education occurs within the secondary school system, but it also falls within adult education and career and technical education.

One tool for providing a comprehensive view of education is through longitudinal studies, which can monitor individual students' progress through the education system and transitions into the workforce. These studies can incorporate multiple components (i.e., of students, parents, teachers, and administrators), while also measuring change over time and student outcomes, such as test scores and academic progress. The data can be used to develop and investigate theories about what makes education effective or ineffective. However, new sequences of surveys start relatively infrequently, and sometimes they are not well timed for monitoring trends or current education issues. NCES might explore ways of more frequently updating surveys to include current topics, even if they do not fit the longitudinal structure. Sometimes others might pay NCES to add modules on special topics, either incorporating a module within a survey (as the National Science Foundation did when adding a teacher transcript request form to the National Education Longitudinal Study of 1988, or by conducting a follow-up survey (as performed by the University of Texas at Austin when conducting a midlife follow-up of High School & Beyond respondents).[9]

---

[8]Daphne Greenberg, "A Vision and Roadmap for Education Statistics," presentation to the National Academies of Sciences, Engineering, and Medicine, August 23, 2021.

[9]See: https://sites.utexas.edu/hsb/ [March 2022].

## Linking to Other Types of Data Relevant to Education

NCES's longitudinal studies provide one kind of linkage—linking data on students over time—but linkages to other databases could also be useful by expanding the types of data that are available, sometimes increasing accuracy by using administrative data rather than self-reports, while lessening respondent burden. Students often receive services outside of schools (sometimes through referrals from the schools) that affect their success in education, and linking to measures of such services provides a more complete picture of the students' situations. For example, 22 percent of states link child care data with social-services data and 16 percent link it with health data.[10] At another level, 30 percent of states link early childhood education programs with workforce data to examine issues such as supply and demand, professional development, and supports to retain an effective early-childhood-education workforce).[11] Additional sources of administrative data on children and families for linkages can be found in an Administration for Children and Families report (Holman et al., 2020).

Linking data might also involve creating partnerships with other agencies and levels of government using alternative types of data. For example, ED collects a great deal of information about family finances through its grant and loan programs (some of which is used by the National Postsecondary Student Aid Study [NPSAS]), and merges student-aid-participant data with Internal Revenue Service tax data to produce employment-outcome statistics for the College Scorecard. Other high-value statistical products could be developed with other datasets. For example, the Department of Health and Human Services has individual-level information on Medicaid, Medicare, and quarterly earnings and unemployment insurance (in the National Directory of New Hires) and aggregate information on other human-services programs administered by states. The Department of Agriculture holds aggregate data on participants in the Supplemental Nutrition Assistance Program and school lunch programs that states administer. The Department of the Treasury's Office of Tax Analysis has expressed interest in collaborating with other federal agencies, and its data, along with data related to unemployment insurance, might be used to better link education with workforce outcomes. The U.S. Department of Labor maintains a Registered Apprenticeship Program, which may provide a valuable supplement to the data that NCES collects from schools and colleges. Privacy concerns can occur when data are shared across agencies, but mechanisms for protecting privacy can be employed.

---

[10] Carlise King, "Early Childhood Data Integration Goals and Trends," presentation to the National Academies of Sciences, Engineering, and Medicine, August 6, 2021.

[11] Ibid.

NCES might also consider ways of making its data more linkable to support the work of others. For example, conducting evaluations (other than on methodological issues) is outside the scope of NCES, but NCES survey data might be used to better support the extraction of specialized subsets of schools or colleges that could be used in evaluations. NCES already supports such work in the sense of providing CCD and IPEDS, but NCES also collects more detailed information about school practices in survey systems such as the National Teacher and Principal Survey (NTPS), SSOCS, ECLS, and the High School Longitudinal Study of 2009 that might be useful to researchers desiring more detailed data about schools when selecting study participants. Allowing the use of these survey systems to support sampling would raise issues of access to restricted-use data, and NCES would need to review its systems for protecting confidentiality.

### Document the Broader Educational Environment

Much of what happens in education is affected by the educational environment, which might be broadly defined as including administrative infrastructure (e.g., workforce development, curricula, finance and management, and school context), educational tools (e.g., use of technology and online teaching), and comparative data (e.g., international data). NCES is already actively conducting research in these areas, but much remains to be done.

**Administrative Infrastructure**

A core task for the education system is the development and maintenance of the teaching workforce and supplemental staff, which includes teacher training, recruiting, hiring, school placement, addressing turnover across schools, and improving retention in education. Teacher education and skills, credentials, and certifications—especially for high-need areas such as special education—are all very important. Other high-priority topics for NCES include teacher and staff diversity, the representativeness of teachers and staff of the community and school population, the teacher pipeline, and teacher compensation. NCES already collects data in these areas through the NTPS and the Beginning Teacher Longitudinal Study; additionally, Baccalaureate and Beyond includes questions for those interested in becoming teachers. NCES has tracked the representativeness of teachers in its reports (NCES, 2020), but more data on the training and hiring of teachers would be useful.

Curricula are another important part of the administrative infrastructure. Curricula are a challenging area to study because they vary from state to state and between schools. Still, this variation presents an opportunity for research. NCES can serve an important role in curricular studies in several ways. First, it can continue to create and update classification systems, which help to systematize data from school transcripts and allow studies of course taking on topics such as science, technology, engineering, and math (STEM) education and career and technical education/vocational education.

Second, NCES can continue to produce detailed curricular and pathway data through studies such as the High School Transcript Study (HSTS). These data allow researchers to examine students' progress through secondary and postsecondary education, and support policy analysis (e.g., examining the impact of high school graduation requirements on students' course taking and achievement [Chaney et al., 1997]). The alignment of high school mathematics curricula with existing labor-market needs is an example of an area in which detailed curricular and pathway data would be helpful. Some have expressed concern that the mathematics skills taught in the algebra-geometry pathway in years 3 and 4 of high school are little used by most people, while the mathematics of data science is regularly used and, if more fully incorporated into high school curricula, could help many students build more useful labor market skills.[12] Studies such as HSTS help to measure which pathways students follow and allow researchers to evaluate the outcomes of those various pathways.

Third, as in the Trends in International Mathematics and Science Study, NCES can support deeper investigations of curricula, not only measuring which courses students take, but also delving deeper into topics including how advanced the curricula are, the time spent on the curricula, and the degree of focus on topics. Such data can also be used to address equity, including whether curricular changes might ameliorate the underrepresentation of women and minorities within STEM.[13]

Another component of administrative infrastructure deserving additional NCES attention is funding and expenditures for students, K–12 schools, and postsecondary institutions. NCES collects finance data on states and school districts (but not individual schools) through the U.S. Census Bureau's F-33 survey,[14] which is released in the CCD; on college costs through IPEDS; and on student finances through NPSAS. NCES could deepen its finance and expenditure data collection to investigate the impact of various school-funding formulas and approaches, resource disparities, and effective resource use. In addition, there is a growing focus on the cost of postsecondary education, and students' decisions on whether to attend college and which colleges to attend are greatly affected by the cost

---

[12] Jo Boaler, "Mathematics Is a Subject in Need of Change," presentation to the National Academies of Sciences, Engineering, and Medicine, August 23, 2021.
[13] Ibid.
[14] See: https://nces.ed.gov/ccd/f33agency.asp [March 2022].

of higher education. NCES could do more to capture data on the cost of postsecondary education, and the Center might also consider collecting school-level finance data.

Finally, NCES could collect additional data on school context, which involves many concepts related to students' learning environments. For example, school context data includes state policy contexts, school sectors or types (e.g., charter, magnet, private, virtual, and traditional public schools), school climate, geospatial differences (such as distance to students, geographic location [e.g., state], and urbanicity). Schools may also employ tools such as wraparound services, trauma-informed discipline, student engagement in discipline, peer models, and peer practice, which all contribute to school context. Some aspects of school context are so diverse that it is difficult for surveys or other traditional data systems to properly characterize them. Additional research is required in these areas to determine the types of data that would be most useful and the best modes to obtain them.

Note that topics involving administrative infrastructure are often interrelated with equity issues—a top priority. Schools with high poverty levels tend to have teachers who are less experienced (Gagnon and Mattingly, 2012), and higher turnover rates (NCES, 2021d). They also tend to have fewer financial resources and learning environments that are less supportive. Thus, collecting data on these topics helps with the goal of addressing equity.

**Acquiring and Using Appropriate Tools**

Access to and use of technology is another highly important area, and one that is rapidly changing. From 1994 to 2000, NCES conducted annual surveys of public schools to measure their access to the internet, at which point access had become almost universal (98%); similarly, the ratio of students to instructional computers decreased to 5:1, though schools with the highest poverty levels had fewer computers per student with access to the internet (Cattagni and Farris, 2001). By 2020–2021, 45 percent of schools reported having a computer for each student (Gray and Lewis, 2021). While access to computers and the internet has been increasing rapidly across the U.S. population, the types of equipment and access among the poor, both at the elementary/secondary level and the postsecondary level, continues to be an equity issue. The panel applauds NCES's efforts to monitor issues such as access and recommends that such research be continued with refined measures to better document individual student differences.

The uses of technology have also changed greatly. While schools may once have had computers in the absence of the training or tools to make full use of them, in 2020–2021, 47 percent of schools reported that their teachers used technology for classroom work that would not otherwise be possible (Gray and Lewis, 2021). NCES may both benefit from and be of value to other federal agencies that are conducting technology-related research. For example, the Office of Planning, Evaluation and Policy Development within the U.S. Department of Education sponsored a study of digital-learning resources for instructing English learners (Zehler et al., 2019), and NCES could both advise other federal agencies on research approaches and adapt its own approaches based on what is learned. Professional development is another important technology-related issue. As technology continues to advance and new tools are developed, teachers will need to be instructed in their use. NCES has been active in measuring the use of technology, through both specialized surveys and more general surveys that include questions on technology use. This is an area in which NCES will need to be nimble to stay current, as old questions become outdated and new questions develop.

In addition to being a subject of research, technology can also be a tool for collecting and disseminating new types of data. When students interact with digital learning tools, data can be collected to monitor student learning and what facilitates it. NAEP collects data on digital NAEP test-takers, measuring how long students spend on each question and how that correlates with response accuracy.[15] IES has created a competition called XPRIZE to encourage the collection and analysis of such data,[16] and supports SEERNet as another research tool.[17] Though NCES does not conduct evaluations, it can and should create data systems to facilitate research.

Another aspect of technology worthy of special attention is the rapid transition to online education. Even prior to the COVID-19 pandemic, online education was growing rapidly in postsecondary and adult education, and this growth has further increased with the pandemic, making inroads into elementary and secondary education (Lederman, 2021; NCES, 2021g; U.S. Census Bureau, 2021f). Though online education may not work for all students, some students and parents prefer it, and some school districts are opting to create permanent online options (Lurye, 2021).

Online education raises a host of issues. For example, online education can improve equity by making content, courses, and modes of instruction more broadly available, but this potentially positive impact may be muted or inequity may even increase if disadvantaged groups lack the technology, expertise, or infrastructure to make full use of online education. Online education also changes the way education is performed: at the simplest level, this might include the ability to rewatch a lecture or teaching session; it affects how test security is enforced and how cheating is prevented; and it

---

[15] See: https://www.nationsreportcard.gov/process_data/ [March 2022].
[16] See: https://www.xprize.org/challenge/digitallearning [March 2022].
[17] https://seernet.org/ [March 2022].

may eventually allow virtual reality to replace student labs. NCES will need to stay nimble to monitor the key issues that arise. Currently, NCES collects relatively little information on online education. Some topics concerning online education are evaluative in nature and outside of NCES's mandate; however, NCES can actively monitor online education that is currently in place, assess how extensively it is used, and determine who uses it.

### Developing Cross-State and International Comparisons of the Educational Environment

The U.S. system of delegating education to states and localities results in tremendous diversity in curricula, policies, and practices. Although that diversity may sometimes complicate education research, it also represents an opportunity for experimentation. By tracking the diversity of educational environments, NCES can both provide preliminary data that might be used to examine the impacts of various policies and practices, and also help researchers to design specialized samples for investigating education issues. To date, NCES has not been strongly involved in monitoring state and local policy differences, though NAEP is designed to provide state-level statistics for some states and these data have supported research on education reform (Grissmer et al., 2000). NCES also supports the SLDS. By increased monitoring of differences across states and localities, NCES can supply valuable data.

International studies expand researchers' abilities to make comparisons across cultures and education systems. The panel applauds NCES's participation in international studies. International comparisons also provide important challenges. For example, some countries sample in ways that generate a misleading view of an entire nation. Additionally, the United States is much more heterogeneous than many other countries, and there are important differences in the way education is managed between countries (i.e., the United States has no national curriculum, and states, localities, and private institutions set their own standards and agendas). When participating in international studies, NCES needs to document these types of differences and indicate how they interact with the research findings.

### Congressional Mandates

Almost half of the topics examined (52 topics, or 46%) are mandated by Congress as areas for NCES to collect data. These mandates place obvious constraints upon NCES, and they do not always correspond with the panel's ranking of importance. Some of these mandates extend back for decades, and NCES may wish to explore with Congress whether needs for some types of data have changed, perhaps because of changing priorities or because better alternatives are now available. NCES might also reexamine whether some data collections are overly comprehensive. There may be situations in which data collections on mandated topics could be reduced in scope, still meet the mandates, but leave more resources for other topics.

> **CONCLUSION 3-1: Congressional mandates constrain NCES's data collection priorities yet may no longer reflect what is important for understanding contemporary education.**

> **RECOMMENDATION 3-2: NCES should revisit priorities mandated by Congress and, where appropriate, make recommendations for changes.**

# 4

# Expand Engagement and Dissemination for Greater Mission Impact

As part of the charge given to the National Academies of Sciences, Engineering, and Medicine, the panel was asked to recommend a future portfolio of activities, including desirable changes to data governance and statistical programs, and ways to increase the impact of education statistics produced by NCES. As the nation's principal statistical agency focused on education and related topics, NCES interacts with stakeholders ranging from Congress and the White House to students and their families. The panel considers NCES's stakeholders to include:

- The Department of Education (ED) including the Institute of Education Sciences (IES);
- State education agencies (SEAs);
- Local education agencies (LEAs);
- Education practitioners, such as teachers and education administrators;
- Education consumers, such as students, parents, families, and employers;
- Congress and the President;
- Other federal agencies, especially the principal statistical agencies;
- Other data-holding agencies and organizations;
- State and local policy makers and the policy community;
- The civil rights-monitoring community;
- Advisory boards and professional associations; and
- Researchers and academia.

These stakeholders have varying needs, but common themes include access to data; data products that are useful, timely, and user friendly; feedback from users on data needs; data governance and standards setting; and technical assistance and guidance. While NCES cannot be all things to all stakeholders, it can strategically focus on high-value activities that result in multiple beneficial outcomes. NCES also produces population-level statistics on education for the nation, and the panel suggests that this core role continue. This chapter addresses methods by which NCES could increase its impact through engagement with stakeholders; incorporating user feedback into products and services; expanding its role in data governance and facilitating data access; enabling SEAs to build data-linkage infrastructure; and promoting and delivering products that are accessible, actionable, and timely.

In October 2021, the NCES commissioner introduced a draft stakeholder map (Figure 4-1), which provides a useful perspective of NCES's stakeholders along two dimensions: criticality to mission and level of engagement.[1] The panel finds this approach useful, though one might argue about the placement of some of the stakeholders within the map. One issue is whether the map is meant to be descriptive of current stakeholders or to reflect preferred stakeholder relationships. Another issue is that the role of a stakeholder depends on whether that stakeholder is viewed as a consumer of NCES products or as a contributor to those products. For example, other federal statistical agencies do not currently play a large role with respect to NCES's mission but partnering with such agencies could create valuable linkages with other types of education-relevant data. Data scientists could potentially be valuable in providing alternative types of data and alternative sources that may limit the need to conduct surveys. It is interesting that the map lists families but not students (who are perhaps meant to be incorporated within families in some cases). The list does not include employers, who are stakeholders both in terms of wanting qualified employees and more specifically in terms of their interest in vocational education. The panel recommends that these issues be addressed in NCES's strategic-planning process.

## CREATE ENGAGEMENT FEEDBACK LOOPS TO ENSURE RELEVANCE OF PRODUCTS AND SERVICES

### Engage Broadly for Continuing Feedback

It is challenging for NCES to fully understand the needs of its many stakeholders. NCES has created and participated in many forums, in which it

---

[1] Peggy Carr, NCES, "Partnership, Innovation, and Equity: A Vision for NCES Now and into the Future," presentation at the Association of Public Data Users, October 21, 2021.

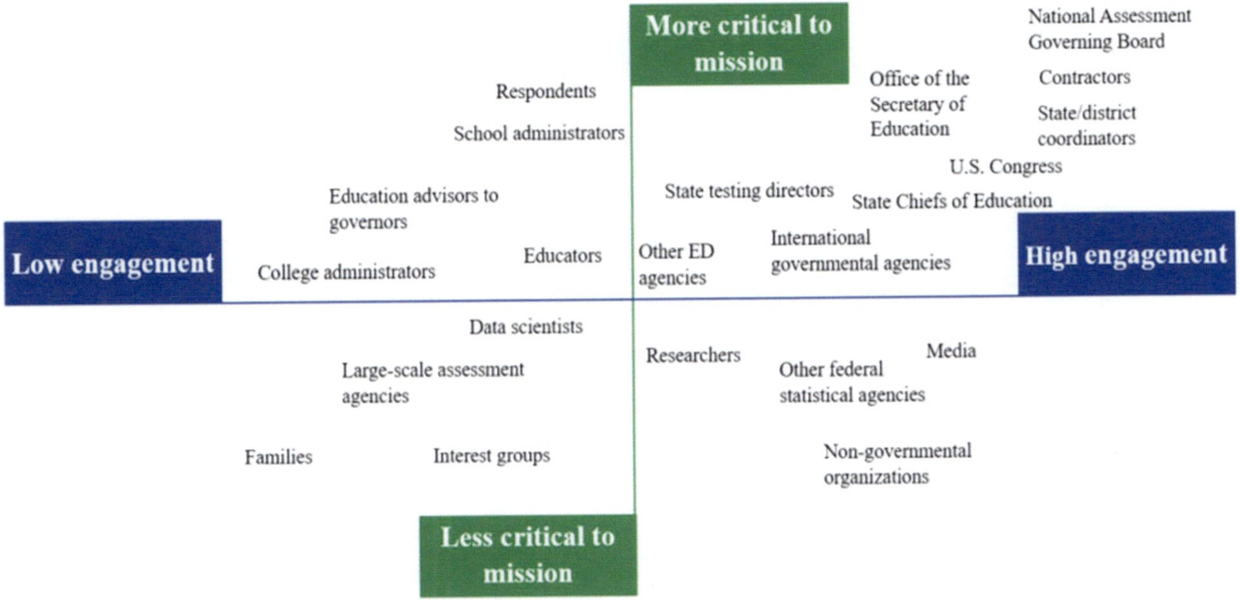

**FIGURE 4-1** NCES stakeholders map.
SOURCE: Peggy Carr, NCES, presentation at the Association of Public Data Users, October 21, 2021.

both provides information and obtains feedback.[2] NCES's efforts are particularly strong with regard to the National Assessment of Educational Progress (NAEP).[3] Additionally, NCES participates in other groups not specifically devoted to NAEP. The National Forum on Education Statistics includes about 100 members, half of whom represent states, with the remainder including representatives from federal offices involved with education data, representatives from education agencies in extra-state jurisdictions, and national organizations with an interest in elementary and secondary education data (NCES, 2021h). These members are presumed to represent the needs and concerns of all 50 states, the District of Columbia, the U.S. territories, and over 13,000 school districts. The National Postsecondary Education Cooperative is charged with developing a research and development agenda focusing primarily on the Integrated Postsecondary Education Data System (IPEDS). NCES works with multiple panels, including a technical review panel for each sample survey data collection, panels coordinated through the National Institute of Statistical Sciences (NISS), a standing panel of K–12 principals to share ideas about new data collections and products, and the NCES Teachers Panel. Additionally, NCES is a member of the Children's Forum, works with several interagency working groups focused on content needs across the federal statistical system, and a group of private-school stakeholders, also including representatives from the ED's Office of Non-Public Education. NCES has collected information from stakeholders for specialized purposes: NAEP collected information from stakeholders, resulting in a Future of NAEP plan of action, and the Ed Tech Equity Framework was developed using stakeholder meetings and panels. Although the Advisory Council on Education Statistics no longer exists[4] and there is no group representing the needs of consumers, such as students, their families, employers, and practitioners, NCES has many avenues for engagement. The panel applauds NCES for its efforts to reach out and listen to stakeholders and encourages NCES to make full use of these resources for improvements to products and services.

---

[2] NCES response to question from the panel, pp. 24–25.

[3] NAEP has the National Assessment Governing Board to set policy, meets with the Council of Chief State School Officers and Council of the Great City Schools on the strategic development of NAEP, funds NAEP state coordinators embedded in state education departments to support NAEP, leads a contracted service center that provides a forum for interaction between NCES and others, has the NAEP Design and Analysis Committee to provide psychometric and large-scale assessment technical support to NCES, has the NAEP Validity Studies Panel to provide input relating to the validity of NAEP, and has standing committees of subject-matter experts for NAEP-assessed topics.

[4] The passage of the Education Sciences Reform Act disbanded the Advisory Council on Education Statistics (established under 20 U.S. Code § 9006) and formed the National Board for Education Sciences (20 U.S. Code § 9516). Available: https://www.govinfo.gov/content/pkg/USCODE-1996-title20/pdf/USCODE-1996-title20-chap71-sec9006.pdf and https://www.law.cornell.edu/uscode/text/20/9516 [March 2022].

NCES conducts some broad, grassroots, technical-assistance efforts that are not well promoted. The Center has a blog that is updated at least monthly, with content generated by a mix of staff and contractors, but the reach of the blog is unclear. The main communication vehicle for sending notifications (via email) when new data or reports are published is IES's Newsflash Subscription Service, which sends information for IES and all of IES's centers.[5] NCES's website provides a form for submitting questions and comments and also provides resources for help with IPEDS, restricted-use data licenses, and general inquiries, but these resources may be more relevant to providing technical assistance as opposed to obtaining feedback.[6] NCES also participates in the American Consumer Satisfaction Index Survey.[7] When using such tools, it is important to obtain actionable information that results in improvements to the Center.

> **RECOMMENDATION 4-1:** NCES should deepen and broaden its engagement with current and potential data users, to gather continuing feedback about their needs and ways that NCES can meet those needs more effectively. This feedback will help NCES shape its efforts to develop and disseminate standards, provide technical assistance, and strengthen its user community.

NCES can leverage existing vehicles to expand its engagement and mission impact in many ways. For example, NCES currently offers Distance Learning Dataset Training (DLDT) (NCES, 2021f) which, while targeted particularly towards new users, provides self-paced, dataset-specific modules to deliver information about studies conducted and data acquired by NCES. DLDT engages its user community via Facebook (3.1K followers[8]), Twitter (24.7K followers[9]), and NCES's blog (number of followers unknown). In 2020, NCES, in collaboration with contractors, created a new user community of graduate students as part of the Coleridge Initiative, by running a trial program to allow students remote access to restricted-use survey data (Schneider, 2021). Another possibility for increasing awareness and use of NCES data might be to coordinate with teachers of applied statistics in education, providing a repository of replication datasets for papers and possibly adding lesson plans.

The panel believes that NCES has a solid foundation for providing technical assistance and supporting new users, but the Center can go further

---

[5] NCES response to question from the panel, pp. 37–38.
[6] See: https://nces.ed.gov/help/webmail/ [March 2022]; https://nces.ed.gov/ipeds/contact-us [March 2022]; https://nces.ed.gov/pubsearch/licenses.asp [March 2022].
[7] NCES response to question from the panel, p. 26.
[8] https://www.facebook.com/EdNCES [March 2022].
[9] https://twitter.com/EdNCES [March 2022].

to consider the impact of the DLDT program and to solicit and incorporate feedback on this program. What do DLDT users think about the program? Are DLDT members representative of NCES usership? Can DLDT usership be broadened? Can successful components of the DLDT model be expanded and less successful components improved? Does NCES employ other mechanisms to engage users? How does NCES collect feedback to understand user needs and how does the Center address such feedback within its strategic priorities? For example, one-on-one stakeholder discussions may reveal that a stakeholder's specific needs are best met outside of NCES, but that NCES may still play an important role in data facilitation. One good example for soliciting and incorporating feedback is the U.S. Department of Agriculture's data-user reviews of the National Household Food Acquisition and Purchase Survey (NASEM, 2020; Wilde and Ismail, 2018).

Many statistical agencies develop ongoing relationships with their user communities. For instance, the U.S. Census Bureau's American Community Survey (ACS) represents a best practice.[10] The ACS Office solicits feedback and questions from all users via email and phone, and it partners with the Population Reference Bureau, which hosts the ACS Data Users Group—a community that shares information, materials, and events.[11] Agencies comparable in size to NCES have developed methods for receiving broad user feedback and/or communicating directly with users via topical webinars or emails announcing product releases, for instance. NCES may consider creating a data-user advisory group to direct the Center's outreach efforts.[12] NCES can also extend its use of technical review panels, such as its Technical Review Panel for IPEDS, which obtains input on IPEDS-related project plans and products and fosters communications with potential data users (RTI International, 2021).

Broad engagement is important for identifying and monitoring current and emerging issues, which drive product and service effectiveness. Ideally, broad engagement will develop into a user community that supports knowledge sharing and spurs innovation among users and NCES. Such a synergy has many positives. When users help each other, the need for NCES to provide technical assistance is lessened. When NCES receives feedback and input, it can more readily adapt to changing needs for education data and services. Finally, as NCES engages a broad community of users, its key role in the education data ecosystem will become prominent.

---

[10] See https://acsdatacommunity.prb.org/ [March 2022].
[11] See https://acsdatacommunity.prb.org/ [January 2022].
[12] For additional ideas for user engagement, see Recommendation 6.7 in NASEM (2021c).

## Engage for Data Acquisition and Best Practices

In addition to ED and IES, other federal, state, nonprofit, and commercial organizations that hold and steward data are also critical stakeholders for NCES. If NCES were to partner strategically with other data-holding organizations, it could share best practices, expand its data holdings, advance evidence building, spur innovation, and create broad mission impact.

RECOMMENDATION 4-2: NCES should actively collaborate with other data-holding federal agencies and organizations to develop useful products and processes, including those that utilize data from alternative sources, to provide timely, policy-relevant insights.

NCES is connected with other federal statistical agencies through the Interagency Council on Statistical Policy, but it could more fully leverage those relationships to advance education statistics and insights. For instance, NCES has partnered with the U.S. Census Bureau to produce the Education Demographic and Geographic Estimates (EDGE) program but has not linked person-level data to the U.S. Census Bureau's vast holdings (U.S. Census Bureau, 2021b,e). There are only two NCES datasets available for use (and potential linkage) in the secure Federal Statistical Research Data Centers run by the U.S. Census Bureau, both fielded by the U.S. Census Bureau on NCES's behalf: the Current Population Survey School Enrollment Supplement and the National Crime Victimization Survey School Crime Supplement.[13] NCES could enhance the value of its data by submitting and enabling more data for linkage and analysis, to gain new insights into education.

The U.S. Census Bureau has multiple joint projects with other federal, state, local, and nonprofit organizations to link data creatively to understand crosscutting issues in demography and social science (U.S. Census Bureau, 2021c).[14] Three such projects involve education data that are not from NCES:

- The Post-Secondary Employment Outcomes project with the University of Texas System, seeking to understand students' earnings, employment, and other outcomes by major field of study, which has now expanded to 11 states (U.S. Census Bureau, 2021d);[15]

---

[13] According to U.S. Census Bureau response to question from the panel, as of December 21, 2021, there was one proposal to use these datasets, and no active or completed projects.

[14] See also U.S. Census Bureau document provided to the panel, "Evidence Building Projects."

[15] See also David Troutman, "University of Texas System Partnership with the U.S. Census Bureau," presentation to the National Academies of Sciences, Engineering, and Medicine, July 9, 2021.

- The Using Multiple Discontinuities to Estimate Broad Effects of Public Need-Based Aid for College project, using state data on financial aid to evaluate the impacts of the Wisconsin Grant on college enrollment, employment, wages, migration, and receipt of social benefits programs;[16] and
- The Outcomes Under the Post-9/11 GI Bill project, studying the return on investment of the post-9/11 GI Bill compared to other GI Bill and veteran benefit programs, using data from the National Student Clearinghouse (a nonprofit data-holding organization) and partnering with the Department of Veterans Affairs.[17]

Multiple federal agencies partner with the U.S. Census Bureau on other joint projects using data linkage or making linked data available. For example, the Economic Research Service has Research Innovation and Development Grants in Economics to develop innovative research on food- and nutrition-assistance issues, and the Department of Housing and Urban Development has deposited Moving to Opportunity and Family Options Study experimental data at the U.S. Census Bureau so that researchers can study long-term outcomes of housing interventions. NCES can increase the value of its data by making more data available to researchers via the U.S. Census Bureau's infrastructure.

The U.S. Census Bureau is not the only agency engaging with other organizations to support data linkage for evidence building and innovative research. The Social Security Administration's statistical agency, the Office of Research, Evaluation and Statistics, runs an extramural research program through its Office of Data Development (Social Security Administration, 2021). The Treasury Department's statistical agency, Statistics of Income, runs its own joint statistical research program (Internal Revenue Service, 2021). The National Center for Health Statistics (NCHS) has a research data center and multiple partnerships using linked data (Centers for Disease Control and Prevention, 2021). The Administration for Children and Families is not a statistical agency, yet it provides access to the National Directory of New Hires data, has multiple research projects involving linked data, and is seeking more opportunities to use and link administrative data to better understand its programs.[18]

Many states and nonprofit organizations also see the benefits of partnering and sharing data. The National Student Clearinghouse, the Manufacturing Institute, Child Trends, and Data Quality Campaign are

---

[16]U.S. Census Bureau document provided to the panel, "Evidence Building Projects."
[17]U.S. Census Bureau document provided to the panel, "Evidence Building Projects."
[18]See, for example: https://www.acf.hhs.gov/opre/project/child-maltreatment-incidence-data-linkages-cmi-data-linkages-2017-2022 [March 2022] and Holman et al. (2020).

all organizations integrating data to understand access to education and student outcomes outside of schooling. The Western Interstate Commission for Higher Education is a multistate partnership for longitudinal data exchange, involving 15 western states and the U.S. Pacific Territories and Freely Associated States (Western Interstate Commission for Higher Education, 2020). Similarly, the Midwest Collaborative, supported by the Coleridge Initiative and the National Association of State Workforce Agencies, aims to exchange data across state lines (Midwest Collaborative, 2020). Due in part to NCES leadership and investment in the Statewide Longitudinal Data Systems (SLDS) Grant Program, Massachusetts integrates data across its education agencies and other government offices to develop longitudinal data on, for example, student and teacher characteristics, student education outcomes, and employment outcomes. All these agencies have partnered with other data-holding agencies to be more useful and valuable to stakeholders.

NCES has many opportunities to support innovative evidence building by combining data with other data-holding agencies. There is vast potential for increased understanding of students, teachers, and schools, as well as other actors and facets of education. Expanding the number of engagements and potential data sources does not mean that NCES itself must produce new product lines from those data—this can be achieved with a relatively high value-to-effort ratio. There are other benefits to partnering in addition to increasing mission impact, such as sharing best practices, providing mutual support, and spurring innovation.

As evidenced by the recent advisory report *Setting Priorities for Federal Data Access to Expand the Context for Education Data* (NISS, 2021c), NCES is seeking to increase the value of its data. The report provides many ideas for federal partnerships to increase the value of NCES's data. NCES is well positioned for increasing its partnerships, as it is already connected to the heads of other statistical agencies and departmental statistical officials through the Interagency Council on Statistical Policy and the Federal Committee on Statistical Methodology. In the panel's opinion, NCES can and should expand its network to support creative evidence building and increase its mission impact.

### Receive and Use the Help of an External Review Body

In addition to engaging broadly, the panel recommends that NCES routinely receive recommendations from experts and address those recommendations. The Advisory Council on Education Statistics used to provide recommendations to NCES.[19] However, the Council was disbanded after the 2002 Education Sciences Reform Act[20] legislation, which moved NCES under the umbrella of IES and established the broader-scoped National Board for Education Sciences (IES, 2021b). While this board still exists, it has been inactive in recent years and is more predominantly focused on other IES centers than was the previous advisory committee, which focused solely on NCES. The panel believes that NCES could benefit greatly from a review body focused solely on reinforcing NCES's strategic goals and helping the Center to meet them.

**RECOMMENDATION 4-3: NCES should explore and establish creative models for a nimble, ongoing consulting body, supplemented by a pool of ad hoc consultants, to help NCES innovate and be accountable for progress on strategic goals.**

To keep the consulting body nimble and flexible, the panel recommends that the body not be subject to Federal Advisory Committee Act (FACA) regulations. The body might contain a set of regular members with knowledge of the full scope of NCES's activities, to provide strategic advice and accountability, along with additional and varying participants (e.g., NISS, 2021b) depending on the particular expertise necessary at a given time. The consulting body would have moral but not statutory authority with regard to NCES, and might also at times provide backing when NCES faces difficult decisions. The goal is a continuing relationship between NCES and the consulting body, in which the consulting body provides advice, helps with strategic planning, addresses special needs as they arise, and supports NCES's decision making. The consulting body would also serve as a source of innovative ideas, helping to prevent insularity and providing motivation and support for continual improvement. Examples of the potential work of the consulting body follow, along with examples of similar kinds of activities, some from FACA committees.

When used properly, an external consulting body is a valuable ongoing resource for NCES, particularly as the Center adapts to maintain relevance (NASEM, 2021b, Principle 1). The Scientific and Public Affairs Advisory Committee within the American Statistical Association (ASA) could serve this role, as could a special committee created in coordination with the ASA specifically for this purpose. The Council of Professional Associations on Federal Statistics is another potential source of a review body.

---

[19] See: https://www.govinfo.gov/app/details/USCODE-1996-title20/USCODE-1996-title20-chap71-sec9006/summary; repealed 2002: https://www.law.cornell.edu/uscode/text/20/9001 [March 2022].

[20] See: https://www.law.cornell.edu/uscode/text/20/chapter-76/subchapter-I [March 2022].

A consulting body is an additional source of stakeholder input and can provide advice, support, validation, and accountability to help NCES stay on target and implement its strategic goals. With enough information (e.g., costs, users, uses, level of effort, beneficiaries) the consulting body can assist NCES with decisions, including prioritizing and deprioritizing data collections. Importantly, the review body can validate NCES's decisions and serve as a key ally, providing reinforcement to NCES in the wake of difficult or controversial decisions.

Many federal agencies have formal advisory committees, most, but not all, of which fall under FACA regulations. Importantly, such boards are only as useful as the agency chooses to make them. Successful agency/advisory committee relationships are characterized by true interaction, discussion, and mutual feedback. The Federal Economic Statistics Advisory Committee is one example. This committee advises the Bureau of Economic Analysis (BEA), the U.S. Census Bureau, and the Bureau of Labor Statistics (BLS), and handles "statistical methodology and other technical matters related to the collection, tabulation, and analysis of federal economic statistics."[21] BEA also works well with its BEA Advisory Committee, which focuses on "the development and improvement of BEA's national, regional, industry, and international economic accounts, especially in areas of new and rapidly growing economic activities arising from innovative and advancing technologies."[22] In the panel's opinion, the BEA Advisory Committee has been instrumental in supporting BEA's exploration of alternative data sources for measuring new and emerging economic topics.

The NCHS Board of Scientific Counselors, although subject to FACA, is a particularly good example of a successful advisory committee. The Board of Scientific Counselors advises NCHS on "goals and objectives, strategies, and priorities," "statistical and epidemiological research and activities that focus on various health issues" and "about opportunities for NCHS programs to examine and employ new approaches to monitoring and evaluating key public health, health policy, and welfare policy changes."[23] The scope of NCHS's board could be the appropriate scope for an NCES review board.

A more deeply engaging and helpful model is that of the Energy Information Administration (EIA), whose Committee on Energy Statistics advisory board is run via the ASA.[24] The structure of the Committee on Energy Statistics' work is unusual because members engage with EIA staff directly in the

---

[21] See: https://apps.bea.gov/fesac/ [March 2022].
[22] See: https://www.bea.gov/beaacm [March 2022].
[23] See: https://www.cdc.gov/nchs/about/bsc.htm [March 2022].
[24] See: https://www.eia.gov/about/stakeholders.php; and https://ww2.amstat.org/committees/commdetails.cfm?txtComm=CCNARS03 [March 2022].

early phases of projects. This means that EIA staff must be open with information and ideas before they typically feel comfortable sharing with external stakeholders. It can be challenging to find staff who are willing to work with outside academics and experts in this intimate way. EIA has found that once staff agree to participate in this joint project, the rewards are multifold. For example, review board members collaborate with staff as they build and develop ideas for projects, so that the members' advice has greater impact on the success of the results. Staff members develop in-house expertise and institutional knowledge. Moreover, staff and members typically become very engaged. Using this model, review board members often report great satisfaction from helping EIA—more than they would if presented with a project in the late stages. In fact, review board members, not EIA staff, often present projects at committee meetings.

EIA's review board, a non-FACA committee, is a good model for NCES. NCHS's board may be a good model for leveraging a standard FACA advisory committee. Regardless of the model chosen, NCES's programs, staff development, culture of innovation, and relationship building would greatly benefit from a nimble consulting body that could help the Center make decisions and meet its goals.

## EXPAND NCES'S ROLE ENABLING DATA ACCESS TO SERVE AND ENGAGE STAKEHOLDERS

### Facilitate Data Access and Use

The panel finds that NCES focuses heavily on its primary data collections and products to achieve mission impact. However, as discussed above, NCES can expand the value of existing data products by providing key services that have high return on investment of effort. Further, the Foundations for Evidence-Based Policymaking Act of 2018 (Evidence Act)[25] effectively expanded NCES's mission to include data governance and facilitation for evidence-building purposes. The panel strongly encourages NCES to expand its role as a data facilitator in the education data ecosystem.

> **CONCLUSION 4-1: NCES can expand its impact by providing leadership and expertise to facilitate responsible data use and access. NCES can help organizations develop capacity to integrate and analyze education data and other data, to produce actionable analyses.**

NCES can maximize its mission impact by expanding its role in data governance (i.e., in helping create the processes and metrics to aid the use of

---

[25] See: https://www.congress.gov/bill/115th-congress/house-bill/4174/text [March 2022].

information). NCES already performs aspects of data governance, in terms of setting standards for data, statistics, and privacy for state data providers, and as part of ED's Data Governance Board. The Common Education Data Standards program is critical in setting standards for state data systems and works closely with agency governance leads throughout the nation. NCES also issues licenses for use of restricted data. NCES can expand its governance role by assisting states and other organizations in data linkage.

NCES can streamline data linkage, prepare and curate data for ease of linkage, develop data-sharing agreement and proposal templates, and simplify data-access processes. NCES can also guide state and local data providers in data infrastructure (e.g., by vetting data-sharing projects and analysts), while simultaneously considering secure-access environments, data content, and output products (the "Five Safes" [Desai et al., 2016; Wikipedia, 2021b]). NCES can also refer to the Advisory Committee on Data for Evidence Building's recommendations for establishing a national secure data service (Advisory Committee on Data for Evidence Building, 2021) as another valuable source for best practices in data facilitation and infrastructure.

Expanding NCES's data governance role will require internal resources, but the value of facilitating responsible data access with strong governance will provide high return on NCES's investment. By increasing data access, more external analysts can participate in evidence building for decision making. Moreover, by setting standards for data and governance processes, NCES can better manage data quality and transparency in data design and provenance—two of NCES's strengths. Eventually, NCES can create a virtuous cycle, as its initial investments lead to a stronger data-governance and facilitation role in the broader education data ecosystem.

### Leverage NCES's Strengths to Support State and Local Education Agencies

As noted throughout this study, NCES can invest internal resources to activate external resources as a force multiplier, for broader mission impact. To maximize use of external resources, NCES needs to align these resources to its strategic plan. The panel finds that NCES is underutilizing its ability to engage the states in achieving the Center's strategic goals.

**RECOMMENDATION 4-4: NCES should strengthen state capacity to link data across systems, adopt shared data standards, and provide actionable information to state and local education agencies to help improve student learning outcomes. NCES can leverage its Statewide Longitudinal Data Systems Grant Program to achieve this goal.**

Like most federal statistical agencies, NCES influences its data collections and secondary data acquisitions, including its state and local data providers, by setting standards and governance processes. Unlike many of its sister agencies, NCES has substantial financial influence via its SLDS grants. As part of implementing its strategic plan, the panel suggests that NCES be thoughtful about the goals and outcomes of SLDS awards, to align others' resources to the Center's goals. NCES can then circulate these intentions to the states and award those proposals that meet the criteria.

The panel finds that certain strategic activities may be particularly high value for broadening NCES's mission impact. In the panel's opinion, NCES should support SEAs in observing shared data standards and governance processes. NCES should also support infrastructure investments for states and state consortiums that want to integrate data for evidence building. This includes prioritizing states' evidence-building and data-linkage capacity and identifying high-value linkages with data systems across other social domains (e.g., justice, health, well-being), both across states and with other government agencies.

Importantly, the panel finds that LEAs often lack resources such as data analysts and managers. LEAs need data access and technical assistance. To address these gaps, NCES could award SLDS grants for states to share data with LEAs, facilitate LEAs' access to data for evidence building, and provide technical assistance. SEAs could also offer analytic assistance, using state and local data to help agencies diagnose and prioritize issues faced in their schools, measure implementation and impact of programs or policy changes, and perform predictive modeling of the results of such changes. SLDS grants could facilitate collaborations among regions or groups of LEAs and could also generate products and tools useful to LEAs and SEAs. This would be a large task given the lack of a national curriculum or common standards, but NCES could be a catalyst for creating standards. Such tools might be offered to other states and localities, to scale their impact. In other words, NCES could capitalize on the existing SLDS infrastructure to maximize its reach and impact.

Another way to mobilize states to conduct high-value activities is to fund a data and statistics liaison at each state, possibly through SLDS grants, who would help to coordinate between state personnel and NCES. This general model already exists at NCES, as NCES-funded state-level coordinators for NAEP, and a review of the NAEP state coordinator role might help to create NCES state coordinators. Ideally, a state liaison for data and statistics would focus on the building and maintenance of data systems, data analysis, data collection, and reporting.[26] The liaison could execute data-governance procedures in terms of standards, data-access

---

[26] Carrie Conaway, testimony provided to the panel, "NCES-funded position in SEAs."

processes and security, building and testing high-quality data linkages, and collecting longitudinal data.[27] The liaison could also produce estimates and other analyses for local areas, produce federally required reports, and support new NCES data collections, such as quick-response surveys.[28] A structure of liaisons might also facilitate cross-state collaboration. While NCES is advised to establish such liaison positions as soon as possible, the activities of the liaisons need to align with NCES's strategic plan, to increase the Center's effectiveness with relatively minor investments of internal resources.

**Partner with External Researchers and Analysts for Evidence Building**

As described in the Evidence Act:

- Statistical agencies are presumed to be able to access any data asset held by any executive agency for the purpose of developing evidence, with limitations.[29]
- Statistical agencies must expand access to their data for the purposes of developing evidence, while also protecting the data from inappropriate access and use.[30]
- Statistical agencies must establish an agency-level process adhering to the Standard Application Process (established by the director of the Office of Management and Budget) so that "agencies, the Congressional Budget Office, state, local, and Tribal governments, researchers, and other individuals, as appropriate, may apply to access" data for evidence building.[31]

To support NCES's expanded role in data governance and evidence building, NCES can leverage its existing data-licensing program to further expand access to data while also directing and participating in research and analysis.

**RECOMMENDATION 4-5: NCES, in collaboration with the Institute of Education Sciences, should establish a joint statistical research program that includes matching internal staff with highly qualified**

---

[27]Ibid.
[28]Ibid.
[29]44 U.S. Code § 3581 – Presumption of accessibility for statistical agencies and units. Available: https://www.law.cornell.edu/uscode/text/44/3581 [March 2022].
[30]44 U.S. Code § 3582 – Expanding secure access to CIPSEA data assets. Available: https://www.law.cornell.edu/uscode/text/44/3582 [March 2022].
[31]44 U.S. Code § 3583 – Application to access data assets for developing evidence. Available: https://www.law.cornell.edu/uscode/text/44/3583 [March 2022].

external researchers, statisticians, and data scientists to develop new data analyses, tools, and publications.

ED will make faster progress in its evidence-building efforts by both broadening the community of researchers and policy makers who can access data for analytics and by signaling important topics, such as those for which ED especially wants data. For that purpose, we recommend that NCES establish a joint statistical research program (JSRP) for external researchers and fellows. By establishing a JSRP aspect to its data-licensing program, NCES can provide data access to external analysts, while also collaborating with those analysts to learn about the Center's datasets. A JSRP can be used to improve methods, evaluate data quality and fitness for purpose, study trends, and understand questions and emerging issues. External analysts can contribute innovative ideas, benefiting NCES staff and supporting a learning-centered environment. Ultimately, a JSRP builds research, analysis, and evidence on important topics in education. Examples of other statistical agencies' JSRPs and similar programs have been discussed, including those of Statistics of Income; the Office of Research, Evaluation, and Statistics; the Economic Research Service; NCHS; and the U.S. Census Bureau (for examples of criteria for access, see U.S. Census Bureau, 2021a). Another example is the BLS's collaborative Senior Research Fellow Program, conducted in conjunction with the ASA and funded by a grant from the National Science Foundation (Bureau of Labor Statistics, 2021).

In addition to joint research, the panel feels that NCES can and should expand and modernize its data-licensing program to further increase responsible data access for evidence building. Data licensing is often somewhat ad hoc, in that researchers request licenses to pursue research with little relationship to NCES's priorities. Such requests pose little burden on NCES other than license administration, and NCES has an interest in maintaining such licensing to promote the Center as a source of quality data. At the same time, NCES could promote specific types of data-access applications, in which the highest-priority topics and questions for evidence building (e.g., America's Datahub Consortium, 2021; U.S. Environmental Protection Agency, 2022) have been jointly determined by the commissioner of NCES (ED's statistical official) and the commissioner of the National Center for Education Evaluation and Regional Assistance (NCEE) (ED's evaluation officer). By doing so, the evidence developed will build on previous research to advance knowledge on a subject, rather than resulting in an expanded but disconnected set of analyses. NCES could further encourage such research through a secondary analysis grant program, such as its former program to promote the use of NAEP,[32] or other IES grant program[33] with criteria designed to encourage the desired research.

Both broadening the size of the research community using licensed data and increasing the diversity of such users could benefit NCES. Current licensees tend to be R1 elite universities, but increasing diversity could generate new perspectives and unique uses of data. Similarly, NCES might consider expanded licensing for graduate students, who might use the data for their dissertations. Generally NCES does not allow graduate students to obtain licenses except through a sponsoring professor but, during the COVID-19 pandemic, NCES ran a trial program to give graduate students online remote access to data through a program called the Coleridge Initiative. This and related approaches might be explored further. Graduate students tend to be more diverse than faculty, so increasing their access could increase the diversity of NCES's data users and add new perspectives.

To fully leverage a strategic, extramural research program, the panel suggests that NCES establish requirements for external researchers to share what they learn with NCES and NCEE, so that external research projects will still support NCES's learning and innovation. Additionally, external projects can feed back into IES's information systems and contribute to broad dissemination tools, such as NCEE's What Works Clearinghouse, or other dissemination venues, such as NCES or NCEE webinars.[34]

The goal of increasing data licensing is not only to increase the number of individuals working with licensed data, but also to create a community of users who share research results and best practices. Such a community could provide internal support to data users while increasing the visibility of NCES's data and facilitating participation of new users.

NCES could also expand its analytic reach by partnering with other agencies that have similar extramural research programs. In these partnerships, the panel recommends that NCES set the strategic analytic agenda and require feedback on the data and analyses performed. Such collaborations could aid NCES both by leveraging external federal resources and best practices to expand the Center's extramural research program, and by leveraging external analytic resources to expand education evidence building.

---

[32] See IES's NAEP Secondary Analysis Grants Program awards from 2002 to 2007: https://ies.ed.gov/funding/grantsearch/index.asp?mode=1&sort=1&order=1&searchvals=&SearchType=or&checktitle=on&checkaffiliation=on&checkprincipal=on&checkquestion=on&checkprogram=on&checkawardnumber=on&slctAffiliation=0&slctPrincipal=0&slctYear=0&slctProgram=40&slctGoal=0&slctCenter=0&FundType=1 [March 2022].

[33] See: https://ies.ed.gov/funding/overview.asp [March 2022].

[34] See: https://ies.ed.gov/ncee/wwc/ [March 2022].

# IMPROVE DISSEMINATION, FOCUSING ON ACCESSIBILITY AND USEFULNESS

## Ensure Accessibility and Usability of NCES's Products and Tools

Multiple studies have assessed NCES's products, tools, and website for usability and recognition of NCES's role (NISS, 2021a; NISS, 2021c; NISS, 2020; NISS, 2016). The panel finds this area in need of further improvement. The panel applauds NCES's efforts to make complex data available to the public via tools such as the College Navigator (NCES, 2021c). However, in recent years, people have come to expect higher standards in terms of user accessibility and internet search capabilities. For example, compare NCES's College Navigator to ED's College Scorecard (U.S. ED, 2021a), both of which serve a similar audience: students and their families. The latter has a simple layout and is easy to read and use, with toggles or tabs to control search options.

Improving data accessibility requires thoughtful review and modernization of key resources directed at general audiences. To support equity and inclusion, government agencies need to be transparent and accessible to the populations they serve. In terms of mission impact, NCES would benefit from applying accessible, human-centered design to its website, products, and tools. Sometimes, rather than creating new tools itself, NCES might make use of others' efforts by certifying systems that meet high standards, if this is allowed within NCES's mandate. IES's What Works Clearinghouse does something similar in assessing the quality of evaluations.

**CONCLUSION 4-2: NCES can improve the accessibility and usability of its products, tools, website, and other dissemination platforms to allow a broader range of audiences to benefit from its products.**

NCES can also extend its impact by ensuring that its website, statistical products, and tools are accessible to diverse audiences, particularly those that lack data and analysis resources, such as many state and local school districts and consumers (e.g., students, parents, employers). To reach these audiences, NCES needs to communicate the existence of its products while also providing products and tools in user-friendly, inclusive formats on an intuitive website that allows users to find information easily.

Accessibility means more than applying 508 compliance (U.S. General Services Administration, 2021a,b) so that people with disabilities can perceive and understand web content. Today, accessibility includes usability, which means applying human-centered design, so that products are easy for everyone to use and understand (University of Washington, 2021; Henry et al., 2016). Language can factor into accessibility, in terms of both inclusivity for non-English speakers and a reading level that supports ease of use. The panel suggests engaging experts to design accessible products and a website that accounts for the ways people, including those with disabilities, currently search for and digest online information. The goal is to build and broaden NCES's general user base while also making data discovery and access easier for even its more tech-savvy users.

Web usability can be difficult to address because, for people who are knowledgeable, everything may seem easy to find. For novices who are less familiar with NCES and its products, however, finding desired material can be much more difficult. Specifically, NCES's website is organized around surveys and programs, while a novice user might want to search by topic area. To understand the experience of new users, NCES could both talk to users about their needs and assess their processes when asked to find specific information on the Center's website.[35] Eye-tracking technology can reveal the foci of users' attention as they search for information. Examples of well-designed websites, at varying levels of complexity, could guide NCES's website usability efforts.[36]

Developing more application programming interfaces (APIs) (i.e., software that provides a way of submitting requests for data and obtaining results, as when checking the weather from one's phone) could also help users identify and access data. For example, the Urban Institute's Education Data Portal project provides most of NCES's administrative data in API format for ready access and adds further value by harmonizing variables for easy comparison across datasets and time.[37] College Navigator could possibly be run through an API, or topical searches could be addressed through an API. NCES might sponsor a hackathon or competition to promote the development of APIs, which, at the same time, could further promote NCES.

### Create Actionable Products and Tools for Local and State Agencies

The content of products and tools is also important for building a broad user base. Individual stakeholders have unique needs in terms of content, quality of information, and timeliness—what is relevant and useful for one group may not be for others. NCES can build its user base, both by creating useful tools and by making well-documented, reliable data available to developers who can customize the data for the unique purposes of stakeholders.

---

[35] For additional ideas for engaging users on accessibility and usability, see Recommendation 6.7 in NASEM (2021c).
[36] See: The Opportunity Atlas at https://www.opportunityatlas.org/; the Stanford Education Data Archive at https://edopportunity.org/; and ED's Common Education Data Standards at https://ceds.ed.gov/Default.aspx [March 2022].
[37] See: https://educationdata.urban.org/documentation/ [March 2022].

Practitioners within LEAs want to understand their school districts in context, for example, by comparing themselves to the rest of the nation or to schools with similar demographics. These practitioners want to understand how similar or different their LEAs are and what actions can be taken to improve their schools and student outcomes. However, many practitioners within LEAs, and to a lesser extent SEAs, often lack data-analysis skills and tools for even the initial step of selecting comparable districts or schools. This means that pure data summaries, without explanatory text, have limited usefulness. Even short briefs containing descriptive statistics and light explanatory text may not suffice to help practitioners understand their LEAs or SEAs in comparison to others, let alone help them to take steps to improve. Providing tools to easily select and examine comparable districts or schools could be very helpful.

Timeliness, in which information is available when it needs to be used in decision making, is another dimension of usefulness. As with accessibility, the definition of timeliness has shifted. In this new era of fast and available (but questionable-quality) data, the careful preparation, collection, processing, and dissemination of high-quality survey data and analyses can seem slow, unresponsive, and irrelevant. There are conflicting priorities and incentives for data that adhere to rigorous methods, standards, and quality compared to data that are timely and relevant. For practitioners and policy makers, the tradeoff often favors timeliness and relevance, even if information is approximated or of moderate quality.

**RECOMMENDATION 4-6: NCES should release data and data products that are useful, actionable, and timely for local and state education agencies and other stakeholders. To increase timeliness, NCES, in collaboration with the Institute of Education Sciences, should review and revise its internal and external quality assurance processes.**

To assist state and local school districts that have few resources for data analysis, NCES needs to deliver products that help LEAs improve their districts' schools and student outcomes. Products such as NCES's Public School District Finance Peer Search (NCES, 2021i) need to be extended to other topics and could be improved by the addition of analytic features, tools, or templates that provide statistical testing for samples.[38] Products that include links to curated resources to assist LEAs with researching interventions can directly address NCES's usefulness and actionability.

The NISS reports (2021a,c) provide additional examples of products and services that could increase the usefulness of NCES's data for LEAs,

---

[38] See, for example, U.S. Census Bureau's Statistical Testing Tool. Available: https://www.census.gov/programs-surveys/acs/guidance/statistical-testing-tool.html [March 2022].

such as localized summary statistics and/or model estimates for "schools like ours." Expanding on these ideas, the panel sees value in a tool that would allow districts to input key student demographics (e.g., exam or graduation statistics) to produce estimated, localized, score-distribution percentiles to contextualize data. This would require NCES (or its contractors) to model state data with those key demographics. For infographics, briefs, and practitioner-oriented products, NCES could partner with NCEE to provide resources or search terms from the What Works Clearinghouse that may be relevant to the topic at hand.[39] Such collaboration has the added benefit of cross-promoting IES products and tools to boost both centers. Table 4-1 provides ideas for improving current products and services for various stakeholders' needs.

Regarding timeliness, the panel recommends that NCES consider three things: stakeholders, operations, and review processes. NCES is encouraged to engage with practitioners, policy makers, and other stakeholders on their needs, as expectations for timeliness vary by stakeholder and have changed over time. The panel urges NCES to revisit the timeliness of each of its existing products, to determine if the degree of timeliness suits the product's target audience.

To further improve timeliness, NCES could assess its data collection and processing procedures, which could include exploring acceptable quality tradeoffs to decrease lag time. The panel understands the challenges inherent in balancing high response rates, completeness, quality-assurance processes, and timely dissemination. NCES should consider whether producing quick, crude estimates (appropriately caveated) could sometimes prove useful and informative. These estimates could be followed by refined estimates providing necessary, high-quality data. At times, NCES produces multiple versions of its data (as with the 2015–2016 National Teacher and Principal Survey),[40] and this could be done more often—estimates can often be revised with minimal ill effects. When BEA produces the Gross Domestic Product, a leading economic indicator, it releases this indicator and then later revises it. Similarly, BLS produces employment statistics every month that are frequently revised after publication. The COVID-19 pandemic reinforced NCES's ability to perform fast, high-quality work, such as the School Pulse Panel (NCES, 2021l). The panel urges NCES to assess its collections to determine which purposes can tolerate, with transparency, a slightly reduced level of data quality with the potential for revision.

Another way to improve timeliness involves staggered data releases, which prioritize the release of high-priority content that is most useful when timely, followed by more detailed information as it becomes available. By

---

[39] See: https://ies.ed.gov/ncee/wwc/ [March 2022].
[40] NCES response to question from the panel, p. 58.

**TABLE 4-1** Current NCES Products and Services, Stakeholders, and Known and/or Anticipated Needs

| Stakeholder(s) | Brief Description of Product/Service | Examples of Current Products, Services, or Topics | Known and/or Anticipated Needs |
|---|---|---|---|
| Policy makers, Congress, congressional staff, media | Short briefs and infographics with light analytic text, collection and analysis of time-sensitive data for specific policy purposes | Statistics in Brief, special requests, School Pulse Panel | Decreasing text, using more graphics, lowering reading level, maintaining and expanding infrastructure and supports |
| Students, families | Tools for finding, researching, and selecting schools | NCES's school and district search tools, College Navigator | Modernized, usable, information suited for user-driven translations to non-English languages (e.g., Google Translate), information grouped by topic area for novice users, search engine optimization, school climate survey data |
| Local school and district administrators | Tools for putting test scores, school climate measures, and other data into context | NAEP School Profiles | Adding analytic features, tools, or templates that provide statistical testing for samples; links to curated resources that can serve as starting points for researching interventions; small(er) area estimates; data on teacher workforce and retention |

| Stakeholder(s) | Brief Description of Product/Service | Examples of Current Products, Services, or Topics | Known and/or Anticipated Needs |
|---|---|---|---|
| Researchers, academics, graduate students, IES staff, other federal statistical agencies, private sector | High-quality, representative, accessible data; standards, classification systems, and guidance | Restricted-use data licenses, DataLab, geocodes for linkages, user-support materials, Common Education Data Standards, Classification of Secondary School Courses, School Codes for the Exchange of Data | Application programming interfaces, new data linkages, remote access (expanding on trial program) |
| State chiefs of education | Funding for states to collect and maintain statewide longitudinal data systems; tested, vetted measures and/or instruments that can be used at the state and local levels | Statewide Longitudinal Data Systems Grant Program, School Climate Surveys | State-level liaisons |
| U.S. Department of Education, domestic and international leaders and policy makers, media, nongovernmental organizations | Acquisition, analysis, processing, and maintenance of data that allows for international comparisons | International Activities Program (surveys combined with assessments) | Automated scoring, automated item generation, natural language processing of international data including social media |

using this approach, NCES would not be trading off data quality, but rather strategically prioritizing releases for greater product impact. NCES could even use staggered or first-release data to its benefit. For example, states usually release a first-look dataset that is left open to edit by districts. The state of Ohio, like most states with unit record systems, regularly collects both K–12 and higher education data from LEAs and institutions of higher education but allows for data corrections to ensure accuracy and data quality. NCES may consider scenarios in which it is advantageous to involve SEAs, LEAs, and other data providers in data-quality processes, iterating between first releases and revisions.

Additionally, NCES, in collaboration with IES, is advised to conduct a top-to-bottom review of both NCES's and IES Standards Review Office's[41] quality-assurance processes, to revise the review procedure for products requiring more timeliness. NCES is encouraged to consider ways to embed transparency about quality tradeoffs (see Appendix E for detailed information on NCES and IES review processes). NCES has a more extensive review process than any other center in IES or many other statistical agencies (IES Standards and Review Office, 2006).[42] In principle, both NCES and IES would benefit from fewer layers of review, to issue timely, relevant, rigorous analyses and products that inform decision making.

Together, NCES and IES should consider the roles and relevance of each reviewer, to determine whether each is necessary and provides meaningful feedback, or whether certain reviewers could be limited to particular aspects of review. For instance, the commissioner could mainly conduct sensitivity reviews instead of full reviews.[43] As another example, after a product has been approved by a branch chief and an associate commissioner, it undergoes methodological review by four to five people—a senior mathematical statistician leads the review, a research associate and two research assistants usually conduct technical review, and the chief statistician signs off (IES Standards and Review Office, 2006). In comparison, methodological reviews for the U.S. Census Bureau's Social, Economic, and Housing Statistics Division products are conducted by one mathematical statistician in parallel with the branch chief's review.

Products need various levels of reviewer expertise. For instance, a conference presentation or working paper with the author's disclaimer may not need the same level of review as an official report with a press release. Experimental products that are transparent about their quality and methods may not need a high level of review. Twenty-one percent of NCES's products underwent external review in the last 3 years.[44] Considering that the median time to issue an IES disposition memo is 1 week for internal reviews and 6 weeks for external reviews (Table E-3), IES (and thus NCES) may want to consider when and if external reviewers are needed (see exemptions

---

[41] The Education Sciences Reform Act of 2002 (20 U.S. Code § 9501 et seq.) requires IES to have a peer review process. See: https://ies.ed.gov/director/sro/, and https://ies.ed.gov/director/sro/ppt/Scientific_Peer_Review.pptx [March 2022].

[42] For example, BEA released updated guidelines in 2019 that reduced the number of individuals required to approve most products. Also, the U.S. Census Bureau's Social, Economic and Housing Statistics Division considers it acceptable to use peer reviewers outside of the author's branch but internal to the agency.

[43] Currently, "many products also receive a full review at the commissioner's level." NCES response to question from the panel, p. 35.

[44] External review is conducted by experts outside of IES from "across a wide range of substantive and methodological fields." IES document provided to the panel, "Peer Review of IES Reports," p. 1.

from peer review in U.S. OMB [2004]). In some statistical agencies, such as the U.S. Census Bureau, peer reviewers can come from other units within the agency.

In the panel's opinion, NCES and IES would benefit from a careful consideration of ways to match the review process to the product, focusing on the desired outcomes of review (e.g., timely, relevant, high quality). Tradeoffs to be considered include not only the quality and timeliness of the product, but also effects on staff. Long reviews frequently depress staff morale, inhibit a culture of innovation, and prevent or delay engagement with stakeholders.

# 5

# Transform Internal Structure and Operations to Align with and Directly Support the Strategic Plan

As NCES expands its audience and adapts its value proposition, its organizational structure must evolve to fulfill the Center's new strategic goals. This chapter addresses the second element in the Statement of Task for this study: consider current and future priorities, operations, and staffing, including the use of contractors. Both NCES's current and future operations, staffing, and use of contractors were reviewed to help NCES identify elements that are working well and those that are problematic now or may become so. This included reviews of publicly available information as well as other information provided by NCES upon request. The key findings are provided in this chapter, with additional detail provided in Appendixes D and E.

Detailed recommendations for staffing, size, use of contractors, and budget implications are dependent on the strategic plan outlined in Chapter 2, and so cannot be fully specified in this report. This chapter will explore various options and their implications that will need to be considered as the Center develops and implements its strategic plan.

## ORGANIZATIONAL STRUCTURE

In 2013, NCES and the Institute of Education Sciences (IES) were reorganized (see Easton, 2012).[1] Some activities (e.g., Performance Information Management Service and ED*Facts*) were moved to NCES from the Office

---

[1] IES document provided to the panel, "Reorganization within the Institute of Education Sciences."

of Planning, Evaluation, and Policy Development (OPEPD). NCES's four divisions, which were organized along topical and methodological dimensions, were replaced with divisions organized by data source. Reasons for the reorganization, as offered in a memorandum from the IES director, included "efficiencies and improvements in both data quality and customer service, as well as reductions in customer and stakeholder burden" (Easton, 2012, p. 1).

NCES was reorganized around three divisions, each with a distinct focus: administering and reporting on formal assessments, performing longitudinal and crosscutting surveys, and collecting administrative statistics from state education agencies and postsecondary institutions (Figure 5-1). Outside those divisions, teams within the Office of the Commissioner perform functions that are crosscutting across specific collections or programs, such as annual reporting, statistical standards, and confidentiality. The expertise and management needed for each program predominantly exist within the division carrying out that program.[2] Human resources, hiring, and information technology (IT) management are all currently managed out of IES's front office.

## BUDGET

Among 13 officially recognized federal statistical agencies in the United States, NCES has the third largest budget (U.S. OMB, 2020; see Appendix D). The American Statistical Association (ASA) has performed several detailed analyses of NCES's staffing and budget (e.g., American Statistical Association et al., 2021; Pierson, 2021; Elchert and Pierson, 2020), which this study largely replicated and extended independently, using internal data provided by IES and NCES.

The statistics program accounts for about 35 percent of NCES's overall budget.[3] From fiscal years (FYs) 2003–2021, statistics appropriations have remained largely flat in absolute terms—fluctuating between $89M and $112M (see Appendix D, Figure D-2). Meanwhile, the appropriations for national assessment programs have increased substantially in the same time period—from $90M in FY 2003 to $165M today.

## REIMBURSABLE WORK

NCES performs little reimbursable work overall, and the exact amount of reimbursable work varies from year to year depending on what specific

---

[2]NCES response to question from the panel, p. 39.

[3]The statistics units count includes the Administrative Data Division, Sample Surveys Division and its predecessors, Statistical Standards and Data Confidentiality Staff, Annual Reports and Information Staff, and the Office of the Commissioner. IES document provided to the panel, "IES & NCES Historical FTE Data and IES Appropriations Historical"; NCES response to question from the panel, pp. 7–10.

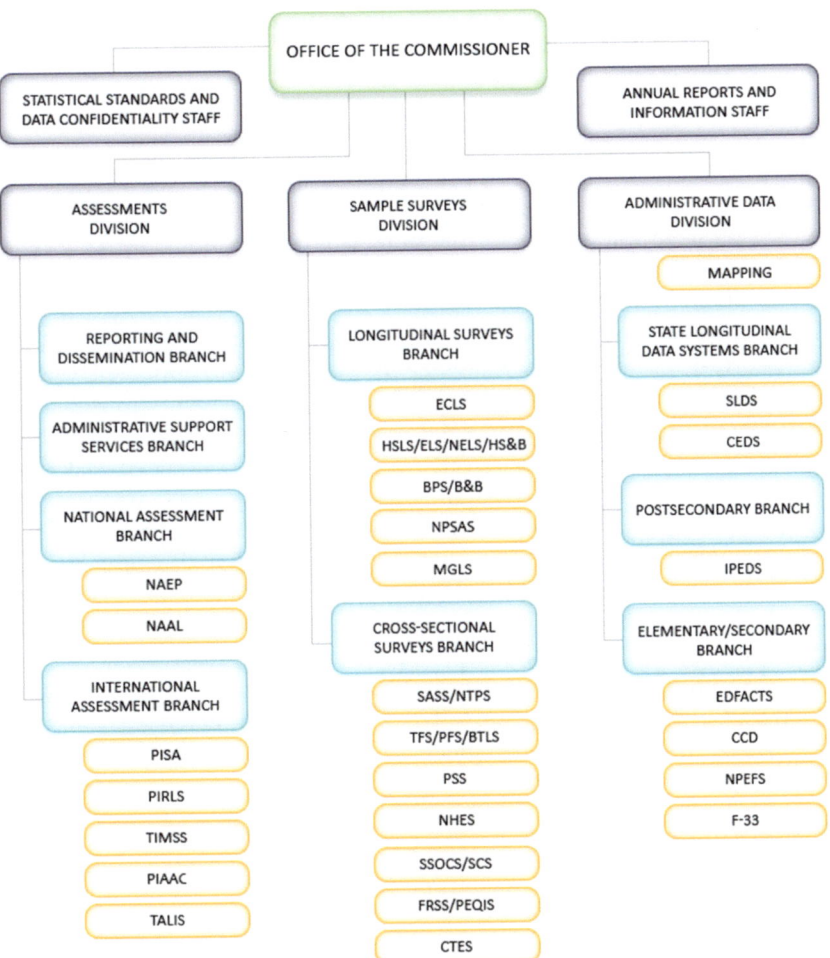

**FIGURE 5-1** NCES organizational structure as of December 2021.
SOURCE: https://nces.ed.gov/about/ [March 2022].

collections occur each year. In FYs 2019 and 2020, NCES received $6.3M in reimbursables from other federal agencies (U.S. OMB, 2020). The largest consistent reimbursable funding is passed in entirety through an interagency agreement (IAA) to the U.S. Census Bureau for the Small Area Income and Poverty Estimates program.[4] Currently, there is no reimbursable arrange-

---

[4] NCES response to question from the panel, p. 6.

ment between the Department of Education (ED) program offices and NCES for handling ED*Facts*.[5]

## STAFF CHARACTERISTICS

NCES staffing levels have dropped precipitously over time, particularly in the last 2 years. In FY 2021, NCES's staff of 90 full-time equivalent (FTE) employees were responsible for the same workload handled by 95 FTEs in FY 2019 and 113 FTEs in FY 2015.[6] NCES's current workforce is mostly (65%) at the GS-14 and GS-15 levels. Statisticians (job series GS-1530) make up the majority of NCES staff.[7] Managing contracts is an increasingly large part of staff workload. Daily, NCES staff must develop, plan, oversee, direct, review, and assess work performed by contractors.[8] Consequently, NCES tends to hire and retain employees with the technical expertise and specialized work experience to effectively perform contracted tasks and, as a result, NCES currently has a lesser capacity than most large statistical agencies to hire, train, and develop junior, inexperienced staff.

Current and former NCES employees report that, because NCES is a small agency, most staff work across multiple projects and divisions. Figure 5-2 provides a snapshot into the distribution of NCES's workforce across its organizational units. Of the 90 total FTEs that NCES currently employs, 32 are organized into assessment units and the remaining 58 are organized in statistics units.[9] A full examination of how NCES staff work across projects, divisions, and functions would require fact finding that is beyond the scope of this report.

---

[5]NCES provided additional context for why there is no reimbursable aspect to ED*Facts*: "ED*Facts* is one of ED's major information technology investments. Every year, funding decisions on all major IT investments are made by a central ED body (the Investment Review Board) and funds are marked to support the investments accordingly. IES/NCES is recognized as the point of contact (POC) implementing and managing ED*Facts*." NCES response to question from the panel, p. 7.

[6]IES document provided to the panel, "IES & NCES Historical FTE Data and IES Appropriations Historical."

[7]NCES document provided to the panel, "NCES Organizational Chart with Job Series Positions."

[8]NCES response to question from the panel, p. 17.

[9]Also noted in Chapter 1 and Appendix D, the assessment units count includes the Assessments Division, a new branch established in 2013 comprising staff who work(ed) primarily on international studies, plus one FTE from across multiple employees located in the Office of the Commissioner who work on assessments for some of their time.

# TRANSFORM INTERNAL STRUCTURE AND OPERATIONS

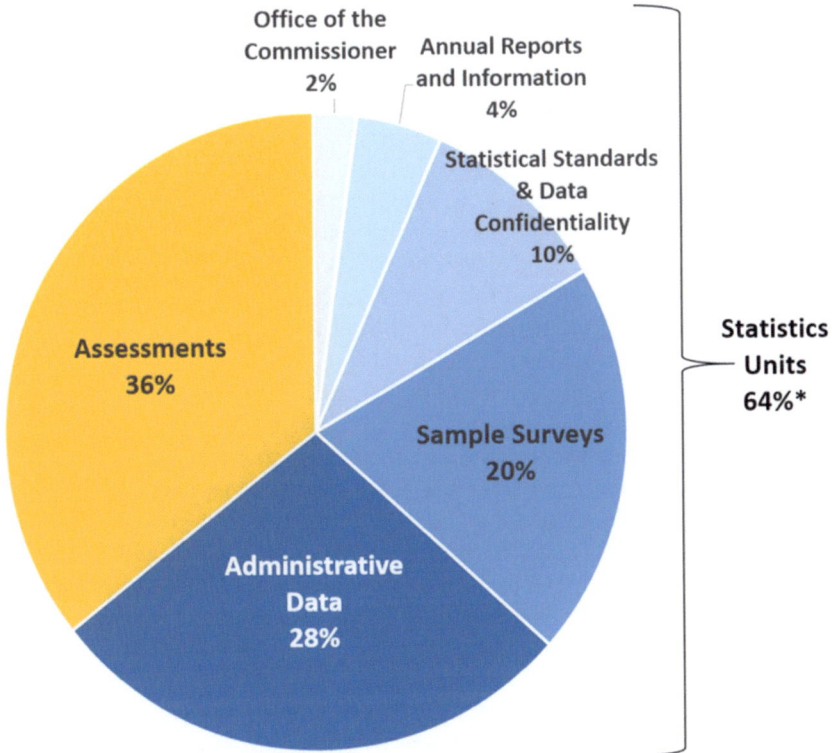

**FIGURE 5-2** Distribution of NCES staff into organizational units.
SOURCE: IES document provided to the panel, "IES & NCES Historical FTE Data and IES Appropriations Historical."
NOTES: The organization of staff into statistics and assessment units does not align with program appropriations (Figure D-2). For example, staff who work primarily on international studies are organized in assessment units, while the program dollars for the international studies collections have always come from the statistics budget appropriation. The organization of full-time equivalents does not fully reflect the functional roles of the staff. Vacant positions are not represented. (See also Appendix D, Table D-2.)
*Statistics units are shown in varying shades of blue.

## STAFF TURNOVER

It is generally believed that NCES is understaffed (American Statistical Association et al., 2021; Elchert and Pierson, 2020).[10] For at least 18 years, NCES has faced a declining staffing budget. Between FYs 2003–2021,

---

[10] See also: https://ies.ed.gov/director/remarks/5-24-2021.asp [March 2022].

NCES experienced a net loss of 23 FTE (20%; see Appendix D, Table D-2). Over the same period, NCES faced multiple new unfunded mandates, such as the Geospatial Data Act, and an expansion in mission under the Foundations for Evidence-Based Policymaking Act of 2018 (Evidence Act). NCES's annual net attrition rate averaged 4.5 percent from the start of FY 2018 to the end of FY 2021 (see Appendix D, Table D-3). At this rate, by FY 2032 NCES's workforce will be half the size it started with in FY 2018. Within NCES, the statistics units experienced a net loss of 25 FTEs (30%) from FYs 2003–2021 (see Appendix D, Table D-2).[11,12] The assessment units had a net gain of 2 FTEs (7%) in the same period.

Our analysis found structural and operational mechanisms that partially explain this downward trend in staffing. NCES has temporary hiring authority to hire FTEs into temporary positions for 3 years and to extend for 3 years maximum, after which time NCES, vis-a-vis IES, must post a competitive position within IES and recompete for that job. This hiring authority is intended for use in the federal government when an agency needs specialized expertise for a short-term project. As a result of the temporary hiring authority, NCES has lost staff and/or staff have lost wages between the end of the extension and the beginning of the new permanent position, resulting in a net loss of both staff and productivity over time, a substantially increased administrative burden, and decreased staff morale. Shifting an agency's vacated positions back into a larger, often competitive, centralized pool is not an uncommon practice in the federal government.

The Senate's FY 2022 appropriations report creates a separate appropriation for IES that is distinct from ED's program administration account, which has funded IES since its inception, and leaves the door open for increasing NCES staffing in the future:

> ESRA required IES, in carrying out its mission, to compile statistics, develop products, and conduct research, evaluations, and wide dissemination activities in areas of demonstrated national need and ensure that such activities conform to high standards of quality, integrity, and accuracy and are objective, secular, neutral, and nonideological and are free of partisan political influence. To better support this statutory mission, the Committee provides an appropriation for administrative expenses directly to IES.

---

[11] The organization of staff into statistics and assessment units does not align with program appropriations and does not fully reflect the functional roles of staff.

[12] NCES-initiated reorganizations have changed the structure of NCES several times since 2002. For example, as part of the 2013 reorganization, six staff who worked primarily on international studies were moved from the Early Childhood, International, and Cross-cutting Division into a newly formed branch of the Assessments Division. The Administrative Data Division was added as part of the statistics units by FY 2015. Today, the statistics units include all subunits except for the Office of the Commissioner and the Assessments Division (see Appendix D, Table D-2).

Previously, administrative expenses for IES were supported from the appropriation for Program Administration under the control of the Secretary. The Committee recommendation is $67,527,000, an increase of 23 percent from comparable fiscal year 2020 spending (U.S. House of Representatives Committee on Appropriations, 2021, p. 275).

## AVERAGE NUMBER OF U.S. DOLLARS MANAGED BY EACH AGENCY EMPLOYEE

As noted above, NCES's staff has declined while the statistics and Statewide Longitudinal Data Systems Grant Program appropriations have remained flat (see Appendix D, Table D-2, Figure D-2). Overall, each NCES staff member managed an average of $2.8 million dollars in FY 2021 (see Appendix D, Table D-1). NCES had the largest average number of dollars managed by each staff member[13] of all 13 federal statistics agencies.

Figure 5-3 compares all 13 federal statistical agencies on the average number of U.S. dollars managed by each employee, based on the total number of employees in FY 2020. As shown, the average number of dollars managed per employee was nearly three times larger for NCES ($2.8M) than each of the next three largest agencies on this measure.[14]

## USE OF CONTRACTORS

NCES accomplishes its mission by contracting out much of the Center's work (Pierson, 2021; Elchert and Pierson, 2020). NCES has 43 staff (48%) who serve as contracting officer's representatives (CORs) or administer IAAs in addition to other duties. On average, each COR or IAA administrator manages 3.7 IAAs or contracts (see Appendix D, Table D-4). Many of NCES's data collections are conducted by contractors. Data analyses and writing, including NCES's blog and conference presentations, are generated by a mix of staff and contractors.[15] The 2019 report for the Confidential Information Protection and Statistical Efficiency Act

---

[13] Also noted in Appendix D, Table D-1, this is the average number of dollars calculated as direct funding in FY 2020 divided by the number of FTE permanent staff—sometimes called the budget-to-staff ratio. It is used to express the average number of dollars managed by each agency staff member.

[14] NCES has a budget-to-staff ratio of approximately $2.75M per FTE—more than seven times the median ratio for the 13 principal federal statistical agencies—according to ASA-compiled data for the 13 federal statistical agencies (Pierson, 2021).

[15] For two recent examples, see American Association for Public Opinion Research (2021) Annual Conference Abstract Book (Available: https://www.aapor.org/AAPOR_Main/media/MainSiteFiles/AAPOR-2021-Conference-Program-5421.pdf [March 2022]) and the Federal Committee on Statistical Methodology Fall 2020 Program (Available: https://copafs.org/fcsm-fall-2020-conference-program/ [March 2022]).

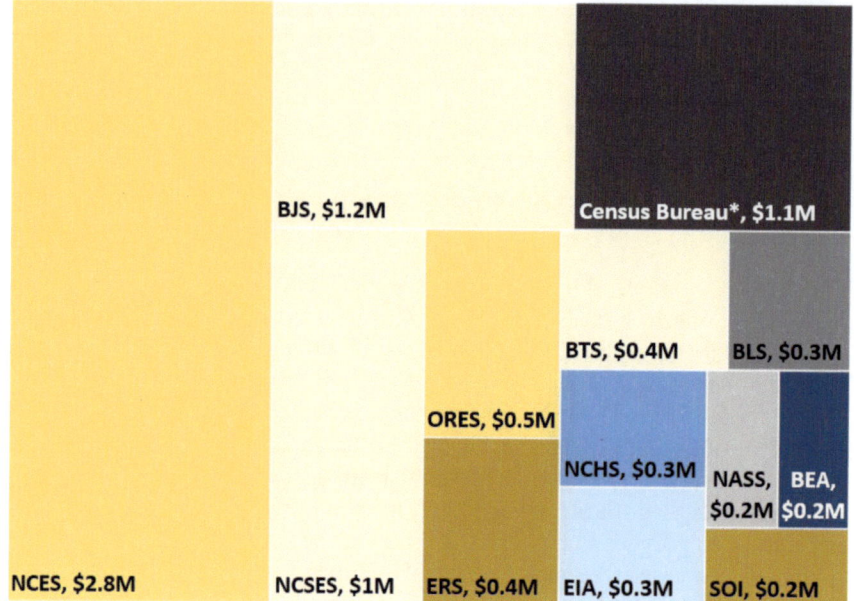

**FIGURE 5-3** Average number of U.S. dollars ($) managed by each agency employee.
SOURCE: U.S. OMB (2020), Appendix Tables 3a (Staffing Levels) and 1a (Direct Funding for Statistical Programs, 2018–2020).
NOTES: The size of each box indicates the average number of U.S. dollars (millions) managed by each agency full-time permanent employee. This is the average number of dollars calculated as direct funding in FY 2020 divided by number of FTE permanent staff, sometimes called the budget-to-staff ratio. It is used to express the average number of dollars managed by each agency staff member (see also Appendix D, Table D-1).

Colors are used to group agencies according to their size in FTEs (small, medium, large). Grey denotes large statistical agencies (more than 1,000 FTEs) and includes U.S. Census Bureau,* BLS, and NASS. Blue denotes medium statistical agencies (200–1,000 FTEs) and includes BEA, NCHS, and EIA. Yellow denotes small statistical agencies (less than 200 FTEs) and includes ERS, SOI, NCES, ORES, BTS, NCSES, and BJS. Gradations within each color group further differentiate workforce size with darker gradients representing larger agencies within a given group and lighter gradients representing smaller agencies.

*FY 2020 is a decennial census year.

shows 1,743 "contractor agents" for NCES involved in non-National Assessment of Educational Progress (NAEP) data collection and management, with another 411 working on design and planning, processing, documentation, and analysis, and 234 more providing IT support for data collections.[16,17] It is less clear how heavily NCES currently relies on contractors for activities such as maintaining key stakeholder relationships.

Compared to other federal statistical agencies, NCES is particularly lopsided with respect to contractors versus FTEs (U.S. OMB, 2020). Managing contractors is a primary function of many NCES employees.[18] Historically, the contractor staff has been heavily embedded into NCES, and at various times, contractual requirements have stipulated colocation with NCES staff at the Center's offices.[19] At times, this model has benefited NCES by allowing the Center to supplement staff quickly, without disrupting mandated operations. In the past, this arrangement also created a pipeline of vetted new staff who could fill vacated or newly created FTE slots. However, particularly when combined with sustained staffing losses, this model can result in knowledge loss over time.

## RESOURCES FOR STAKEHOLDER ENGAGEMENT, COMMUNICATION, AND DISSEMINATION

NCES has several long-standing channels for outreach and communications.[20] The NewsFlash system remains at the center of NCES's channels and is used for releases or significant updates. Many studies, assessments, and collections have also established outreach models to connect with their specific stakeholders. Except for communications related to NAEP, formal communications with the press, Congress, or other parts of ED are mainly coordinated through IES. Within NCES, no obvious person(s) or office(s) currently exists for growing and replenishing the Center's users and

---

[16] The non-NAEP data collections include: Baccalaureate and Beyond Longitudinal Study, Early Childhood Longitudinal Study, Fast Response Survey System, High School and Beyond Longitudinal Survey, High School Longitudinal Study, Middle Grades Longitudinal Study, National Household Education Survey, National Teacher and Principal Survey, Progress in International Reading Literacy Study, Program for International Student Assessment, School Survey on Crime and Safety, and Trends in International Mathematics and Science Study.

[17] NCES document provided to the panel, "2019 Report to OMB on the NCES Implementation of the Confidential Information Protection and Statistical Efficiency Act (CIPSEA) in 2019."

[18] NCES response to question from the panel, p. 17.

[19] See, for example, Federal Contract Opportunity for Education Statistics Support Institute Network ED-IES-11-R-0058, posted May 19, 2011. Available: https://govtribe.com/opportunity/federal-contract-opportunity/education-statistics-support-institute-network-essinedies11r0058 [March 2022].

[20] NCES response to question from the panel, pp. 37–38.

stakeholders, understanding the evolving needs of users and stakeholders, or innovating to meet those needs.

## INTRADEPARTMENTAL OPERATIONS, SUPPORT, AND RELATIONS

Human resources, hiring, and IT management are all currently managed out of IES's front office. Many of NCES products also require IES internal or external reviews (see Appendix E). Over the course of this study, IES reviews were frequently cited as a barrier to timeliness. According to a recent article by the ASA (Pierson, 2021, paragraph 5):

> NCES has also lost autonomy and stature over the past two decades, undermining its ability to produce objective education statistics. NCES was moved under the newly created IES in 2002; its advisory panel was disbanded; and part of its budget, hiring, and contracting control was transferred to the IES director. A few years later, NCES's authority to promise data confidentiality was weakened by the Patriot Act. In 2012, Congress removed the requirement of Senate confirmation of the commissioner, and there have since been several proposals to remove presidential appointment of the NCES commissioner. Finally, IES's work to build its profile comes with diminishment of NCES's profile.

Some unique features of the intradepartmental operations and relationships between NCES, IES, and ED were revealed during fact finding and deliberations for this study. First, NCES's funding structure is different from that of other federal statistical agencies: like all IES centers, NCES's FTE allocation is set by IES. Second, while there were many anecdotal reports of NCES's value and utility to ED, NCES does not seem to get much, if any, formal recognition for its contributions to that work, which can create the perception that NCES's value does not align with the actual work of NCES for ED. IES currently lists itself as the main producer of many NCES publications and products, in many cases not citing NCES as the responsible producer. For example, The College Scorecard is currently produced by the OPEPD, under the department's chief data officer. However, NCES led the collaboration to merge student-level data held by ED's student aid office with annual Internal Revenue Service income tax data (managed by the Social Security Administration) to produce aggregate earnings data, by school, for students who received federal student loans and grants. This work laid the foundation for the College Scorecard. The NCES staff person who led the effort took this function with him when he moved to OPEPD. Compared to other federal statistical agencies, NCES provides significant technical assistance to ED (see Chapter 2).[21]

---

[21] NCES response to question from the panel, p. 14.

## KNOWLEDGE RETENTION

The issue of knowledge retention came up frequently in the panel's work, particularly when discussing use of contractors. NCES's contractors are increasingly relied upon to analyze data and write reports, which effectively reduces the ability of NCES's staff to learn from the data and turn that knowledge into subsequent surveys or other data-collection designs. It was beyond the scope of this study to systematically examine knowledge retention at NCES. However, one proxy measure of knowledge loss is NCES's annual employee turnover rate, which has ranged from 9 to 11 percent since FY 2018 (see Appendix D, Table D-3).[22] This suggests that even if NCES backfilled all vacancies, the staff as a whole is losing 9–11 percent of its institutional knowledge each year. Also, in gathering information about staffing, use of contractors, and other operational characteristics, the panel gathered anecdotal information suggesting that the combined effects of staffing losses and increasing reliance on contractors are endangering NCES's ability to retain knowledge and fully leverage the Center's resources. When the contractors have institutional knowledge not shared by NCES staff, there is a risk of losing that institutional knowledge completely if contracts and/or contractors change.

## NCES'S STRUCTURE AND OPERATIONS—CONCLUSIONS

While IES initially conceived of NCES's current organization by data source as providing a "more rational and coherent organization structure" (Easton, 2012, p. 1), this study leads the panel to conclude that NCES's structure is a barrier to the innovation, blended data, and cross-fertilization that will be central to the Center's future success.

**CONCLUSION 5-1: NCES's current organizational structure, with statistical programs separated by data source type (sample surveys and administrative data), contributes to silos that limit innovation.**

In the panel's opinion, NCES should explore organizational and program-management structures that, at a minimum, promote blending of data sources and other innovations, insightful evidence building by education topic, and staff teamwork and cross-fertilization. Additionally, given the importance of growing and organizing NCES's users and stakeholders, understanding stakeholders' evolving needs, and innovating to meet those needs, NCES may also want to consider creating both a small innovation unit to assist with components design, study, and implementation of new

---

[22] This includes internal transfers from NCES to elsewhere in ED.

approaches and a small unit dedicated to promotion, external engagement, and integration of feedback into products and services. This would accelerate the necessary transition from siloed products based on data sources to a focus on educational topics and the types of questions, evidence, and diverse data sources needed to inform those topics. The panel considered the advantages and disadvantages of various organizational structures and program-management features (see Box 5-1):

- Scenario 1: Reorganize by topic or school level.
  - Advantages: This may be a more intuitive organizational structure for new audiences, potentially making it easier for new stakeholders to navigate NCES.
  - Disadvantages: This structure alone is not likely to promote cross-fertilization of data sources.
- Scenario 2: Adopt a matrix organizational structure along two dimensions: data source and topic or school level.
  - Advantages: This arrangement has the same advantages as Scenario 1 but would also promote cross-fertilization of data sources.
  - Disadvantages: This may be a difficult organizational structure to adopt within the federal government context. This structure is not necessarily more efficient.
- Scenario 3: Separate NAEP from NCES.
  - Advantages: Separation would remove the structural constraints of a statistical agency from assessment activities, allowing for a "richer interpretation of the [assessment] results that can easily transcend the comfort level of a statistical agency."[23]
  - Disadvantages: A joint statement by the ASA and four other research and statistics organizations argues that "severing the important link of education inputs to what students learn and removing the legal guarantees of independence accorded a statistical agency for those assessment activities" (American Statistical Association et al., 2021, p. 3) is one of the challenges NCES faces in 2021. Staff currently work across these two programs, so separating them could further reduce staff and agency capacity. Additionally, such an arrangement would exacerbate the issue of silos by data source and further limit innovation.

**CONCLUSION 5-2: NCES's current overreliance on contractors and its high turnover rate endanger the Center's ability to retain institutional knowledge and build internal capabilities needed to meet its strategic goals.**

---

[23] See: https://ies.ed.gov/director/remarks/5-12-2020.asp [March 2022].

> **BOX 5-1**
> **Internally Organizing to Support a Bold Strategic Plan—Bureau of Transportation Statistics**
>
> In October 2020, the Bureau of Transportation Statistics (BTS) made its new strategic plan available to the public (Bureau of Transportation Statistics, 2020). The plan concisely states the Bureau's vision and priorities; it also provides specific, concrete information about how the Bureau is organized and operates in service of the plan. In contrast to NCES's current organizational structure, with three primary divisions that are grouped by data source (i.e., assessments, surveys, administrative data; see NCES, 2021b), BTS is organized by topic and function. In addition to its substantive offices, BTS also has leadership staff dedicated to the functions of public affairs and technology, who are included in the Office of Director.

While the precise mission needs to be refined as part of the strategic plan, any realistic operationalization of that mission will depend on a competent, stable, and adequate workforce. When a position is vacated at NCES, the Center does not automatically get a backfill. As a result, at least 12 NCES programs have been discontinued and/or put on hiatus, citing lack of staff (e.g., there are no staff to oversee the contractors).[24] These facts suggest that, if NCES is to successfully fulfill its promise and vision, additional support is needed to curb a deteriorating staffing situation. At the very least, NCES needs staff with the time and skills to advocate for its resource needs, including staff to support strategic-planning activities.

## OPPORTUNITIES FOR LEVERAGING CONTRACTORS AND OTHER NONTRADITIONAL MECHANISMS FOR BUILDING AGENCY CAPACITY, RETAINING KNOWLEDGE, AND ENHANCING RESILIENCE

In the short term, NCES's contracting model may provide valuable opportunities because contracts are useful for getting new things done quickly. If used appropriately, contractors could make NCES much nimbler. For example, capitalizing on opportunities provided by 21st-century advances in data collection, both within and outside the federal government, (e.g., web scraping, natural language processing, social media, data linking) will require skilled personnel who are dedicated to these functions. NCES has a profound shortage of data scientists and other staff; therefore, without

---
[24] NCES response to question from the panel, pp. 30–32.

the use of contractors, NCES may not realistically be able to rapidly increase its capabilities or capacity in areas that require sampling statisticians, assessment development experts, survey methodologists and statisticians, and data analysts and scientists.[25]

There are, however, disadvantages to heavy reliance on contracts. Staff with technical expertise are needed to manage contractors, even though managing contractors itself is nontechnical, which means that staff are underutilized.[26] Communication between staff and contractors can be very slow, delaying operations. When established contracts constrain the scope of work, heavy use of contractors can result in the inability to adapt, or can cause delays due to contract modifications needed to make operational changes. Finally, there may be "perverse incentives" for contractors to avoid modernizing processes or improving quality and products.[27]

Based on the advantages and disadvantages of using contractors, it may be useful for NCES to consider the following questions in its strategic-planning activities:

- What functions can contractors effectively assume (and not assume) in the short and long term?
- What functions should, with time and support, be brought in-house (e.g., NISS, 2021a)?
- To what extent can contracts be used to build staffing pipelines, retain existing institutional knowledge, and build internal capabilities?

Another creative way to build staff capabilities and capacity is by establishing senior level and senior technical positions, which are not subject to Senior Executive Service caps.[28] The U.S. Census Bureau and Energy Information Administration were among the first statistical agencies to make use of Senior Level and Senior Technical positions; this strategy has since been introduced to other agencies, such as the Bureau of Justice Statistics. Establishing such positions is one of several nontraditional tools that NCES could consider as it builds its technical (e.g., data science) capabilities.

---

[25] NCES response to question from the panel, p. 18.
[26] Lynn Woodworth, "National Center for Education Statistics: A Vision of Education Statistics," presentation to the National Academies of Sciences, Engineering, and Medicine, May 26, 2021.
[27] Woodworth, p. 6.
[28] See U.S. Office of Personnel Management, Policy, Data, Oversight: Senior Executive Service. Available: https://www.opm.gov/policy-data-oversight/senior-executive-service/scientific-senior-level-positions [March 2022].

Another nontraditional staffing arrangement that would be advantageous for NCES to leverage is the Intergovernmental Personnel Act (IPA) Mobility Program, which "provides for the temporary assignment of personnel between the federal government and state and local governments, colleges and universities, Tribal governments, federally funded research and development centers, and other eligible organizations."[29] According to the Office of Personnel Management, "agencies do not take full advantage of the IPA program which, if used strategically, can help agencies meet their needs for 'hard-to-fill' positions."[30] Fellowships are another useful mechanism for increasing headcount and, if integrated with staff, fellowships are useful for developing the capabilities of an organization's workforce. Other federal statistical agencies have found user groups to be an invaluable resource for building internal capacity without necessarily adding headcount. Each of these mechanisms can work as force multipliers, replenishing and renewing an agency's workforce.

Finally, when the program office receives a greater benefit from NCES services than does NCES, an argument can be made for reimbursable arrangements. Additionally, reimbursable work may be one way for NCES to get more resources and staff without using its IES allocations. Reimbursable arrangements also provide a mechanism for documenting and assessing future value and priorities.

As a note of caution, other organizations have suffered from attempting to substitute a researcher or statistician with a data scientist; it is tempting to assume that a data scientist will easily acquire the necessary statistical expertise and content knowledge. In reality, understanding educational tests, psychometrics, and related measurements is a skillset that requires years of training and experience to employ effectively. Similarly, content expertise in areas such as adult literacy or early childhood education requires an advanced degree and years of professional experience in relevant settings, such as classrooms. Fortunately, NCES is housed within IES—an institute that possesses deep content expertise in extremely diverse contexts. By expanding and cultivating partnerships within IES, NCES will be better positioned to identify and integrate the specialized content expertise needed to supplement and inform the Center's technical work. Such partnerships, however, need to be actively curated by NCES.

---

[29] See U.S. Office of Personnel Management, Policy, Data, Oversight: Hiring Information, Intergovernment Personnel Act. Available: https://www.opm.gov/policy-data-oversight/hiring-information/intergovernment-personnel-act/ [March 2022].

[30] Ibid.

## EVALUATE POSSIBLE ORGANIZATIONAL STRUCTURES AND FEATURES AS PART OF STRATEGIC PLANNING

Organizational recommendations are often dependent on an organization's strategic plan. However, some important activities can happen as part of the strategic-planning process and others can happen independently.

**RECOMMENDATION 5-1: NCES should utilize contractors and creative staffing arrangements to work collaboratively with staff to build internal capacity. To enhance resilience, NCES should also explore greater use of flexible contract types, stronger incentives for contractors to adopt cost-effective innovations, and performance-based requirements.**

The panel recommends that NCES establish a process for systematically reviewing its contract activities and functions, with an eye towards identifying those that need to be insourced within the Center to meet NCES's medium- and long-term strategic objectives. In addition, future contracts need to be written such that information from contracted activities flows into NCES's brain trust to build the Center's capacity. Such contracts may require high levels of integration and coordination across activities and functions. NCES may benefit from master agreements that are indefinite delivery, indefinite quantity[31] and that issue task orders for which qualified vendors compete, in lieu of separate contracts for distinct chunks of work. This approach could both reduce the burden of writing and managing individual contracts and could generate a vetted bench of candidates that the Center could draw from when necessary. The panel further recognizes that the model of "renting" contract staff, who are embedded within and function as Center staff, has historically been beneficial and could be continued in some form in the future.

NCES will need to carefully consider which activities it wants to contract out versus complete in-house. Whether and how hiring practices change depends on NCES's new strategic plan. Adjusting the contractor-to-FTE ratio or shifting from temporary hires to a larger, often competitive, centralized pool of applicants will take time and may have fiscal and legal ramifications. The National Institute of Statistical Science's graphics report (NISS, 2021a) discusses phases of bringing interactive visualization expertise in-house and offers an example of the actions NCES could consider when a skills gap exists. Supporting this perspective, a recent retail trade study used firm-level data available at the U.S. Census Bureau to

---

[31]Federal Acquisition Regulation § 16.504. Available: https://www.acquisition.gov/far/16.504 [March 2022].

examine the evolution of business operations (Ding et al., 2020). The study found that, in recent years, large manufacturing firms have tended to move towards in-house professional services (including scientific and professional services) rather than outsourcing. These firms find that insourcing saves money, makes the firms more nimble, and keeps innovations in-house.

Regardless, as discussed in Chapter 2, NCES should seek to better integrate its work with IES and avoid being siloed from the remainder of IES. Currently, IES conducts evaluative work that is outside of NCES's authority but that could be supported by NCES in terms of data and statistical expertise, and IES has offices, such as the new data sciences group, that provide many opportunities for collaboration. The panel advises that NCES, in collaboration with IES, explore ways to bring together grant-making authority and contracts for producing statistical products, such that IES and its centers can work collaboratively with NCES to generate ideas, test those ideas in the research space, and subsequently operationalize those ideas.

# 6

# Summary of Recommendations

Education is changing in ways that create both challenges and opportunities. These changes have crucial implications for NCES, which is charged by Congress to take a key leadership role. However, critical factors restrain NCES from filling this intended role. For example, NCES has experienced a severe decline in full-time equivalent employees, operates under multiple constraints and unfunded mandates, is not entirely in control of its future, and lacks a unified strategic plan to guide it through difficult priority decisions.

The panel proposes a bold vision of NCES as a leader in the education data ecosystem. This report reflects the panel's efforts to reimagine what NCES can be, with each recommendation playing a role in manifesting that vision. This report cannot take the place of strategic planning, which will require an intensive self-examination and review of the education environment by NCES, working together with consultants. Instead, this report provides a blueprint of key issues and ways that NCES may seek to resolve them.

The panel provides 5 conclusions and 15 recommendations, with the fundamental recommendations being the most critical for organizational transformation. While NCES is the primary actor, some recommendations require collaboration with other actors, such as the director of the Institute of Education Services (IES) and the secretary of education. A listing of recommendations and conclusions by theme follows (see also Figure 6-1).

The goal of this chapter is to provide readers with a single listing of all recommendations and conclusions. Readers are strongly encouraged to review the individual chapters in which the recommendations and conclusions

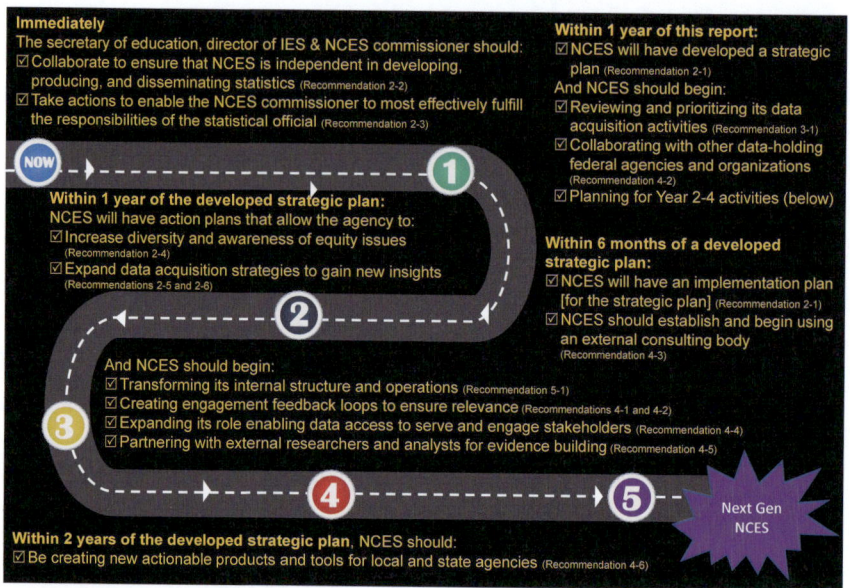

FIGURE 6-1 Roadmap with milestones and goalposts.
NOTE: Recognizing that not everything can be done at once, this graphic is intended to help prioritize the recommendations in terms of which actions must be taken first, and to illustrate what might be accomplished over the next 5 years. A final set of milestones will depend on the work of the strategic-planning effort.

are discussed in detail. The first digit of each recommendation and conclusion indicates the chapters in which the evidence, context, and examples are provided (e.g., Recommendation 4-2 is discussed in Chapter 4). For example, Chapter 3 discusses those areas in which NCES provides strong measures relating to equity and those areas where it does not, and Chapter 4 provides example of how other federal statistical agencies can produce more timely results by incorporating fewer layers of review.

## COMPLETE LISTING OF RECOMMENDATIONS AND CONCLUSIONS

### Fundamental Recommendations

Theme: Develop a Strong Strategic Plan to Make Tough Decisions

> RECOMMENDATION 2-1: To direct its future, NCES should develop and implement a bold strategic plan that incentivizes innovation and creative partnerships and that will produce relevant, timely, and reliable

statistical products to assist education decision makers at every level of government. NCES should develop and begin implementation of the plan within 1 year of the release of this report.

This panel is not the first to recommend a strategic-planning effort, and NCES has, in many ways, acted strategically. However, the country faces important challenges, such as improving equity and navigating changes in the education system that include new technologies, a movement to education outside of the traditional system, and increased use of online teaching. New data are also becoming available, with the growing use of administrative data and other big data, and there is great demand for evidence for decision making. Meanwhile, NCES faces budgetary challenges that have contributed to the discontinuation of some of its surveys. These challenges are best addressed strategically rather than piecemeal.

**Theme: Support and Empower NCES to Set Its Own Priorities**

RECOMMENDATION 2-2: The secretary of education, director of the Institute of Education Sciences, and NCES commissioner should collaborate to ensure that NCES is independent in developing, producing, and disseminating statistics.

NCES's role is somewhat ambiguous. As with many statistical agencies, it is situated within another agency, but it sometimes lacks the administrative authority common to those other agencies.

**Theme: Maximize NCES's Unique Value for Evidence Building**

RECOMMENDATION 2-3: The secretary of education, director of the Institute of Education Sciences, and NCES commissioner should immediately take actions to enable the NCES commissioner to most effectively fulfill the responsibilities of the statistical official delineated in the Foundations for Evidence-Based Policymaking Act of 2018 and to support evidence-building needs across the Department of Education.

Given the position of the NCES commissioner as the Department of Education's (ED's) statistical official, the Center needs to exercise that role more fully, while working collaboratively with IES and ED.

### Theme: Adapt to the Changing World of Education by Increasing Diversity and Awareness of Equity Issues

RECOMMENDATION 2-4: NCES should proactively embed diversity, equity, inclusion, and accessibility in all areas of its work and organization, to adapt and serve contemporary communities of the changing world of education.

The country will best succeed if it makes full use of its available resources. NCES can play a valuable role in providing data on inequity that researchers and policy makers can use to find solutions. More fundamentally, as the nation's premier education statistical agency, NCES has the responsibility of continually ensuring its collections, methods, and products accurately measure contemporary diverse populations and reflect their lived experiences. NCES should be thoughtful about diversity, equity, and accessibility considerations throughout the data life cycle, from data collection through analysis and publication. NCES will benefit from cultivating diversity within its own organization, supported by a culture of inclusivity.

### Theme: Expand Data-Acquisition Strategies to Gain New Insights

RECOMMENDATION 2-5: To improve its efficiency, timeliness, and relevance, NCES should continually explore alternative data sources for potential use in data and statistical products, conduct studies on the quality of these sources and their fitness for use, and expand responsible access to data from multiple sources and linkage tools. Testing and adoption of new data-science methods for harnessing alternative data should be done in collaboration with other federal statistical agencies, as well as with other components of the Institute of Education Sciences that are actively exploring ways to strengthen the impact of these techniques.

Data science, along with the country's movement towards digitizing much of its data, provides new opportunities for research, sometimes allowing greater depth, accuracy, and timeliness than survey research. Rather than choose between data science and survey research, each can complement the other.

RECOMMENDATION 2-6: For primary collections, NCES should modernize standard language on consent and planned usage, to permit secure secondary uses that enable high-quality follow-up studies, such as through privacy-protected linkages with other data sources.

Currently, NCES's data are constrained by difficulties associated with its use. Maintaining privacy is critical, but NCES can still look for ways to make data more readily available for secondary uses, to expand the data's value.

## Additional Recommendations and Conclusions

### Theme: Prioritize Topics, Data Content, and Statistical Information to Increase Relevance

RECOMMENDATION 3-1: NCES should conduct a top-to-bottom review of its data-acquisition activities, to prioritize topics most relevant to understanding contemporary education, and to discontinue activities that are disproportionately costly and burdensome relative to their value.

During this time of budgetary challenges, it is critical to conduct a comprehensive evaluation of which research activities are needed, and how they complement each other.

CONCLUSION 3-1: Congressional mandates constrain NCES's data collection priorities yet may no longer reflect what is important for understanding contemporary education.

RECOMMENDATION 3-2: NCES should revisit priorities mandated by Congress and, where appropriate, make recommendations for changes.

Roughly half of NCES's research topics are mandated by Congress, with some of the mandates having existed for decades. NCES should work with Congress to determine which mandates remain important.

### Theme: Expand Engagement and Dissemination for Greater Mission Impact

*Create engagement feedback loops to ensure relevance of products and services*

RECOMMENDATION 4-1: NCES should deepen and broaden its engagement with current and potential data users, to gather continuing feedback about their needs and ways that NCES can meet those needs more effectively. This feedback will help NCES shape its efforts to develop and disseminate standards, provide technical assistance, and strengthen its user community.

NCES has several mechanisms for engaging with stakeholders, particularly with regard to the National Assessment of Educational Progress (NAEP). Working to build non-NAEP stakeholder outreach could make NCES more effective and its data more widely used.

> **RECOMMENDATION 4-2:** NCES should actively collaborate with other data-holding federal agencies and organizations to develop useful products and processes, including those that utilize data from alternative sources, to provide timely, policy-relevant insights.

Other agencies often have data that are highly relevant to education, and working with those agencies could expand the usefulness of data that NCES already collects. Further, NCES might learn useful data-handling practices from other agencies, and the Center has its own strengths to share, particularly with regard to survey research and standards.

> **RECOMMENDATION 4-3:** NCES should explore and establish creative models for a nimble, ongoing consulting body, supplemented by a pool of ad hoc consultants, to help NCES innovate and be accountable for progress on strategic goals.

A body subject to Federal Advisory Committee Act regulations would probably not exhibit the required nimbleness. Rather, NCES needs both regular members who are knowledgeable of the full scope of NCES's activities and who can provide strategic advice and accountability along with periodic access to experts in specialized areas as the need arises.

## *Expand NCES's role enabling data access to serve and engage stakeholders*

> **CONCLUSION 4-1:** NCES can expand its impact by providing leadership and expertise to facilitate responsible data use and access. NCES can help organizations develop capacity to integrate and analyze education data and other data, to produce actionable analyses.

By helping to set standards for collecting, processing, and analyzing data, NCES can advance the quality and comparability of data collected by non-NCES researchers, creating a larger body of education data and analyses.

> **RECOMMENDATION 4-4:** NCES should strengthen state capacity to link data across systems, adopt shared data standards, and provide actionable information to state and local education agencies to help improve student learning outcomes. NCES can leverage its Statewide Longitudinal Data Systems Grant Program to achieve this goal.

SUMMARY OF RECOMMENDATIONS                                                      *129*

One way to support the states is to create state NCES coordinators, as NCES has already done for NAEP. This would help states create shareable data that can benefit all states, while also lessening the development work within individual states.

*Partner with external researchers and analysts for evidence building*

RECOMMENDATION 4-5: NCES, in collaboration with the Institute of Education Sciences, should establish a joint statistical research program that includes matching internal staff with highly qualified external researchers, statisticians, and data scientists to develop new data analyses, tools, and publications.

By doing this, NCES can expand the use of its data while also creating a feedback mechanism that will help NCES remain current in meeting researchers' needs and support education evidence building.

*Improve dissemination, focusing on accessibility and usefulness*

CONCLUSION 4-2: NCES can improve the accessibility and usability of its products, tools, website, and other dissemination platforms to allow a broader range of audiences to benefit from its products.

RECOMMENDATION 4-6: NCES should release data and data products that are useful, actionable, and timely for local and state education agencies and other stakeholders. To increase timeliness, NCES, in collaboration with the Institute of Education Sciences, should review and revise its internal and external quality assurance processes.

NCES is often slow to release data, and the many layers of review that NCES and IES require are one reason for this. NCES can learn from other federal statistical agencies who have shortened their review processes, staggered their data releases, or issued revised estimates.

**Theme: Transform the Internal Structure and Operations to Align with and Directly Support the Strategic Plan while Incentivizing Innovation, Experimentation, and Continuous Learning**

CONCLUSION 5-1: NCES's current organizational structure, with statistical programs separated by data source type (sample surveys and administrative data), contributes to silos that limit innovation.

By creating mechanisms to increase collaboration, share multiple types of data, and align data collections to collectively meet NCES's key priorities, NCES can promote greater cross-fertilization of ideas and more complete final products.

**CONCLUSION 5-2: NCES's current overreliance on contractors and its high turnover rate endanger the Center's ability to retain institutional knowledge and build internal capabilities needed to meet its strategic goals.**

Compared to other statistical agencies, NCES stands out in its great reliance on outside contractors, while its own staff has decreased in size. Though the use of outside contractors has often been useful, NCES has a diminished capacity even to monitor its contractors, let alone to provide leadership.

**RECOMMENDATION 5-1: NCES should utilize contractors and creative staffing arrangements to work collaboratively with staff to build internal capacity. To enhance resilience, NCES should also explore greater use of flexible contract types, stronger incentives for contractors to adopt cost-effective innovations, and performance-based requirements.**

Contractors bring valuable skills and knowledge, and NCES should make full use of contractors to strengthen its own internal operations, rather than becoming dependent on them. Employing various types of contracts may provide NCES more flexibility in how contractors are used.

## FINAL THOUGHTS

This is an opportunity that should not be lost. There is a great need for more and better data about education, and NCES is in a prime position to address that need. Doing so will require changes both within NCES and in NCES's role relative to IES and ED. In the panel's opinion, NCES should be nimble, regularly reassessing its priorities, monitoring changes in education, and responding to changes in data availability. While NCES is already performing aspects of the recommended actions, the Center can push further to fully embody each recommendation. Realizing all the fundamental recommendations will result in the substantial organizational transformation needed to attain the vision. These changes will be challenging, sometimes painful, and will require readiness for innovation. Ultimately, the investments NCES makes into its organization in the coming years will result in the reestablishment of NCES as a leader in the education data ecosystem.

# References

Advisory Committee on Data for Evidence Building. (2021). Advisory Committee on Data for Evidence Building: Year 1 Report. Available: https://www.bea.gov/system/files/2021-10/acdeb-year-1-report.pdf [March 2022].

Alessa, A., and Faezipour, M. (2018). A review of influenza detection and prediction through social networking sites. Theoretical Biological and Medical Modeling, 15(2). Available: https://doi.org/10.1186/s12976-017-0074-5.

America's Datahub Consortium. (2021). Opportunities. Available: https://www.americasdatahub.org/opportunities/ [March 2022].

American Association for Public Opinion Research. (2021). Data Collection, Measurement, and Public Opinion During a Pandemic: Abstract Book. 76th Annual Data Collection, Measurement, and Public Opinion During a Pandemic Conference. May 11–14, 2021. Virtual meeting. Available: https://www.aapor.org/AAPOR_Main/media/MainSiteFiles/2021-Abstract-Book_Draft-043021.pdf [March 2022].

American Psychological Association. (2021). APA Style: Bias-Free Language. Available: https://apastyle.apa.org/style-grammar-guidelines/bias-free-language [March 2022].

American Statistical Association, American Educational Research Association, Council of Professional Associations on Federal Statistics (COPAFS), Population Association of America/Association of Population Centers, Consortium of Social Science Associations. (2021). National Center for Education Statistics: Priorities for the 117th Congress and 2021–2025 Administration. Washington, DC: U.S. Department of Education. Available: https://www.amstat.org/docs/default-source/amstat-documents/pol-nces_priorities-2021plus.pdf [March 2022].

Backes, B., Holzer, H., and Velez, E.D. (2015). Is it worth it? Postsecondary and employment outcomes of disadvantaged students. IZA Journal of Labor Policy, 4, 1. Available: https://izajolp.springeropen.com/articles/10.1186/s40173-014-0027-0 [March 2022].

Biden, J.R., Jr. (2021). Memorandum on Restoring Trust in Government Through Scientific Integrity and Evidence-Based Policymaking (January 27, 2021). Available: https://www.whitehouse.gov/briefing-room/presidential-actions/2021/01/27/memorandum-on-restoring-trust-in-government-through-scientific-integrity-and-evidence-based-policymaking/ [March 2022].

Brown, K.S., Ford, L., and Ashley, S. (2021). Ethics and Empathy in Using Imputation to Disaggregate Data for Racial Equity: Recommendations and Standards Guide. Washington, DC: Urban Institute. Available: https://www.urban.org/sites/default/files/publication/104512/ethics-and-empathy-in-using-imputation-to-disaggregate-data-for-racial-equity_1.pdf [March 2022].

Bureau of Labor Statistics. (2021). Office of Survey Methods Research: ASA/NSF/BLS Senior Research Fellow Program. Available: https://www.bls.gov/osmr/asa_nsf_bls_fellowship_info.htm [March 2022].

Bureau of Transportation Statistics. (2022). Bureau of Transportation Statistics Strategic Plan, updated February 24, 2022. Available: https://www.bts.gov/learn-about-bts-and-our-work/bts-strategic-plan-0 [March 2022].

Carr, E.W., Reece, A., Kellerman, G., and Robichaux, A. (2019). The value of belonging at work. Harvard Business Review. Available: https://hbr.org/2019/12/the-value-of-belonging-at-work [March 2022].

Cattagni, A., and Farris, L. (2001). Internet access in U.S. public schools and classrooms: 1994–2000. Statistics in Brief. National Center for Education Statistics, U.S. Department of Education. Available: https://nces.ed.gov/pubs2001/2001071.pdf [March 2022].

Centers for Disease Control and Prevention. (2021). National Center for Health Statistics: NCHS Data Linkage Activities. Available: https://www.cdc.gov/nchs/data-linkage/index.htm [March 2022].

Chaney, B., Burgdorf, K., and Atash, N. (1997). Influencing achievement through high school graduation requirements. *Educational Evaluation and Policy Analysis,* 19, 229–244.

Chetty, R., Hendren, N., and Katz, L. (2016). The effects of exposure to better neighborhoods on children: New evidence from the Moving to Opportunity experiment. American Economic Review, 106(4), 855–902.

Coleridge Initiative. (2022). About the Multi-State Postsecondary Dashboard. Available: https://coleridgeinitiative.org/projects-and-research/multi-state-post-secondary-dashboard/ [March 2022].

Couper, M.P. (2013). Is the sky falling? New technology, changing media, and the future of surveys. Survey Research Methods, 7(3), 145–156. Available: https://doi.org/10.18148/srm/2013.v7i3.5751.

Crafts, J., Kindlon, A., and Chaney, B. (2016). "Qualitative Framework for Iterative Development of NCSES's Microbusiness Survey." Presentation at 2016 International Conference on Questionnaire Design, Development, Evaluation, and Testing (QDET2). November 12, 2016. Available: https://ww2.amstat.org/meetings/qdet2/OnlineProgram/ViewPresentation.cfm?file=303209.pptx [March 2022].

de la Cruz, G.P. (2011). A Review of the August 2008 CPS Migration Supplement Automated Questionnaire. Working Paper POP-WP092. Available: https://www.census.gov/library/working-papers/2011/demo/POP-twps0092.html [March 2022].

Desai, T., Ritchie, F., and Welpton, R. (2016). Five Safes: Designing Data Access for Research. Working Paper. Available: http://csrm.cass.anu.edu.au/sites/default/files/rsss/Ritchie_5safes.pdf [March 2022].

Ding, X., Forty, T.C., Redding, S.J., and Schott, P.K. (2020). Structural Change Within Versus Across Firms: Evidence from the United States. Working Paper. Available: https://faculty.tuck.dartmouth.edu/images/uploads/faculty/teresa-fort/DFRS_Structural_Change.pdf [March 2022].

# REFERENCES

Eggleston, C. and Fields, J. (2021). Census Bureau's Household Pulse Survey Shows Significant Increase in Homeschooling Rates in Fall 2020. U.S. Census Bureau. Available: https://www.census.gov/library/stories/2021/03/homeschooling-on-the-rise-during-covid-19-pandemic.html [March 2022].

Elchert, D., and Pierson, S. (2020). National Center for Education Statistics faces program cuts. Amstat News. American Statistical Association. Available: https://magazine.amstat.org/blog/2020/06/01/nces-faces-program-cuts/ [March 2022].

Ellis, R., Virgile, M., Holzberg, J.L., Nelson, D.V., Edgar, J., Phipps, P., and Kaplan, R. (2018). Assessing the Feasibility of Asking About Sexual Orientation and Gender Identity in the Current Population Survey: Results from Cognitive Interviews. Working Paper RSM2018-06. Available: https://www.census.gov/library/working-papers/2018/adrm/rsm2018-06.html [March 2022].

Executive Order 13985 of January 20, 2021, Advancing Racial Equity and Support for Underserved Communities Through the Federal Government, 86 Federal Register 7009 (January 25, 2021). Available: https://www.federalregister.gov/documents/2021/01/25/2021-01753/advancing-racial-equity-and-support-for-underserved-communities-through-the-federal-government [March 2022].

Executive Order 13994 of January 21, 2021, Ensuring a Data-Driven Response to COVID-19 and Future High-Consequence Public Health Threats, 86 Federal Register 7189 (January 26, 2021). Available: https://www.federalregister.gov/documents/2021/01/26/2021-01849/ensuring-a-data-driven-response-to-covid-19-and-future-high-consequence-public-health-threats [March 2022].

Executive Order 14000 of January 21, 2021, Supporting the Reopening and Continuing Operation of Schools and Early Childhood Education Providers, 86 Federal Register 7215 (January 26, 2021). Available: https://www.federalregister.gov/documents/2021/01/26/2021-01864/supporting-the-reopening-and-continuing-operation-of-schools-and-early-childhood-education-providers [March 2022].

Executive Order 14035 of June 25, 2021, Diversity, Equity, Inclusion, and Accessibility in the Federal Workforce, 86 Federal Register 34593 (June 30, 2021). Available: https://www.federalregister.gov/documents/2021/06/30/2021-14127/diversity-equity-inclusion-and-accessibility-in-the-federal-workforce [March 2022].

Flores, J.G., and Alonso, C.G. (1995). Using focus groups in educational research: Exploring teachers' perspectives on educational change. Evaluation Review, 19(1), 84–101.

Gagnon, D., and Mattingly, M.J. (2012). Beginning Teachers are More Common in Rural, High-Poverty, and Racially Diverse Schools. Carsey Institute. Available: https://scholars.unh.edu/cgi/viewcontent.cgi?article=1172&context=carsey [March 2022].

Gray, L., and Lewis, L. (2021). Use of Educational Technology for Instruction in Public Schools: 2019–20 (NCES 2021-017). Washington, DC: National Center for Education Statistics. U.S. Department of Education. Available: https://nces.ed.gov/pubsearch/pubsinfo.asp?pubid=2021017 [November 2021].

Grissmer, D., Flanagan, A., Kawata, J., and Williamson, S. (2000). Improving Student Achievement: What State NAEP Test Scores Tell Us. RAND. Available: https://www.rand.org/pubs/monograph_reports/MR924.html [March 2022].

Grodsky, E., Doren, C., Hung, K., Muller, M., and Warren, J.R. (2021). Continuing education and stratification at midlife. Sociology of Education, 94, 341–360.

Haber, J.R. (2021). Sorting schools: A computational analysis of charter school identities and stratification. Sociology of Education, 94, 43–64.

Hansen, R. (2019). New data available on prevalence of recognized student acceptance groups. National Center for Education Statistics Blog. Available: https://nces.ed.gov/blogs/nces/post/new-data-available-on-prevalence-of-recognized-student-acceptance-groups [March 2022].

Henry, S.L., Abou-Zahra, S., and White, K. (Eds.) (2016). Accessibility, Usability, and Inclusion. World Wide Web Consortium: W3C Web Accessibility Initiative. May 6, 2016. Available: https://www.w3.org/WAI/fundamentals/accessibility-usability-inclusion/ [March 2022].

Hiebert, J., Stigler, W.J., Jacobs, J.K., Bogard Givvin, K., Garnier, H., Smith, M., Hollingsworth, H., Manaster, A., Wearne, D., and Gallimore, R. (2005). Mathematics teaching in the United States today (and tomorrow): Results from the TIMSS 1999 video study. Educational Evaluation and Policy Analysis, 27, 111–132.

Holman, D., Pennington, A., Schaberg, K., and Rock, A. (Eds.). (2020). Compendium of Administrative Data Sources for Self-Sufficiency Research. OPRE Report 2020-42. Washington, DC: Office of Planning, Research, and Evaluation, Administration for Children and Families, U.S. Department of Health and Human Services. Available: https://www.acf.hhs.gov/sites/default/files/documents/opre/lto_data_compendium_032020_508.pdf [March 2022].

Indiana University. (2022). The Carnegie Classification of Institutions of Higher Education: Basic Classification Description. Available: https://carnegieclassifications.iu.edu/classification_descriptions/basic.php [March 2022].

IES (Institute of Education Sciences). (2021a). Funding Opportunities: Education Research Grant Programs. Available: https://ies.ed.gov/funding/ncer_progs.asp [March 2022].

IES. (2021b). National Board for Education Sciences. Available: https://ies.ed.gov/director/board/ [March 2022].

IES. (2021c). What Works Clearinghouse. Available: https://ies.ed.gov/ncee/wwc/ [March 2022].

IES Standards and Review Office. (2006). Procedures for Peer Review of Reports. Available: https://ies.ed.gov/director/pdf/SRO_reports_peerreview.pdf [March 2022].

Internal Revenue Services. (2021). SOI Tax Stats–Joint Statistical Research Program. Available: https://www.irs.gov/statistics/soi-tax-stats-joint-statistical-research-program [March 2022].

Irwin, V., Wang, K., Cui, J., Zhang, J., and Thompson, A. (2021). Report on Indicators of School Crime and Safety: 2020. Washington, D.C.: NCES. Available: https://nces.ed.gov/pubs2021/2021092.pdf [May 2022].

Jensen, E.B. (2013). A Review of Methods for Estimating Emigration. Working Paper 101. Available: https://www.census.gov/content/dam/Census/library/working-papers/2013/demo/POP-twps0099.pdf [March 2022].

Lederman, D. (2021). Detailing last fall's online enrollment surge. Inside Higher Ed, September 16, 2021. Available: https://www.insidehighered.com/news/2021/09/16/new-data-offer-sense-how-covid-expanded-online-learning [March 2022].

Lurye, S. (2021). Some districts plan for new full-time virtual schools to outlast the coronavirus pandemic. Washington Post, November 8. Available: https://www.washingtonpost.com/education/2021/11/08/virtual-schools-new-equity/ [March 2022].

Midwest Collaborative. (2020). Midwest Collaborative Spring Convening Report of Proceedings. Available: https://coleridgeinitiative.org/wp-content/uploads/2020/04/Midwest_Spring_Summary_Report.pdf [March 2022].

NASEM (National Academies of Sciences, Engineering, and Medicine). (1986). Creating a Center for Education Statistics: A Time for Action. Washington, DC: The National Academies Press. Available: https://doi.org/10.17226/19230.

NASEM. (2018). Improving Health Research on Small Populations: Proceedings of a Workshop. Washington, DC: The National Academies Press. Available: https://doi.org/10.17226/25112.

NASEM. (2019a). Monitoring Educational Equity. Washington, DC: The National Academies Press. Available: https://doi.org/10.17226/25389.

NASEM. (2019b). Using Models to Estimate Hog and Pig Inventories: Proceedings of a Workshop. Washington DC: The National Academies Press. Available: https://doi.org/10.17226/25526.

NASEM. (2020). A Consumer Food Data System for 2030 and Beyond. Washington, DC: The National Academies Press. Available: https://doi.org/10.17226/25657.

NASEM. (2021a). A Satellite Account to Measure the Retail Transformation: Organizational, Conceptual, and Data Foundations. Washington, DC: The National Academies Press. Available: https://doi.org/10.17226/26101.

NASEM. (2021b). Principles and Practices for a Federal Statistical Agency: Seventh Edition. Washington, DC: The National Academies Press. Available: https://doi.org/10.17226/25885.

NASEM. (2021c). Transparency in Statistical Information for the National Center for Science and Engineering Statistics and All Federal Statistical Agencies. Washington, DC: The National Academies Press. https://doi.org/10.17226/26360.

NASEM. (2022). Measuring Sex, Gender Identity, and Sexual Orientation. Washington, DC: The National Academies Press. https://doi.org/10.17226/26424.

National Center for Special Education Research. (2021). Pre-Elementary Education Longitudinal Study (PEELS). Available: https://ies.ed.gov/ncser/projects/peels/ [March 2022].

National Safety Council. (2022). Feeling Safe at Work. Available: https://www.nsc.org/getmedia/9f80b60f-05f0-4300-927f-58d1d83429ff/nsm-wk3-tipsheet.pdf [March 2022].

NCES (National Center for Education Statistics). (2018). Status and Trends in the Education of Racial and Ethnic Groups. Washington, DC: U.S. Department of Education, Institute of Education Sciences. Available: https://nces.ed.gov/programs/raceindicators/ [March 2022].

NCES. (2020). Race and Ethnicity of Public School Teachers and Their Students. Available: https://nces.ed.gov/pubsearch/pubsinfo.asp?pubid=2020103 [March 2022].

NCES. (2021a). 2017–2018 National Postsecondary Student Aid Study, Administrative Collection (NPSAS:18-AC): First Look at Student Financial Aid Estimates for 2017–2018 (NCES 2021-476). Washington, DC: U.S. Department of Education, Institute of Education Sciences. Available: https://nces.ed.gov/pubs2021/2021476.pdf [March 2022].

NCES. (2021b). About Us. Navigator. Washington, DC: U.S. Department of Education. Available: https://nces.ed.gov/about/ [March 2022].

NCES. (2021c). College Navigator. Washington, DC: U.S. Department of Education, Institute of Education Sciences. Available: https://nces.ed.gov/collegenavigator/ [March 2022].

NCES. (2021d). Digest of Education Statistics: 2019 (Table 210.30). Washington, DC: U.S. Department of Education, Institute of Education Sciences. Available: https://nces.ed.gov/programs/digest/d19/tables/dt19_210.30.asp?current=yes [March 2022].

NCES. (2021e). Digest of Education Statistics: 2020. Washington, DC: U.S. Department of Education, Institute of Education Sciences. Available: https://nces.ed.gov/programs/digest/2020menu_tables.asp [March 2022].

NCES. (2021f). Distance Learning Dataset Training. Washington, DC: U.S. Department of Education. Available: https://nces.ed.gov/training/datauser/#/ [March 2022].

NCES. (2021g). Fast Facts: Distance Learning. Washington, DC: U.S. Department of Education. Available: https://nces.ed.gov/fastfacts/display.asp?id=79 [March 2022].

NCES. (2021h). Member List: State/Local Education Agency Representatives by State. Washington, DC: U.S. Department of Education. Available: https://nces.ed.gov/forum/member_state.asp [March 2022].

NCES. (2021i). Public School District Finance Peer Search. Washington, DC: U.S. Department of Education, Institute of Education Sciences. Available: https://nces.ed.gov/edfin/search/search_intro.asp [March 2022].

NCES. (2021j). Race/Ethnic Enrollment in Public Schools. Washington, DC: U.S. Department of Education, Institute of Education Sciences. Available: https://nces.ed.gov/programs/coe/indicator/cge [March 2022].

NCES. (2021k). Revenues and Expenditures for Public Elementary and Secondary School Districts: FY 19 (NCES 2021-304). Washington, DC: U.S. Department of Education, Institute of Education Sciences. Available: https://nces.ed.gov/pubs2021/2021304.pdf [March 2022].

NCES. (2021l). School Pulse Panel: Overview. Washington, DC: U.S. Department of Education. Available: https://nces.ed.gov/surveys/spp/ [March 2022].

NCES. (2021m). Statewide Longitudinal Data Systems Grant Program. Washington, DC: U.S. Department of Education. Available: https://nces.ed.gov/programs/slds/ [March 2022].

NCES. (2022a). College Affordability Views and College Enrollment (NCES 2022-057). Washington, DC: U.S. Department of Education, Institute of Education Sciences. Available: https://nces.ed.gov/pubs2022/2022057.pdf [March 2022].

NCES. (2022b). ED School Climate Surveys (EDSCLS). Washington, DC: U.S. Department of Education. Available: https://nces.ed.gov/surveys/edscls/index.asp [March 2022].

NCES. (2022c). High School and Beyond (HS&B). Washington, DC: U.S. Department of Education. Available: https://nces.ed.gov/surveys/hsb/ [March 2022].

NCES. (2022d). High School Longitudinal Study of 2009 (HSLS:09). Washington, DC: U.S. Department of Education. Available: https://nces.ed.gov/surveys/hsls09/ [March 2022].

NCES. (2022e). Program for International Student Assessment (PISA). Washington, DC: U.S. Department of Education. Available: https://nces.ed.gov/surveys/pisa/ [March 2022].

NCES. (2022f). Trends in International Mathematics and Science Study (TIMSS). Washington, DC: U.S. Department of Education. Available: https://nces.ed.gov/timss/overview.asp [March 2022].

NISS (National Institute of Statistical Sciences). (2016). Integrity, Independence, and Innovation: The Future of NCES. Washington, DC: U.S. Department of Education. Available: https://www.niss.org/research/integrity-independence-and-innovation-future-nces [March 2022].

NISS. (2020). Post-COVID Surveys. Washington, DC: U.S. Department of Education. Available: https://www.niss.org/research/post-covid-surveys [March 2022].

NISS. (2021a). Innovative Graphics for NCES Online Reports. Washington, DC: U.S. Department of Education. Available: https://www.niss.org/research/innovative-graphics-nces-online-reports [March 2022].

NISS. (2021b). National Center for Education Statistics Report Library. Washington, DC: U.S. Department of Education. Available: https://www.niss.org/nces-report-library [March 2022].

NISS. (2021c). Setting Priorities for Federal Data Access to Expand the Context for Education Data. Washington, DC: U.S. Department of Education. Available: https://www.niss.org/research/setting-priorities-federal-data-access-expand-context-education-data [March 2022].

Pierson, S. (2021). State of the education data infrastructure: What three experts have to say about the National Center for Education Statistics. Amstat News. Available: https://magazine.amstat.org/blog/2021/09/01/nces/ [March 2022].

Rock, D., and Grant, H. (2016). Why diverse teams are smarter. Harvard Business Review. Available: https://www.agileleanhouse.com/lib/lib/Topics/Teams/Why%20Diverse%20Teams%20Are%20Smarter.pdf [March 2022].

Rock, D., Grant, H., and Grey, J. (2016). Diverse teams feel less comfortable—and that's why they perform better. Harvard Business Review. Available: https://purplebeach.com/wp-content/uploads/2020/01/HBR_diverseteamsfeellesscomfortable-2.pdf [March 2022].

RTI International. (2021). Technical Review Panel: Reports and Suggestions from Past IPEDS Technical Review Panels. Available: https://edsurveys.rti.org/ipeds_trp/ [March 2022].

Schneider, M. (2021). Reflecting on Three Years at IES. Institute of Education Sciences. April 7. Available: https://ies.ed.gov/director/remarks/4-7-2021.asp [March 2022].

Schwabish, J., and Feng, A. (2021). Do No Harm Guide: Applying Equity Awareness in Data Visualization. Washington, DC: Urban Institute. Available: https://www.urban.org/sites/default/files/publication/104296/do-no-harm-guide.pdf [March 2022].

Shernoff, D.J., Csikszentmihalyi, M., Schneider, B., and Steele Shernoff, E. (2014). Student engagement in high school classrooms from the perspective of flow theory. Pp. 475–494 in Applications of Flow in Human Development and Education. Dordrecht: Springer.

Social Security Administration. (2021). Research, Statistics & Policy Analysis. Washington DC: Social Security Administration. Available: https://www.ssa.gov/policy/extramural/index.html [March 2022].

Torres, A., Kelley, C., Kelley, S., Piña, G., Garcia-Baza, I., and Griffith, I. (2021). An analysis of digital media data to understand parents' concerns during the COVID-19 pandemic to enhance effective science communication. Journal of Creative Communications, 16(2). Available: https://journals.sagepub.com/doi/full/10.1177/09732586211000281.

U.S. Census Bureau. (2021a). Apply for Access. Washington, DC: U.S. Census Bureau. Available: https://www.census.gov/about/adrm/ced/apply-for-access.html [March 2022].

U.S. Census Bureau. (2021b). Census Bureau Administrative Inventory. Washington, DC: U.S. Census Bureau. Available: https://www2.census.gov/about/linkage/data-file-inventory.pdf [March 2022].

U.S. Census Bureau. (2021c). Data Linkage Infrastructure Projects. Washington, DC: U.S. Census Bureau. Available: https://www.census.gov/about/adrm/linkage/projects.html [March 2022].

U.S. Census Bureau. (2021d). Longitudinal Employer-Household Dynamics: Post-Secondary Employment Outcomes (PSEO). Washington, DC: U.S. Census Bureau. Available: https://lehd.ces.census.gov/data/pseo_experimental.html [March 2022].

U.S. Census Bureau. (2021e). Restricted-Use Data. Washington, DC: U.S. Census Bureau. Available: https://www.census.gov/programs-surveys/ces/data/restricted-use-data.html [March 2022].

U.S. Census Bureau. (2021f). Week 30 Household Pulse Survey: May 12–May 24. Washington, DC: U.S. Census Bureau. Available: https://www.census.gov/data/tables/2021/demo/hhp/hhp30.html [March 2022].

U.S. Census Bureau. (2021g). What are Experimental Data Products? Washington, DC: U.S. Census Bureau. Available: https://www.census.gov/data/experimental-data-products.html [March 2022].

U.S. Department of Labor. (2021). Employment and Training Administration: Federal Employment Data Exchange System (FEDES). Available: https://www.dol.gov/agencies/eta/performance/fedes [March 2022].

U.S. Department of Education (ED). (2013). Office for Civil Rights, Resolution Agreement: South Carolina Technical College System OCR Compliance Review No. 11-11-6002. Available: https://www2.ed.gov/about/offices/list/ocr/docs/investigations/11116002-b.html [March 2022].

U.S. ED. (2020). U.S. Department of Education Data Strategy. Available: https://www.ed.gov/sites/default/files/cdo/ed-data-strategy.pdf [March 2022].

U.S. ED. (2021a). College Scorecard. Available: https://collegescorecard.ed.gov/ [March 2022].

U.S. ED. (2021b). Open Government Initiative at ED. Available: https://www.ed.gov/open/plan/nces [March 2022].

U.S. ED. (2021c). Protecting Student Privacy. Available: https://studentprivacy.ed.gov/about-us [March 2022].

U.S. Environmental Protection Agency. (2022). National Aquatic Resource Surveys Data Analysis Innovation Challenge. Available: https://www.epa.gov/innovation/national-aquatic-resource-surveys-data-analysis-innovation-challenge/ [March 2022].

U.S. General Services Administration. (2021a). IT Accessibility Laws and Policies. Washington, DC: U.S. Access Board. Available: https://www.section508.gov/manage/laws-and-policies/ [March 2022].

U.S. General Services Administration. (2021b). Section 508.gov: Buy. Build. Be Accessible. Available: https://www.section508.gov/ [March 2022].

U.S. House of Representatives Committee on Appropriations. (2021). Explanatory Statement for Department of Labor, Health and Human Services, and Education, and Related Agencies Appropriations Bill, 2022. Washington, DC: U.S. Congress. Available: https://www.appropriations.senate.gov/imo/media/doc/LHHSREPT_FINAL3.PDF [March 2022].

U.S. OMB (U.S. Office of Management and Budget). (2004). Final Information Quality Bulletin for Peer Review. OMB Memorandum M-05-03. Available: https://obamawhitehouse.archives.gov/sites/default/files/omb/assets/omb/memoranda/fy2005/m05-03.pdf [March 2022].

U.S. OMB. (2008). Statistical Policy Directive No. 4: Release and dissemination of statistical products produced by federal statistical agencies. 73 Federal Register 12625 (March 7, 2008). Available: https://www.govinfo.gov/content/pkg/FR-2008-03-07/pdf/E8-4570.pdf [March 2022].

U.S. OMB. (2014a). Guidance for Providing and Using Administrative Data for Statistical Purposes. OMB Memorandum M-14-06. Available: https://obamawhitehouse.archives.gov/sites/default/files/omb/memoranda/2014/m-14-06.pdf [March 2022].

U.S. OMB. (2014b). Statistical Policy Directive No. 1: Fundamental responsibilities of federal statistical agencies and recognized statistical units. 79 Federal Register 71609 (December 2, 2014). Available: https://www.govinfo.gov/content/pkg/FR-2014-12-02/pdf/2014-28326.pdf [March 2022].

U.S. OMB. (2016). OMB Circular A-108, Federal agency responsibilities for review, reporting, and publication under the Privacy Act. 81 Federal Register 94424 (December 23, 2016). Available: https://www.whitehouse.gov/omb/information-regulatory-affairs/privacy/ [March 2022].

U.S. OMB. (2019a). Improving Implementation of the Information Quality Act. OMB Memorandum M-19-15. Available: https://www.whitehouse.gov/wp-content/uploads/2019/04/M-19-15.pdf [March 2022].

U.S. OMB. (2019b). Phase 1 Implementation of the Foundations for Evidence-Based Policymaking Act of 2018: Learning Agendas, Personnel, and Planning Guidance. OMB Memorandum M-19-23. Available: https://www.whitehouse.gov/wp-content/uploads/2019/07/M-19-23.pdf [March 2022].

U.S. OMB. (2020). Statistical Programs of the United States Government: Fiscal Years 2019/2020. Statistical and Science Policy Office, Office of Information and Regulatory Affairs. Washington, DC: U.S. Government Printing Office. Available: https://www.whitehouse.gov/wp-content/uploads/2020/12/statistical-programs-20192020.pdf [March 2022].

U.S. OMB. (2022). The Interagency Council on Statistical Policy's recommendation for a standard application process (SAP) for requesting access to certain confidential data assets. 87 Federal Register 2459 (January 14, 2022). Available: https://www.federalregister.gov/documents/2022/01/14/2022-00620/the-interagency-council-on-statistical-policys-recommendation-for-a-standard-application-process-sap [March 2022].

University of Washington. (2021). What Is the Difference Between Accessible, Usable, and Universal Design? University of Washington. Available: https://www.washington.edu/doit/what-difference-between-accessible-usable-and-universal-design [March 2022].

# REFERENCES

Westat. (2016). Evaluation of the Illinois Network for Advanced Manufacturing: Final Report. Bethesda, MD: PTB & Associates. Available: https://www.skillscommons.org/bitstream/handle/taaccct/15660/William%20Rainey%20Harper%20College%20-%20Final%20Evaluation%20Report.pdf?sequence=1&isAllowed=y [March 2022].

Western Interstate Commission for Higher Education. (2021). Multistate Longitudinal Data Exchange. Boulder, CO: Western Interstate Commission for Higher Education. Available: https://www.wiche.edu/key-initiatives/multistate-longitudinal-data-exchange/ [March 2022].

Wikipedia. (2021a). Data Governance. Available: https://en.wikipedia.org/wiki/Data_governance [March 2022].

Wikipedia. (2021b). Five Safes. Available: https://en.wikipedia.org/wiki/Five_safes [March 2022].

Wikipedia. (2022). Validity (statistics). Available: https://en.wikipedia.org/wiki/Validity_(statistics) [March 2022].

Wilde, P., and Ismail, M. (2018). Review of the National Household Food Acquisition and Purchase Survey (FoodAps) from a Data User's Perspective. Available: https://www.ers.usda.gov/media/9776/foodaps_datauserperspective.pdf [March 2022].

Zehler, A.M., Miyaoka, A., Chaney, B., Orellana, V., Vahey, P., Gibney, D.T., Yee, K., and Yilmazel-Sahin, Y. (2019). Supporting English Learners Through Technology: What Districts and Teachers Say About Digital Learning Resources for English Learners. U.S. Department of Education, Office of Planning, Evaluation and Policy Development, Policy and Program Studies Service. Available: https://www2.ed.gov/rschstat/eval/title-iii/180414.pdf [March 2022].

# Appendix A

# Glossary of Terms and Acronyms Used in This Report

| | |
|---|---|
| 508 compliance | Federal agencies' responsibilities under Section 508 of the Rehabilitation Act to make websites, documents, and products accessible to people with disabilities. |
| Accessibility | When "[a] person with a disability is afforded the opportunity to acquire the same information, engage in the same interactions, and enjoy the same services as a person without a disability in an equally effective and equally integrated manner, with substantially equivalent ease of use" (U.S. ED, 2013). |
| Administrative records | Administrative data are defined in varying ways, but traditionally refer to data collected by governments for other than statistical purposes (e.g., through the process of administering a program). See Appendix B for more detail. |
| Alternative data sources | Includes administrative data as well as other data from sources and technologies currently available (e.g., commercial data, web-scraped data, processing of video or audio data) and those that may become available in the future. These sources are alternative to the collection of data using surveys and censuses, the traditional federal statistical approaches (though many of the traditional approaches have relied on |

| | |
|---|---|
| | administrative data for frames, imputations, and other uses). |
| API | Application programming interface. |
| ASA | American Statistical Association. |
| ATES | The Adult Training and Education Survey, a module on the National Household Education Survey, collected data on adults ages 16–65 not enrolled in high school, focusing on nondegree credentials and work experience programs. See Table B-1 for more detail. |
| B&B | The Baccalaureate and Beyond Longitudinal Study, which "examines students' education and work experiences after they complete a bachelor's degree, with a special emphasis on the experiences of new elementary and secondary teachers. Following several cohorts of students over time, B&B looks at bachelor's degree recipients' workforce participation, income and debt repayment, and entry into and persistence through graduate school programs, among other indicators" (Table B-1). |
| BEA | Bureau of Economic Analysis. |
| BJS | Bureau of Justice Statistics. |
| BLS | Bureau of Labor Statistics. |
| Blue Book | Informal name for the *Statistical Programs of the United States Government,* an annual publication of the U.S. Executive Office of the President, Office of Management and Budget, which summarizes U.S. government statistical activities. |
| BPS | "Each cycle of the Beginning Postsecondary Students Longitudinal Study (BPS) follows a cohort of students who are enrolled in their first year of postsecondary education. The study collects data on student persistence in, and completion of, postsecondary education programs [including postsecondary transcript studies], their transition to employment, |

# APPENDIX A

143

|  |  |
|---|---|
| | demographic characteristics, and changes over time in their goals, marital status, income, and debt, among other indicators" (Table B-1). |
| BTLS | Beginning Teacher Longitudinal Study. See Table B-1 for more detail. |
| BTS | Bureau of Transportation Statistics. |
| CCD | Common Core of Data. |
| CDO | Chief data officer. |
| CEDS | "The Common Education Data Standards (CEDS) are a national, collaborative effort to develop voluntary, common education data standards for a key subset of K–12 (e.g., demographics, program participation, course information) and K–12-to-postsecondary education transition variables" (Table B-1). |
| CIP | "The Classification of Instructional Programs (CIP) provides a taxonomic scheme that supports the accurate tracking and reporting of postsecondary fields of study and program completions activity in IPEDS. An important product of the CIP effort is the crosswalk of CIP program codes to the Standard Occupational Classification (SOC) system, which is referred to as the CIP-SOC Crosswalk" (Table B-1). |
| CIPSEA | The Confidential Information Protection and Statistical Efficiency Act |
| COR | Contracting officer's representative. |
| CPS | Current Population Survey, a labor force survey collected by the Bureau of Labor Statistics. NCES co-sponsors the October Supplement to the CPS. See Table B-1 for more detail. |
| CTE | Career and technical education. |
| Data governance | "Data governance is a term used on both a macro and a micro level. The former is a political concept |

and forms part of international relations and internet governance; the latter is a data management concept and forms part of corporate data governance" (Wikipedia, 2021a).

Diversity          The presence of differences that may include race and ethnicity, gender identity, (dis)ability, religion, sexual orientation, socioeconomic status, language, Veteran status, age, and other intersubjective categories that historically have served to systematically and differentially allocate material resources and symbolic value to various members of society. This includes differences in life experiences and often includes populations that have been and remain underrepresented and marginalized in the broader society.

DOL                Department of Labor.

ECLS-B             Early Childhood Longitudinal Study: Birth Cohort (2001), longitudinal survey of children from birth through kindergarten. Initial collection in 2001. There were four interviews at age 9 months, 2 years, preschool, and kindergarten. See Table B-1 for more detail.

ECPP               Early Childhood Program Participation, a module of the National Household Education Survey. See Table B-1 for more detail.

ED                 Department of Education.

EDGE               Education, Demographic and Geographic Estimates program. See Table B-1 for more detail.

EDSCLS             "ED School Climate Surveys (EDSCLS) are a suite of survey instruments that were developed for schools, districts, and states by NCES. This NCES effort extends activities to measure and support school climate by ED's Office of Safe and Healthy Students (OSHS). Through EDSCLS, schools nationwide have access to survey instruments and a survey platform that allows for the collection and reporting of school

APPENDIX A

climate data across stakeholders at the local level. The surveys can be used to produce school-, district-, and state-level scores on various indicators of school climate from the perspectives of students, teachers, non-instructional school staff, principals, and parents/guardians. NCES also developed psychometric benchmarks to enable meaningful comparisons between student subgroups and between schools" (NCES, 2022b).

| | |
|---|---|
| Education data ecosystem | The dynamic system of education data sources and producers, methods, products, services, and consumers and their mutually reinforcing interrelationships. |
| EIA | Energy Information Administration. |
| ELS | Education Longitudinal Study (2002), one of a series of six longitudinal studies following middle- or high-school students through school and sometimes beyond. Depending on the survey, the data include surveys of students, parents, teachers, school administrators, student assessments in math and English, and high school transcripts. |
| EO | Evaluation Officer. |
| Equity | The "process of ensuring processes and programs are impartial, fair, [just,] and provide equal possible outcomes for every individual. It is about deconstructing the systems that do not treat people the way they should and would want to be treated" (National Safety Council, 2022, p. 1). |
| ERS | Economic Research Service. |
| ESRA | Education Sciences Reform Act of 2002, established the Institute of Education Sciences (IES), with the National Center for Education Statistics as one of IES's centers. |
| Evidence | The collection, compilation, processing, analysis, and dissemination of an available body of facts, signs, or objects indicating whether a belief or proposition is |

true or valid. U.S. law on confidential information protection and statistical efficiency defines evidence as "information produced as a result of statistical activities conducted for a statistical purpose" (44 U.S. Code § 3561(6). Available: https://www.law.cornell.edu/uscode/text/44/3561). The U.S. Office of Management and Budget provides additional guidance that evidence includes "four interdependent components…: foundational fact finding, policy analysis, program evaluation, and performance measurement. Each of these components informs and directs the others, and many evidence-building activities may be hard to categorize because they organically include more than one component" (OMB, 2019b, p. 13).

| | |
|---|---|
| Evidence Act | Foundations for Evidence-Based Policymaking Act of 2018. |
| Experimental data | Experimental data are typically collected through an experimental or quasi-experimental design in attempt to determine a causal relationship. Randomized controlled trials are often considered the gold standard for generating experimental data. |
| FEDES | Federal Employment Data Exchange System, a program of the Employment and Training Administration (ETA) of the Department of Labor. The system was suspended as of February 2018, but ETA was working with the Office of Personnel Management and the Department of Defense to establish the necessary protocols for the exchange of wage data. The system was intended to provide state agencies with an efficient way to include federal employment information in performance and evaluation reports required by federal and state law and regulations, and data were to be exchanged quarterly between participating states and participating federal agencies (U.S. Department of Labor, 2021). |
| FRSS | Fast Response Survey System, which conducted multiple surveys per year on special topics sometimes |

APPENDIX A

|  |  |
|---|---|
|  | requested by NCES and sometimes by other ED agencies. The survey respondents have included public and private elementary and secondary schools, elementary and secondary school teachers and principals, local education agencies, public libraries, and school libraries. The system ended in 2021 because of staffing issues at NCES. See Table B-1 for more detail. |
| FTE | Full-time equivalent, with respect to employees. |
| FY | Fiscal year. |
| HS&B | High School and Beyond Longitudinal Survey (1982 and planned for 2022), two of a series of six longitudinal studies following middle- or high-school students through school and sometimes beyond. Depending on the survey, the data include surveys of students, parents, teachers, school administrators, student assessments in math and English, and high-school transcripts (NCES, 2022c). |
| HSLS | High School Longitudinal Study of 2009, one of a series of six longitudinal studies following middle- or high-school students through school and sometimes beyond. Depending on the survey, the data include surveys of students, parents, teachers, school administrators, student assessments in math and English, and high-school transcripts (NCES, 2022d). |
| HSTS | High School Transcript Study. See Table B-1 for more detail. |
| IAA | Interagency agreement. |
| IAP | International Activities Program. |
| IES | Institute of Education Sciences, parent organization of NCES. |
| Inclusion | The practice of ensuring that people feel a sense of belonging and that everyone, regardless of background, can participate fully in development |

opportunities and decision-making processes that affect their lives.

IPA — Intergovernmental Personnel Act Mobility Program.

IPEDS — "The Integrated Postsecondary Education Data System (IPEDS), established as the core postsecondary education data collection program for NCES, is a system of surveys designed to collect data from all...institutions and educational organizations whose primary purpose is to provide postsecondary education. The IPEDS system is built around a series of 12 interrelated surveys to collect institution-level data in such areas as enrollments, program completions, faculty, staff, finances, and academic libraries" (Table B-1).

IRS — Internal Revenue Service.

LEA — Local education agency.

MGLS2017 — Middle Grades Longitudinal Survey. See Table B-1 for more detail.

NAAL/NALS — The National Assessment of Adult Literacy is "a nationally representative assessment of English literacy among American adults age 16 and older" (Table B-1). It is preceded by the National Adult Literacy Survey (NALS), conducted in 1992.

NAEP — "The National Assessment of Educational Progress (NAEP), also known as 'the Nation's Report Card,' is the only nationally representative and continuing assessment of what America's students know and can do in various subject areas. Since 1969, assessments have been conducted periodically in reading, mathematics, science, writing, U.S. history, civics, geography, and the arts. In addition to tests of students' knowledge, NAEP includes surveys of students, teachers, and principals. NAEP is a congressionally mandated survey" (Table B-1).

NASS — National Agricultural Statistics Service.

APPENDIX A

| | |
|---|---|
| NCEE | National Center for Education Evaluation and Regional Assistance. The commissioner of NCEE is the Department of Education's chief evaluation officer. |
| NCES | National Center for Education Statistics. The commissioner of NCES is the Department of Education's chief statistical official. |
| NCHS | National Center for Health Statistics. |
| NCSER | National Center for Special Education Research. |
| NCSES | National Center for Science and Engineering Statistics. |
| NCVS | National Crime Victimization Survey, a household survey collected by the Bureau of Justice Statistics. See Table B-1 for more detail. |
| NELS | National Education Longitudinal Study of 1988 (NELS:88), one of a series of six longitudinal studies following middle- or high-school students through school and sometimes beyond. Depending on the survey, the data include surveys of students, parents, teachers, school administrators, student assessments in math and English, and high-school transcripts. See Table B-1 for more detail. |
| NHES | National Household Education Survey, conducted for NCES by the U.S. Census Bureau. Consists of modules that address various topics, such as early childhood care and education, family involvement in schools, and homeschooling. See Table B-1 for more detail. |
| NISS | National Institute of Statistical Sciences. |
| NLS | National Longitudinal Study (1972), one of a series of six longitudinal studies following middle- or high-school students through school and sometimes beyond. Depending on the survey, the data include surveys of students, parents, teachers, school administrators, student assessments in math and English, and high-school transcripts. See Table B-1 for more detail. |

| | |
|---|---|
| NPSAS | "The National Postsecondary Student Aid Study (NPSAS) is a comprehensive study [using both student interviews and administrative records] that examines how students and their families pay for postsecondary education. It includes nationally representative samples of undergraduate and graduate students, as well as students attending public and private less-than-2-year institutions, community colleges, 4-year colleges, and major universities. Both students who receive financial aid and those who do not receive financial aid [are sampled]. NPSAS has been conducted every 3–4 years since 1987" (Table B-1). |
| NPSAS:18-AC | National Postsecondary Student Aid Study, Administrative Collection. |
| NSOPF | The National Study of Postsecondary Faculty was "a nationally representative sample of full- and part-time faculty and instructional staff at public and private not-for-profit 2- and 4-year institutions in the United States, designed to provide data about faculty and instructional staff to postsecondary education researchers and policy makers. There are no plans to repeat the study. Rather, NCES plans to provide technical assistance to state postsecondary data systems" (Table B-1). |
| NTPS | The National Teacher and Principal Survey "collects extensive data on American public and private elementary and secondary schools every two to three years….NTPS provides data on characteristics and qualifications of teachers and principals, teacher hiring practices, professional development, class size, and other conditions in schools. NTPS replaces the Schools and Staffing Survey, which was last conducted in the 2011–12 school year" (Table B-1). |
| OMB | U.S. Office of Management and Budget, Executive Office of the President. |
| OPEPD | Office of Planning, Evaluation and Policy Development in the Department of Education. It is the umbrella office for the Office of the Chief Data Officer. |

APPENDIX A

| | |
|---|---|
| OPM | U.S. Office of Personnel Management. |
| ORES | Office of Research, Evaluation, and Statistics, a statistical office in the Social Security Administration. |
| PEELS | The Pre-Elementary Education Longitudinal Study collected data on "the preschool and early elementary school experiences of a nationally representative sample of children with disabilities and the outcomes they achieved, and included children's preschool environments and experiences, their transition to kindergarten, their kindergarten and early elementary education experiences, and their academic and adaptive skills" (National Center for Special Education Research, 2021). This is a NCSER study and NCES issues restricted data licenses for the data and provides publicly available data in its DATALAB tool (National Center for Special Education Research, 2021). |
| PEQIS | Postsecondary Education Quick Information System. See Table B-1 for more detail. |
| PFI | The Parent and Family Involvement in Education (PFI) is a module conducted as part of the National Household Education Survey. See Table B-1 for more detail. |
| PIAAC | Program for the International Assessment of Adult Competencies. See Table B-1 for more detail. |
| PII | Personally identifiable information. |
| PISA | The Program for International Student Assessment is "an international assessment that measures 15-year-old students' reading, mathematics, and science literacy every three years. First conducted in 2000, the major domain of study rotates between reading, mathematics, and science in each cycle" (NCES, 2022e). PISA is conducted by NCES in coordination with the Organisation for Economic Co-operation and Development (NCES, 2022e). |

| | |
|---|---|
| PSS | The Private School Survey, "a biennial universe collection of private elementary and secondary schools. PSS generates biennial data on the total number of private schools, teachers, and students and builds an accurate and complete list of private schools to serve as a sampling frame for NCES surveys of private schools" (Table B-1). |
| PTAC | The Privacy Technical Assistance Center, located in the U.S. Department of Education's Student Privacy Policy Office. It was "established in 2010 a 'one-stop' resource for education stakeholders to learn about data privacy, confidentiality, and security practices related to student-level data systems and other uses of student data" (U.S. ED, 2021c). PTAC provides several services, such as a help desk, training materials, and technical assistance (U.S. ED, 2021c). NCES was a key player in the development of PTAC, a departmentwide initiative under ED's Open Government Plan in 2010 (U.S. ED, 2021b). |
| R1 | A category of the Carnegie Classification of Institutions of Higher Education, indicating U.S. doctoral universities that engage in "very high research activity" (Indiana University, 2022). |
| Randomized controlled trial | Provides one form of experimental data, frequently viewed as the gold standard of experimental data (see Experimental data). |
| RUD license | Restricted Use Data License. NCES uses RUD licenses as a mechanism for making more detailed data available to qualified researchers. |
| SASS | Schools and Staffing Survey, an NCES survey last conducted in 2011–2012 and replaced by the National Teacher and Principal Survey. See Table B-1 for more detail. |
| SCED | School Codes for the Exchange of Data, a course classification system designed to facilitate schools' and districts' maintenance of secondary-level transcript |

# APPENDIX A

|  |  |
|---|---|
|  | data over time and the transfers of those data among districts and states. See Table B-1 for more detail. |
| SCS | School Crime Supplement, a supplement of the National Crime Victimization Survey. See Table B-1 for more detail. |
| SEA | State education agency. |
| SL position | Senior Level position, a "category of high level Federal jobs [that] was established in 1990 to replace GS-16, 17, and 18 of the General Schedule. There are two broad types of SL positions. Most Senior Level employees are in non-executive positions whose duties are broad and complex enough to be classified above GS 15. However, in a few agencies that are statutorily exempt from inclusion in the Senior Executive Service, executive positions are staffed with SL employees" (U.S. Office of Personnel Management, Policy, Data, Oversight: Senior Executive Service. Available: https://www.opm.gov/policy-data-oversight/senior-executive-service/scientific-senior-level-positions [March 2022]). |
| SLDS | Statewide Longitudinal Data Systems Grant Program. |
| SO | Statistical official, as established under the Evidence Act. |
| SOC | Standard Occupational Classification system. |
| SOI | Statistics of Income Division, a statistical office in the Internal Revenue Service. |
| SPP | School Pulse Panel survey. The school pulse panel is a monthly panel study to examine the impact of the coronavirus pandemic on K–12 public schools. It produces nationally representative data with a quick turnaround. SPP is conducted by the U.S. Census Bureau on behalf of NCES. See Table B-1 for more detail. |
| SSA | Social Security Administration. |

| | |
|---|---|
| SSOCS | School Survey on Crime and Safety, a "sample survey of the nation's public schools designed to provide estimates of school crime, discipline, disorder, programs, and policies" (Table B-1). |
| ST position | Senior Technical position. "This unique category of Federal jobs covers non-executive positions classified above the GS-15 level, and involves performance of high-level research and development in the physical, biological, medical, or engineering sciences, or a closely-related field. Many of the Federal Government's most renowned scientists and engineers serve in ST positions" (U.S. Office of Personnel Management, Policy, Data, Oversight: Senior Executive Service. Available: https://www.opm.gov/policy-data-oversight/senior-executive-service/scientific-senior-level-positions [March 2022]). |
| Statistical activities | "The collection, compilation, processing, or analysis of data for the purpose of describing or making estimates concerning the whole, or relevant groups or components within, the economy, society, or the natural environment. [This] includes the development of methods or resources that support those activities, such as measurement methods, models, statistical classifications, or sampling frames" (44 U.S. Code § 3561(10). Available: https://www.law.cornell.edu/uscode/text/44/3561 [March 2022]). |
| Statistical purpose | "The description, estimation, or analysis of the characteristics of groups, without identifying the individuals or organizations that comprise such groups. [This] includes the development, implementation, or maintenance of methods, technical or administrative procedures, or information resources that support [these] purposes" (44 U.S. Code § 3561(12). Available: https://www.law.cornell.edu/uscode/text/44/3561 [March 2022]). |
| STEM | Science, technology, engineering, and mathematics. |
| TIMSS | Trends in International Mathematics and Science Study, which "provides reliable and timely trend |

APPENDIX A

|  |  |
|---|---|
|  | data on the mathematics and science achievement of U.S. students compared to that of students in other countries. TIMSS data have been collected from students at grades 4 and 8 every 4 years since 1995.... TIMSS is sponsored by the International Association for the Evaluation of Educational Achievement and conducted in the United States by the National Center for Education Statistics" (NCES, 2022f). |
| USDA | U.S. Department of Agriculture. |
| Validity | "Validity is the main extent to which a concept, conclusion or measurement is well-founded and likely corresponds accurately to the real world" (Wikipedia, 2022). |
| Web-scraping method | An automated process of collecting data from an online source. Also known as an internet harvesting method. See Appendix B for more detail. |

# Appendix B

# Data Sources and Collection Approaches

This appendix describes selected data sources relevant to this study, including traditional data sources already used by NCES. The primary legacy data source for statistical agencies is data that can be derived only through probability sample surveys, such as longitudinal and cross-sectional surveys. Administrative data have also been extensively used for statistical purposes by federal statistical agencies including NCES, but expansion of their use has been encouraged by the U.S. Office of Management and Budget (U.S. OMB, 2014a). New sources of data include commercial data (available for purchase), data available through web scraping, wearable recording devices, transcribing of video and/or audio recordings, and others. Here, we refer to *alternative data sources* to include administrative data (because new uses are emerging) in addition to commercial/proprietary and web-scraped data, data available from transcription of video and audio recordings, as well as sources/methodologies that may lead to new data in the future. We provide definitions as used in this report; they are not meant to be definitive descriptions for the field of statistics.

This report recommends that NCES expand its use of alternative data sources and new collection methodologies. This has been an active area of research for all statistical agencies in recent years as online data sources proliferate and novel ways to use data sources emerge. This is part of a natural evolution and modernization. New data sources and approaches may provide cost-effective ways to counter some of the challenges with the traditional sample survey approach (e.g., surveys are expensive and time-consuming, respondents may find them burdensome, and achieving high response rates has become more challenging). However, alternative data

## PROBABILITY SAMPLE SURVEYS

In probability sample surveys, some or all members of a population are selected to participate, each with a known probability of selection. When all members are selected, the probability of selection is one and the survey is called a census. An advantage of probability sample surveys is that the tabulated responses represent the entire population, and a measure of accuracy can be calculated. Probability-based surveys form the bulk of government data collections.

Two common types of surveys are *cross-sectional*, in which respondents are surveyed at a single point in time, and *longitudinal*, in which the same respondents are surveyed over multiple points in time with the intention of measuring change over time. A third alternative is *experience* sampling, in which the time period is also part of the sampling. Experience sampling has been useful for capturing "in-the-moment" states of mind and responses to ongoing situations (e.g., a class). Shernoff et al. (2014) provide an interesting example.

Surveys can incorporate a variety of measurements in addition to those obtained from questionnaires: tests or assessments, record collection, classroom observations, and physical measurements, such as blood pressure. Other measurement approaches made possible by technology include studies that involve video (and its coded version), audio (e.g., of classrooms), and text (e.g., syllabi and lesson plans). Hiebert et al. (2005) provide a useful example of a study using video recordings.

As illustrated in Table B-1, NCES has an extensive history of repeated longitudinal surveys, especially of students in grades K–5, secondary, post-secondary (and beyond) NCES longitudinal surveys typically include interviews with students, parents, and teachers, as well as administrative data and transcript study results, based on coding and summarizing transcript information in a consistent way. Additional value is derived from these surveys by the use of selected follow-on studies (sometimes funded by other parties) that target longitudinal survey participants with additional questions at a later date. The follow-on studies of the High School and Beyond (1982) sophomore cohort conducted in 2015 and 2021 are one example.[1]

---

[1] For additional information, see: https://sites.utexas.edu/hsb/ [March 2022].

TABLE B-1 NCES Public Data Sources (Selected)‡

| Level of Education | NCES Products | Survey, Administrative or Other | Characteristics, Topics, etc. | Frequency, Lag Time, etc. | Link |
|---|---|---|---|---|---|
| Pre-K | Early Childhood Longitudinal Survey, Birth Cohort (ECLS-B) | Longitudinal survey | Longitudinal survey of children from birth through K. | Initial collection in 2001. Four interviews at age 9 months, 2 years, preschool, and kindergarten. | https://nces.ed.gov/ecls/birth.asp |
| K–12 | Early Childhood Longitudinal Survey, Kindergarten Cohorts (ECLS-K) | Longitudinal survey | Longitudinal surveys of children from K through grade 8 (1998–99), or from K through grade 5 (2010–11, and 2023–24) | Survey first fielded for grades K–8 beginning in 1998–99, K–5 in 2010–11, and 2023–24. | https://nces.ed.gov/ecls/ |

*continued*

*159*

TABLE B-1 Continued

| Level of Education | NCES Products | Survey, Administrative or Other | Characteristics, Topics, etc. | Frequency, Lag Time, etc. | Link |
|---|---|---|---|---|---|
| K–12 | School Crime Supplement (SCS) to the Bureau of Justice Statistics National Crime Victimization Survey (NCVS) | Cross-sectional survey | NCVS is a household survey that collects information from household members age 12 or older about crime victimization within the last 6 months. The School Crime Supplement (SCS) collects information from students age 12 to 18 about victimization, crime, and safety at school (public, private elementary, middle, and high schools). The SCS asks about school-related topics such as alcohol and drug availability; fighting, bullying, and hate-related behaviors; fear and avoidance behaviors; gun and weapon carrying; and gangs at school. | As of September 2021, SCS data were available for 1989, 1995, 1999, 2001, 2003, 2005, 2007, 2009, 2011, 2013, 2015, 2017, and 2019. | https://nces.ed.gov/programs/crime/surveys.asp |
| K–12 | School Survey on Crime and Safety (SSOCS) | Cross-sectional survey | SSOCS is a sample survey of the nation's public schools designed to provide estimates of school crime, discipline, disorder, programs, and policies. SSOCS is administered to public primary, middle, high, and combined school principals in the spring of even-numbered school years. Due to staffing and funding issues, SSOCS 2022 will be the final collection | Data collected every other year in even numbered years. Most recent data product available in September 2021 was from 2017–2018. However, data used in Report on Indicators of School Crime and Safety (Irwin et al., 2021) | https://nces.ed.gov/surveys/ssocs/ |

| K–12 | Middle Grades Longitudinal Study (MGLS2017) | Longitudinal survey | The Middle Grades Longitudinal Study of 2017–18 (MGLS:2017) follows a nationally representative sample of students as they enter and move through the middle grades. The study is focusing on student growth in mathematics and literacy skills. | Two rounds of collection: first round 2018 (students in 6th grade in 2017), second round 2020. | https://nces.ed.gov/surveys/mgls/ |
|---|---|---|---|---|---|
| K–12 | Secondary Longitudinal Sample Surveys | Longitudinal surveys | A series of six longitudinal studies following middle- or high-school students through school and sometimes beyond. Depending on the survey, the data include surveys of students, parents, teachers, school administrators, student assessments in math and English, and high-school transcripts. NLS:72, HS&B:82, NELS:88, ELS:2002, HSLS:09 and HS&B:22. | New longitudinal series are periodically created to provide updated data. The most recent are ELS:2002, following 10th graders in 2002 and 12th graders in 2004 through secondary and postsecondary years | https://nces.ed.gov/surveys/els2002/ |

*continued*

TABLE B-1 Continued

| Level of Education | NCES Products | Survey, Administrative or Other | Characteristics, Topics, etc. | Frequency, Lag Time, etc. | Link |
|---|---|---|---|---|---|
| K–12 | Fast Response Survey System (FRSS) | Survey system | This system has conducted multiple surveys per year on special topics sometimes requested by NCES and sometimes by other ED agencies using this as a vehicle. The survey respondents have included public and private elementary and secondary schools, elementary and secondary school teachers and principals, local education agencies, public libraries, and school libraries. The system ended recently because of staffing issues at NCES. FRSS was part of a larger project, the Postsecondary Quick Response Information System, which included surveys of postsecondary institutions. | Surveys were conducted on an as-requested basis, sometimes on entirely new topics and sometimes with essentially the same survey repeated over multiple years. The report for the last survey, FRSS 110, was released in November 2021. | https://nces.ed.gov/surveys/frss/ |

163

| | | | | | |
|---|---|---|---|---|---|
| K–12 | Private School Survey (PSS) | Cross-sectional survey | PSS is a biennial universe collection of private elementary and secondary schools. PSS generates biennial data on the total number of private schools, teachers, and students and builds an accurate and complete list of private schools to serve as a sampling frame for NCES surveys of private schools. Information collected includes: religious orientation; level of school; size of school; length of school year, length of school day; total enrollment (K–12); number of high-school graduates, whether a school is single-sexed or coeducational and enrollment by sex; number of teachers employed; program emphasis; existence and type of kindergarten program. | The PSS began with the 1989–90 school year and has been conducted every 2 years since. The most recent data files available in September 2021 were from 2017–18. | https://nces.ed.gov/surveys/pss/ |
| K–12 | National Teacher and Principal Survey (NTPS) | Cross-sectional survey | NTPS collects extensive data on American public and private elementary and secondary schools every 2 to 3 years. Teachers, principals, and schools are components of the NTPS survey system. NTPS provides data on characteristics and qualifications of teachers and principals, teacher hiring practices, professional development, class size, and other conditions in schools. NTPS replaces the Schools and Staffing Survey (SASS) which was last conducted in the 2011–12 school year. | Administered in years 2015–16, 2017–18, 2020–21, replaced the Schools and Staffing Survey (last conducted in 2011–12) | https://nces.ed.gov/surveys/ntps/ |

*continued*

TABLE B-1 Continued

| Level of Education | NCES Products | Survey, Administrative or Other | Characteristics, Topics, etc. | Frequency, Lag Time, etc. | Link |
|---|---|---|---|---|---|
| K–12 | School Pulse Panel (SPP) | Survey, panel | SPP is a monthly panel study to look at the impact of the coronavirus pandemic on K–12 public schools. It will produce nationally representative data with a quick turnaround. Content will be revised quarterly. SPP is conducted by the U.S. Census Bureau on behalf of NCES. | Clearance requested from OMB in June 2021 | https://www.census.gov/programs-surveys/school-pulse-panel.html |
| K–12 | Common Core of Data (CCD) | Survey to collect aggregates from administrative records | CCD is a comprehensive, national database of all public elementary and secondary schools and school districts. Aggregate data reported via EDFacts by state and local education agencies, or schools based on administrative records. Fiscal data collected by the Census Bureau. | Annual nonfiscal data for 2020–21 released June 28, 2021. Annual fiscal data for 2017–18 available in September 2021. | https://nces.ed.gov/ccd/ |

| | | | | |
|---|---|---|---|---|
| K–12 | Education, Demographic and Geographic Estimates (EDGE) | A special tabulation of the U.S. Census Bureau's American Community Survey (ACS) data | The EDGE program uses data from the U.S. Census Bureau's American Community Survey to create indicators of social, economic, and housing conditions for school-age children and their parents for school districts. It uses spatial data collected by NCES and the U.S. Census Bureau to create geographic locale indicators, school point locations, school district boundaries, and other types of data to support spatial analysis. | Updated annually based on 5-year ACS. As of September 2021 data released for 2005–2009 through 2015–2019. Data can be used to link school district-level aggregates of characteristics of school-age children, the parents of school-age children, and the total population to survey data. | https://nces.ed.gov/programs/edge/ |
| K–12 | National Assessment of Educational Progress (NAEP) is a sample survey combined with an assessment. | Survey with assessment | NAEP, also known as "the Nation's Report Card," is the only nationally representative and continuing assessment of what America's students know and can do in various subject areas. Since 1969, assessments have been conducted periodically in reading, mathematics, science, writing, U.S. history, civics, geography, and the arts. In addition to tests of students' knowledge, NAEP includes surveys of students, teachers, and principals. | Reading and mathematics every 2 years, and other subjects periodically. | https://nces.ed.gov/nationsreportcard/ |

*continued*

TABLE B-1 Continued

| Level of Education | NCES Products | Survey, Administrative or Other | Characteristics, Topics, etc. | Frequency, Lag Time, etc. | Link |
|---|---|---|---|---|---|
| K–12 | High School Transcript Studies (HSTS) | Other, a system of collecting and coding transcript data for inclusion in surveys | NCES's HSTS collect information that is contained on the student high school record—i.e., courses taken while attending secondary school; information on credits earned; year and term a specific course was taken; and final grades. When available, information on class rank and standardized scores is also collected. Once collected, information (e.g., course name, credits earned, course grades) is transcribed and standardized (e.g., credits and credit hours standardized to a common metric) and can be linked back to the student's questionnaire or assessment data. NAEP focuses on grades 4, 8, and 12. | Periodic, depending on the survey. | https://nces.ed.gov/surveys/hst/ |

| | | | | |
|---|---|---|---|---|
| K–12 | Civil Rights Data Collection (CRDC) | Collection from administrative records | The U.S. Department of Education (ED) Office for Civil Rights (OCR) collects data from local education agencies on key education and civil rights issues in our nation's public schools through the CRDC. The CRDC collects a variety of information including student enrollment and educational programs and services, most of which is disaggregated by race/ethnicity, sex, limited English proficiency, and disability. | School-level data collected in 2000, 2004, 2006, 2009–2012, 2011–12, 2013–14, 2015–16, 2017–18, 2019–20 (as of September 2021). Recent collections cover all public schools. Information collected by the CRDC is used by OCR as well as other ED offices, policy makers and researchers outside of ED. | https://www2.ed.gov/about/offices/list/ocr/data.html |
| K–12 | Common Education Data Standards (CEDS) | Other, standards | CEDS are a national, collaborative effort to develop voluntary, common education data standards for a key subset of K–12 (e.g., demographics, program participation, course information) and K–12-to-postsecondary education transition variables. The intention is to facilitate the use of common definitions across state data systems. | | https://nces.ed.gov/programs/ceds/ |

*continued*

TABLE B-1 Continued

| Level of Education | NCES Products | Survey, Administrative or Other | Characteristics, Topics, etc. | Frequency, Lag Time, etc. | Link |
|---|---|---|---|---|---|
| K–12 | Classification of Secondary School Courses (CSSC) and Codes for Exchange of Data (SCED) | Other, classification | To analyze student transcript data, NCES developed the CSSC using data from the initial transcript collection in HS&B. In 2007, NCES released SCED, a course classification system designed to facilitate schools' and districts' maintenance of secondary-level transcript data over time and transfer of those data among districts and states. | This taxonomy was also used to code courses from high-school transcript studies throughout the 1980s, 1990s, and 2000s. | See https://nces.ed.gov/pubs2019/2019417.pdf for methodological report. |
| K–12 | Beginning Teacher Longitudinal Study (BTLS) | Longitudinal survey | BTLS was a study of a cohort of beginning public school teachers initially interviewed as part of the 2007-08 Schools and Staffing Survey through the 2011–12 school year. The study was intended to create an unfolding "story" by following this cohort of first-year teachers. | One cohort. Data collected in 2007–08, 2008–09, and 2010–11, 2011–12, and 2012–13. Web says data were released in 2015. But web only has data for the first 3 waves. | https://nces.ed.gov/surveys/btls/ |

| | | | | |
|---|---|---|---|---|
| Universities and colleges | National Postsecondary Student Aid Survey (NPSAS) | Survey | The NPSAS is a comprehensive study that examines how students and their families pay for postsecondary education. It includes nationally representative samples of undergraduate and graduate students, as well as students attending public and private less-than-2-year institutions, community colleges, 4-year colleges, and major universities. Both students who receive financial aid and those who do not receive financial aid participate in NPSAS. NPSAS has been conducted every 3 to 4 years since 1987. Student interviews and administrative records are used to provide exceptional detail concerning student financial aid. The latest data are available for the 2015–16 academic year. Data collection for 2019–20 has ended and data are currently being processed. | Conducted every 3 to 4 years since 1987. Data for 2019–20 ended in January 2021. | https://nces.ed.gov/surveys/npsas/ |

*continued*

TABLE B-1 Continued

| Level of Education | NCES Products | Survey, Administrative or Other | Characteristics, Topics, etc. | Frequency, Lag Time, etc. | Link |
|---|---|---|---|---|---|
| Universities and colleges | Beginning Postsecondary Students (BPS) | Longitudinal survey | Each cycle of BPS follows a cohort of students who are enrolled in their first year of postsecondary education. The study collects data on student persistence in, and completion of, postsecondary education programs (including postsecondary transcript studies), their transition to employment, demographic characteristics, and changes over time in their goals, marital status, income, and debt, among other indicators. BPS tracks students' paths through postsecondary education and helps answer questions of policy interest, such as why students leave school, how financial aid influences persistence and completion, and what percentages of students complete various degree programs. | 1. In-scope students in NPSAS:90 were followed up in 1992, and 1994.<br>2. In-scope students in NPSAS:96 were followed up in 1998 and 2001.<br>3. In-scope students in NPSAS:04 were followed up in 2006 and 2009.<br>4. In-scope students in NPSAS:12 were followed up in 2014 and 2017. | https://nces.ed.gov/surveys/bps/ |

| | | | | |
|---|---|---|---|---|
| Universities and colleges | Baccalaureate and Beyond Longitudinal Study (B&B) | Longitudinal survey | B&B examines students' education and work experiences after they complete a bachelor's degree, with a special emphasis on the experiences of new elementary and secondary teachers. Following several cohorts of students over time, B&B looks at bachelor's degree recipients' workforce participation, income and debt repayment, and entry into and persistence through graduate school programs, among other indicators. It addresses several issues specifically related to teaching, including teacher preparation, entry into and persistence in the profession, and teacher career paths. B&B also gathers extensive information on bachelor's degree recipients' undergraduate experience, demographic backgrounds, expectations regarding graduate study and work, and participation in community service. | 1. NPSAS:93 identified in-scope students who were followed in 1994, 1997, and 2003.<br>2. NPSAS:2000 identified in-scope students who were followed in 2001.<br>3. NPSAS:08 identified in-scope students who were followed in 2009, 2012, and 2018.<br>4. NPSAS:16 identified in-scope students who were followed up in 2017 and 2019. | https://nces.ed.gov/surveys/b&b/ |

*continued*

TABLE B-1 Continued

| Level of Education | NCES Products | Survey, Administrative or Other | Characteristics, Topics, etc. | Frequency, Lag Time, etc. | Link |
|---|---|---|---|---|---|
| Universities and colleges | Integrated Postsecondary Education Data System (IPEDS) | Survey that collects administrative records data | IPEDS, established as the core postsecondary education data collection program for NCES, is a system of surveys designed to collect data from all primary providers of postsecondary education. IPEDS is a single, comprehensive system designed to encompass all institutions and educational organizations whose primary purpose is to provide postsecondary education. The IPEDS system is built around a series of 12 interrelated surveys to collect institution-level data in such areas as enrollments, program completions, faculty, staff, finances, and academic libraries. | Data collected annually in three waves using 12 survey instruments.* | https://nces.ed.gov/ipeds |

| | | | | | |
|---|---|---|---|---|---|
| Universities and colleges | Classification of Instructional Programs (CIP) | Other, classification | CIP provides a taxonomic scheme that supports the accurate tracking and reporting of postsecondary fields of study and program completions activity in IPEDS. An important product of the CIP effort is the crosswalk of CIP program codes to the Standard Occupational Classification (SOC) System, which is referred to as the CIP/SOC Crosswalk. This crosswalk matches postsecondary programs of study that provide graduates with specific skills and knowledge to occupations requiring those skills or knowledge to be successful. | Classifications updated in 1980, 1985, 1990, 2000, 2010, 2020 | https://nces.ed.gov/ipeds/cipcode/Default.aspx?y=56 |

*continued*

TABLE B-1 Continued

| Level of Education | NCES Products | Survey, Administrative or Other | Characteristics, Topics, etc. | Frequency, Lag Time, etc. | Link |
|---|---|---|---|---|---|
| Universities and colleges | Postsecondary Education Quick Information System (PEQIS) | Survey system | PEQIS was established in 1991 to conduct brief surveys of postsecondary institutions or state higher education agencies on postsecondary education topics of national importance as identified by NCES or another part of the department. Surveys were generally limited to two to three pages of questions, with a response burden of about 30 minutes per respondent. Most PEQIS institutional surveys used a previously recruited nationally representative panel of approximately 1,600 institutions. The system has ended because of staffing issues at NCES. PEQIS was part of a larger project (Quick Response Information System) which included surveys concerning elementary and secondary education FRSS. | The most recent PEQIS survey was conducted in 2013, covering the 2012–13 school year. | https://nces.ed.gov/surveys/peqis/ |

| Universities and colleges | National Study of Postsecondary Faculty (NSOPF) | Survey | NSOPF was a nationally representative sample of full- and part-time faculty and instructional staff at public and private not-for-profit 2- and 4-year institutions in the United States, designed to provide data about faculty and instructional staff to postsecondary education researchers and policy makers. There are no plans to repeat the study. Rather, NCES plans to provide technical assistance to state postsecondary data systems and to encourage the development of robust connections between faculty and student data systems so that key questions concerning faculty, instruction, and student outcomes, such as persistence and completion, can be addressed. | Conducted in 1987–88, 1992–93, 1998–99, and 2003–04. | https://nces.ed.gov/surveys/nsopf/ |

*continued*

TABLE B-1 Continued

| Level of Education | NCES Products | Survey, Administrative or Other | Characteristics, Topics, etc. | Frequency, Lag Time, etc. | Link |
|---|---|---|---|---|---|
| Adult education/ career and technical education | Career and Technical Education (CTE) | Other, a data product built from existing NCES collections | *CTE Statistics* is the NCES reporting system for national information on CTE and workforce preparation. The program compiled information from a variety of existing NCES data collections that examine students, schools, teachers, and adults in general. Information is provided on CTE participation and CTE staff in public high schools, the education and work outcomes of public high-school graduates, and on CTE participation, outcomes, and providers at the subbaccalaureate level. Information is also available on adults' occupational certifications and licenses, and on adults' skills. The CTE program was discontinued in 2019 due to staffing shortage. Contracted web tables are still under production, but no staff are assigned to manage the program. | Website provides links to data and reports in three general areas: secondary/high school, postsecondary/college, and adult. | https://nces.ed.gov/surveys/ctes/ |

| Adult education/ career and technical education | National Assessment of Adult Literacy (NAAL) | Survey plus evaluation | The 2003 NAAL is a nationally representative assessment of English literacy among American adults age 16 and older. Sponsored by NCES, NAAL is the nation's most comprehensive measure of adult literacy since the 1992 National Adult Literacy Survey (NALS). NAAL not only provides information on adults' literacy performance but also on related background characteristics that are of interest to researchers, practitioners, policy makers, and the general public. | 2003 | https://nces.ed.gov/naal/ |
|---|---|---|---|---|---|
| Adult education/ career and technical education | Program for the International Assessment of Adult Competencies (PIAAC) | Survey with assessment | PIAAC is a cyclical, large-scale study that was developed under the auspices of the Organisation for Economic Co-operation and Development. The goal of PIAAC is to assess and compare the basic skills and the broad range of competencies of adults around the world. The assessment focuses on cognitive and workplace skills needed for successful participation in 21st-century society and the global economy. | Conducted in 2012, 2014, 2017, and 2021 | https://nces.ed.gov/surveys/piaac/ |

*continued*

TABLE B-1 Continued

| Level of Education | NCES Products | Survey, Administrative or Other | Characteristics, Topics, etc. | Frequency, Lag Time, etc. | Link |
|---|---|---|---|---|---|
| Pre-K, K–12, Lifelong Learning† | International Activities Program (IAP) | Surveys combined with assessments | The IAP supports a variety of activities to make international comparative data available on education and learning. These include the International Early Learning Study, Progress in International Reading Literacy Study, Trends in International Mathematics and Science Study, International Computer and Information Literacy Study, Program for International Student Assessment, and the Teaching and Learning International Survey. Also, listed under adult education, is the Program for the International Assessment of Adult Competencies. Typically these studies combine surveys with assessments. | | https://nces.ed.gov/surveys/international/ |
| All | October Supplement to the Current Population Survey (CPS) | Survey | Selected household member reports for all members of household. Basic CPS: Household membership and characteristics; demographic characteristics; and labor force participation. October Supplement: Basic annual school enrollment for preschool, elementary, secondary, and postsecondary students; and educational background information needed to produce dropout estimates on an annual basis. | Data collected annually by the U.S. Census Bureau on behalf of the Bureau of Labor Statistics and National Center for Education Statistics. | https://nces.ed.gov/surveys/cps/ |

| | | | | |
|---|---|---|---|---|
| All | National Household Education Survey: with modules (NHES) | Cross-sectional survey | NHES is a national household survey system that has been used to collect data on a variety of topics. Surveys are conducted by the U.S. Census Bureau. **Early childhood modules:** Early Childhood Program Participation Survey (ECPP) and, in prior years, in the NHES School Readiness Survey (SR). These are household surveys of families with children from birth through age 6, not yet enrolled in K. **Homeschooling and Parental Involvement in Education:** NHES Parent and Family Involvement in Education (PFI) Survey collects data on homeschooled children in grades equivalent to K–12 as well as collecting data about students who are enrolled in kindergarten through grade 12. **Career/Technical Training Module:** The Adult Training and Education Survey (ATES) module collected data about adults ages 16 to 65 not enrolled in high school. | The SR survey was conducted in 1993 and 2007. The ECPP surveys occurred in 1991, 1995, 2001, 2005, 2012, 2016, and 2019. The next survey is planned for 2023. PFI data were collected in 2012, 2016 and 2019. ATES was collected once in 2016. | https://nces.ed.gov/nhes/; see also a list of previous topics at https://nces.ed.gov/nhes/publications.asp |

SOURCE: NCES document provided to the panel, "List of NCES Programs—Statistics Budget."
NOTES:
‡The table source, a full listing of NCES's statistics budget programs, is available on request from the project's Public Access File. Available: https://www8.nationalacademies.org/pa/information.aspx.
*After a prepublication version of the report was provided to NCES, this sentence was corrected to reflect more accurately how IPEDS is collected.
†After a prepublication version of the report was provided to NCES, this label was corrected to reflect more accurately the levels of education covered by the IAP.

NCES also has an active program of cross-sectional surveys, including household surveys such as the education module of the Current Population Survey, the School Crime Supplement to the National Crime Victimization Survey, and the National Household Education Survey (NHES). NHES targets segments of the population with special modules that have included early childhood education, family involvement in education, homeschooling, and adult education. The National Principal and Teacher Survey is another example of a cross-sectional survey. NCES assessment surveys, such as the National Assessment of Educational Progress, include student tests or assessments embedded in probability sample surveys.

## ADMINISTRATIVE RECORDS

Administrative data traditionally refer to data collected by governments for other than statistical purposes (e.g., through the process of administering a program). Administrative data may include financial data about a program, summary statistics about participants or program features, and highly specific data about individuals, businesses, or institutions. Administrative data about individuals collected by the government are called *a system of records* and must be protected under the Privacy Act of 1974. There are occasional challenges in sharing such data because of consent requirements. Similar rules regarding the protection of lists of individuals have been adopted by many state and local governments, businesses, and institutions. The Office of Management and Budget used the following definition of administrative data:

> "Administrative data,' for purposes of this Memorandum, refers to administrative, regulatory, law enforcement, adjudicatory, financial, or other data held by agencies and offices of the government or their contractors or grantees (including states or other units of government) and collected for other than statistical purposes. Administrative data are typically collected to carry out the basic administration of a program, such as processing benefit applications or tracking services received. These data relate to individuals, businesses, and other institutions" (U.S. OMB, 2014a, p. 4).

Couper (2013, p. 146) describes administrative data as "data provided by persons or organizations for regulatory or other government activities. Users may assume that the data are confidential and used only for the intended purpose by the agency collecting the data." There has been considerable effort within the federal government to identify and facilitate the use of administrative data for statistical purposes. M-14-06 (U.S. OMB. 2014), cited above, furthered that goal.

NCES relies on administrative data collected by state and local agencies. These agencies provide the data NCES needs for its Common Core of

Data and for its Integrated Postsecondary Education Data System. NCES is prohibited by law from compiling a national database of individually identifiable information on individuals,[2] and hence does not take possession of the administrative microdata for individuals; instead, it asks state and local education agencies to provide aggregate information. NCES also plays a key role in assisting other offices within the Department of Education in the collection of administrative data for programmatic purposes.

## OTHER DATA SOURCES

Because of the limitations of traditional data sources, statistical agencies are augmenting those sources with private-sector data and a variety of new data sources and technologies. For agencies compiling information about purchases, sales, or prices, scanner data (available for purchase from the private sector) and credit card transactions or bank data can be valuable.

"Private retailers and manufacturers have a long history of collecting consumer data, often for market research purposes" (NASEM, 2021a, p. 68). Some companies sell proprietary data from standing panels of households. These nonprobability samples of willing participants simulate probability samples by targeting invitations to particular types of people, and by using eligibility criteria and poststratification to guide participation and weight the responses to be representative of the intended population. "Granularity is among the strengths of commercial data, and some data are available on a weekly basis. At the same time, these data are collected for marketing or other purposes, are not nationally representative, are not well documented, and coverage may vary across geographic areas" (NASEM, 2021a, p. 68).

"Data originating from commercial and other sources provide information not available elsewhere" (NASEM, 2021a, p. 68). However, one of the challenges with using these data is determining their quality and coverage, key to understanding how the data can best be used. (See NASEM, 2020, pp. 76–79, for more detail on challenges).

## NONPROBABILITY SAMPLE SURVEYS

With the growth of web surveys has come growth in nonprobability sampling, in which web posts or advertisements ask people to volunteer for a survey, often in return for an incentive. Such surveys can be used to simulate probability samples by targeting invitations to particular types of

---

[2]See 20 U.S. Code § 9572(a) National Database. Available: https://www.law.cornell.edu/uscode/text/20/9572 [March 2022].

people, and by using eligibility criteria and poststratification to guide who is allowed to participate and to weight the responses to be representative of the intended population. As noted above, commercial firms are selling data from nonprobability panels; however, a number of academic institutions have also found those data valuable. Examples include the University of Southern California's Understanding America Survey, which includes some education modules; RAND Corporation's American Educator Panels; and the American School District Panel.

## TRADE ASSOCIATION AND OTHER MEMBERSHIP DATA

Trade associations, professional societies, and other organizations may maintain useful datasets concerning their members or customers. Some may agree to share data for use in research projects, under appropriate conditions. Sometimes these data may be used to develop statistical samples. For example, there is no national list of teachers, but there are professional associations with membership lists, such as the National Education Association and the American Federation of Teachers. However, such frames are not comprehensive and are potentially subject to bias.

## WEB SCRAPING

In a presentation to the National Academies of Sciences, Engineering, and Medicine Panel on A Consumer Food Data System for 2030 and Beyond in 2019 Carma Hogue of the U.S. Census Bureau, defined web scraping as "an automated process of collecting data from an online source. Web crawling is an automated process of systematically visiting and reading web pages." (NASEM, 2020, p. 202).

The U.S. Census Bureau's Economic Directorate has been researching alternative data sources and big-data methodologies, including web scraping, for 4–5 years. They have concluded that their surveys of federal, state, and local governments are most likely to benefit because "much of the data to be collected on surveys are available online. Currently, analysts manually access data from websites. If Census could develop an automated way to scrape that data, it could reduce respondent and analyst burden." (NASEM, 2020, p. 202). In addition, "many private companies have terms of use on their websites that prohibit web scraping and web crawling. Government websites do not tend to have such restrictions." (NASEM, 2020, p. 202)

In terms of education data, districts and schools have increasingly placed important documents containing course offerings, course prerequisites, course registration procedures, school discipline policies, dress codes, event calendars, and more online. Much of this material exists to inform students and parents. However, web scraping could harvest these documents, code them, and prepare data products.

Haber (2021) provides an example of an education-related analysis of charter schools based on web-scraped data. As a very different web-scraping project, the National Agricultural Statistics Service, has explored web extraction to provide early detection of a disease that impacts pig inventories (NASEM, 2019b, p. 37).

## SOCIAL MEDIA

The identification of influenza outbreaks was one of the early uses of analysis of social media communications (e.g., Facebook, Instagram, etc.) for information gathering. Alessa and Faezipour (2018) review these efforts. In their abstract, they state "Many studies have shown that social networking sites can be used to conduct real time analysis for better predictions."

Torres et al. (2021, p. 1) present a more complex, education-related study. The abstract concludes

> The Child Trends News Service sought to broaden access to science-based information to support families during the pandemic through television news, testing whether digital media can be used to understand parents' concerns, misconceptions, and needs in real time. This article presents that digital media data can supplement traditional ways of conducting audience research and help tailor relevant content for families to garner an average of 90 million views per report.

## COGNITIVE INTERVIEWING/TESTING

Cognitive interviewing is often used as a tool in survey development to verify how respondents understand survey questions and whether they can and will answer accurately. For example, "think-aloud" is a common approach, in which the respondent is asked to read the survey question aloud and then verbalize his/her thoughts in preparing an answer. The interviewer both observes the respondent's reactions (e.g., whether the respondent shows hesitation or confusion in responding to the question, and whether the respondent refers to records to obtain a response) and may probe with additional questions, such as why the respondent hesitated or how the respondent interpreted a particular word in the question. Cognitive testing may be used in an iterative manner, using later rounds to test the changes adopted based on earlier rounds.

Crafts et al. (2016) used cognitive interviewing for developing and testing the National Science Foundation's (NSF's) Microbusiness Innovation Science and Technology Survey (later incorporated within NSF's Business

R&D Innovation Survey). They found that, rather than reading and using the definitions of research and innovation provided in the questionnaire, respondents commonly used their own definitions, which were quite different. NSF revised the questionnaire to eliminate those terms, instead breaking definitions into multiple components, each requiring a yes/no response. Additional testing showed that the reformulated questions obtained more accurate responses.

## FOCUS GROUPS

Focus groups are a qualitative research tool used to develop or test a survey questionnaire, or in other research contexts such as to interpret the results from a data collection or simply to examine a topic in depth without any attempt to relate the results to a survey. Unlike an interview, the interaction among focus group participants is an important part of the process (Flores and Alonso, 1995). Focus groups are kept small to encourage participation from all participants. They may be used early in a study as a type of exploratory research, to determine which concepts are important, or later, to help in the interpretation of results.

In an evaluation of a U.S. Department of Labor grant to a consortium of community colleges providing training in advanced manufacturing, one early result was that student retention rates in the program were low (Westat, 2016). Researchers conducted focus groups with students to determine how students felt about retention and program completion, and they found that students sometimes felt their goals were met prior to completing the program, while retention and program completion were of lesser importance to the students. For example, some students found that taking a few courses was sufficient for obtaining a job, and some decided that, once they received outside certification, they no longer needed a college certification.

# Appendix C

# Summary of Data Content Prioritization Process

To investigate the most-needed data content, the panel interviewed experts and stakeholders on the following topics:

- Level of schooling—early childhood education, K–12, higher education, adult education, career and technical education;
- Actors—schools/facilities and administrators, teachers, students, families/parents;
- Characteristics of actors—educational factors, context and conditions, curriculum, instruction, schools and teacher context, students and home context; and
- Outcomes—education outcomes, workforce, other life outcomes.

In those interviews and panel meetings, the panel probed further about:

- Stakeholders;
- Unit of data collection and measures, including:
  - Important outcomes to measure (e.g., educational, social); and
  - Important educational factors, context, and conditions to measure (e.g., disabilities, family socioeconomic status, curriculum, school discipline policy, availability of wraparound services);
- Relevant levels of education (e.g., early education, K–12, postsecondary, lifelong learning);
- Unit of collection/data acquisition (e.g., students, parents, schools/facilities, teachers); and

- Types of products (e.g., in-depth, medium, fast, visualizations), regularity, and intended audiences.

To determine which topics should be given the highest priority, the panel specified four minimum criteria, requiring that each topic meet at least one of the four. These criteria are:

- What sets the (proximal and distal) context for education?
- What constitutes the developmental and social processes and structures of education?
- What are the social and psychological experiences of students, teachers, and administrators in education?
- What are the (interim, short-, and long-term) outcomes of education?

Based on these criteria, the panel identified 112 topics of interest. These topics were then prioritized in two ways: first, and most critically, by the importance or value of the topic, and second, by level of effort required (i.e., whether NCES could reasonably make progress on the topic).

The importance of each topic was evaluated based on the following dimensions:

1. The presence of a legal mandate or restriction;
2. The impact on students and student outcomes, including:
   a. The topic supports understanding of factors affecting student outcomes; and
   b. Analytics result in actionable interventions affecting student outcomes (i.e., factors, areas, and aspects that influence education and educational outcomes and help stakeholders understand how to enhance outcomes of students, assist people, and move the system forward);
3. Balance across life cycle—covers early childhood education and adult education in addition to K–12 and higher education;
4. Sufficient coverage of:
   a. Workers', teachers', and administrators' information linked to learners; and
   b. Institutional information/context linked to learners (this might include the use of online education);
5. Impact on (national or state) policy: whether data on this topic provide information on how education policy and programs relate to other social policies (e.g., housing, labor force, poverty);
6. National importance: economic viability, social cohesion, basic understanding of the preparation of the future workforce; or emerging, isolated, or dispersed topics with broader national implications

APPENDIX C    *187*

   (for education, for the economy, etc.) that are useful to the education community;
  7. Number of interested parties/data users, both key data users (e.g., the White House) and others; and
  8. Whether data products have key uses, such as answering key research questions to fill knowledge gaps (e.g., What data do users need? Can data products help decision making?)

NCES's ability to make progress on each topic was evaluated based on the following:

  9. Would data products on this topic fill a gap in existing data, statistical products, reports, or tools?
  10. Measurement/operationalization feasibility:
     a. Is the topic easy or difficult to measure? (e.g., student learning [difficult] vs. employment [easier but still difficult] vs. student attributes such as age and gender [easiest]).
     b. Do users need population data or good data with a low standard error? Deep detail? Individual records vs. aggregated data? Longitudinal or intergenerational data?
     c. How uniform are the data definitions collected across the domain on institutions or on people?
  11. Would standards set by NCES add value and be worthwhile?
  12. Do administrative data "pre-exist," or would administrative forms and procedures need modification to collect such data appropriately? If data exist, does NCES have access to these data and can the data easily be added to NCES's operations, via data linkage or otherwise?
  13. If NCES collected/acquired the data, would NCES's work add value or duplicate? What is the return on investment?
  14. Can data be delivered to users on time?
  15. Would this topic be *substantially* advanced by NCES's involvement, such as providing an accessible technological solution, facilitating data linkage, or otherwise supporting education entities' access to data infrastructure?

For each of these criteria, the 112 topics were assigned a yes/no determination as to whether the topic met each criterion. Allowing for the division of criteria 2 and 4 into two separate dimensions, and of criterion 10 into three separate dimensions, a topic could meet up to 10 criteria on importance and up to 9 criteria on feasibility.

These criteria and the process used are described here both to document how the panel evaluated potential topics for inclusion in NCES's data collections and as a possible model for NCES as the Center pursues its strategic planning. No attempt is made to assert that the 19 criteria are equal in value, and a variety of weights might be attached to each criterion; some criteria might be considered so important that satisfying just that criterion would be sufficient justification for including a topic, while others might have lesser importance and be insufficient alone. We suggest using the following strategies. First, if a topic fails to satisfy any of the criteria, one might reevaluate the importance of that topic. Second, the degree to which a topic satisfies multiple criteria can be interpreted as a rough measure of the broad importance or feasibility of the topic. Third, the criteria might be used as tools for identifying gaps in current or planned data collections (e.g., could a data collection be modified to more thoroughly address NCES's research priorities?). Clearly, there are reasons to limit any data collection (e.g., cost constraints and concerns about response rates), and we are not suggesting that every data collection be turned into a massive effort. Sometimes, a risk in data-collection development is that everyone has a topic to add. Still, there may be data collections whose utility can be greatly increased with only minor changes. Fourth, to counterbalance the third point, there may be topics so thoroughly covered elsewhere that there is little advantage to adding data items on those topics. Finally, we should emphasize that, in addition to data collection, another way for NCES to provide leadership on these topics is by creating standards and tools that others may use. NCES has done this by creating tools such as the Classification of Instructional Programs and the Department of Education's School Climate Surveys.

# Appendix D

# Comparing Federal Principal Statistical Agencies and Units

**TABLE D-1** Organizational Statistics of the 13 U.S. Principal Statistical Programs and Units, Sorted by Overall Staff Size (FY 2020)

| Principal Statistical Agency or Unit† | Number of Permanent Full-Time Employees | Direct Funding | Average Number of U.S. Dollars ($) Managed by Each Employee‡ | Reimbursable Programs |
|---|---|---|---|---|
| Census* | 6,328 | $7,185.8M | $1.1M | $303.4M |
| BLS | 1,989 | $655.0M | $0.3M | $34.0M |
| NASS | 1,033 | $163.0M | $0.2M | $17.1M |
| BEA | 501 | $108.0M | $0.2M | $2.3M |
| NCHS | 470 | $155.0M | $0.3M | $83.5M |
| EIA | 357 | $118.0M | $0.3M | $1.1M |
| ERS | 158 | $60.5M | $0.4M | $0.0M |
| SOI | 139 | $34.7M | $0.2M | $2.2M |
| NCES | 105 | $296.5M | $2.8M | $6.3M |
| ORES | 79 | $36.8M | $0.5M | $0.9M |
| BTS | 60 | $26.0M | $0.4M | $8.2M |
| NCSES | 56 | $58.0M | $1.0M | $2.0M |
| BJS | 49 | $57.1M | $1.2M | $18.2M |

SOURCE: U.S. OMB (2020), Appendix Tables 3a (Staffing Levels), 1a (Direct Funding for Statistical Programs, 2018–2020), and 2a (Reimbursable and Purchase Programs, 2020).

NOTES:
   *FY 2020 is a decennial census year.
   †The principal statistical agencies or units are sorted in ascending order by "Number of Permanent Full-Time Employees."
   ‡The average number of dollars calculated as direct funding in FY 2020 divided by the number of FTE permanent staff, sometimes called the budget-to-staff ratio, is used to express the average number of dollars managed by each staff member.

TABLE D-2 Detailed Historical Organization of NCES Full-Time Equivalent (FTE) Employees (Select Fiscal Years)

| | FY 2003 | FY 2004 | FY 2007 | FY 2010* | FY 2013 | FY 2015* | FY 2019 | FY 2021‡ | Net Loss/Gain FYs 2003–2021 Number of FTE Employees | Percent Change |
|---|---|---|---|---|---|---|---|---|---|---|
| Statistics Units | 83 | 76 | 81 | 86 | 64 | 77 | 60 | 58 | –25 | –30 |
| Office of the Commissioner–Statistics** | 20 | 16 | 22 | 18 | 9 | 2 | 2 | 2 | –18 | –90 |
| Annual Reports & Information Staff | | | | | 6 | 10 | 5 | 4 | 4 | N/A |
| Statistical Standards & Data Confidentiality Staff | | | | | 9 | 12 | 9 | 9 | 9 | N/A |
| Sample Surveys Division | | | | | 12 | 19 | 19 | 18 | 18 | N/A |
| Administrative Data Division | | | | | | 34 | 25 | 25 | 25 | N/A |
| Elementary/Secondary & Library Studies Division | 21 | 22 | 25 | 24 | 10 | | | | –21 | –100 |
| Postsecondary Division | 21 | 19 | 21 | 26 | 9 | | | | –21 | –100 |
| Early Childhood, International, and Crosscutting Division–Statistics† | 21 | 19 | 13 | 18 | 9 | | | | –21 | –100 |
| Assessment Units | 30 | 27 | 32 | 38 | 35 | 36 | 35 | 32 | 2 | 7 |
| Assessments Division** | 24 | 21 | 26 | 32 | 29 | 36 | 35 | 32 | 8 | 33 |
| Early Childhood, International, and Crosscutting Division–Assessment† | 6 | 6 | 6 | 6 | 6 | | | | –6 | –100 |
| NCES Total | 113 | 103 | 113 | 124 | 99 | 113 | 95 | 90 | –23 | –20 |

*continued*

191

TABLE D-2 Continued

SOURCE: IES document provided to the panel, "IES & NCES Historical FTE Data and IES Appropriations Historical"; NCES response to question from the panel, pp. 7–10.

NOTES: These data represent how NCES staff are organized. All staff are paid indirectly through an allocation of the Department of Education's Salaries and Expenses appropriation. The organization of staff into statistics and assessment units does not align with program appropriations (Figure D-2). For example, staff who work primarily on international studies are organized in assessment units, while the program dollars for the international studies collections have always come from the statistics budget appropriation. The organization of FTEs does not fully reflect the functional roles of the staff. For example, staff located in a statistics unit may also support assessment work. Vacant positions are not represented.

*NCES-initiated reorganizations have changed the structure of NCES several times since 2002, reflected by the "grayed out" areas. Each reorganization resulted in changes in FTE distribution across NCES. For example, from 2010 to 2013, the NCES Office of the Commissioner was divided into three separate teams, leading to a corresponding reduction in the total FTEs assigned to the Office of the Commissioner.

‡The FY 2021 Office of the Commissioner count excludes two fellows who are not paid employees of the federal government.

**In this table, the Office of the Commissioner count includes one FTE across multiple employees who work on assessments for some of their time. The Assessments Division count includes one FTE from across multiple employees located in the Office of the Commissioner.

†As part of the 2013 reorganization, six staff who work primarily on international studies were moved from the Early Childhood, International, and Crosscutting Division into a newly formed branch of the Assessments Division.

**TABLE D-3** Estimated Annual Hiring and Turnover Rates for NCES Full-Time Equivalent (FTE) Employees by Fiscal Year (FY)

| Fiscal Year (FY)* | FTEs (at end of FY) | Hires | Separations | Average FTEs from Prior Year | FY Hire Rate | FY Turnover Rate |
|---|---|---|---|---|---|---|
| 2013 | 98 | N/A | N/A | N/A | N/A | N/A |
| 2014 | 103 | 12 | 11 | 101 | 11.9% | 10.9% |
| 2015 | 113 | 19 | 11 | 108 | 17.6% | 10.2% |
| 2016 | 114 | 6 | 5 | 114 | 5.3% | 4.4% |
| 2017* | 111 | 0 | 5 | 113 | 0.0% | 4.4% |
| 2018 | 101 | 1 | 10 | 106 | 0.9% | 9.4% |
| 2019* | 93 | 0 | 9 | 97 | 0.0% | 9.3% |
| 2020* | 93 | 10 | 9 | 93 | 10.8% | 9.7% |
| 2021* | 91 | 8 | 10 | 92 | 8.7% | 10.9% |

SOURCE: NCES response to question from the panel, pp. 16–17.
NOTES: The annual hiring rate percent is the number of FTE employee hires divided by (the FTE count at the end of the fiscal year + the FTE count at the end of the prior fiscal year)/2. The annual turnover rate percent is the number of FTE employee separations divided by (the FTE count at the end of the fiscal year + the FTE count at the end of the prior fiscal year)/2.
The number of FTE employees at the end of a fiscal year may differ slightly from Table D-2, due to different sources.
*The following events affected hiring and attrition: hiring freeze 1/23/17–4/12/17 (FY 2017), COVID-19 pandemic 3/13/2020–present (FYs 2020–2021), new telework policy (FY 2019), Voluntary Early Retirement Authority and Voluntary Separation Incentive Payment (FY 2019 and FY 2020).

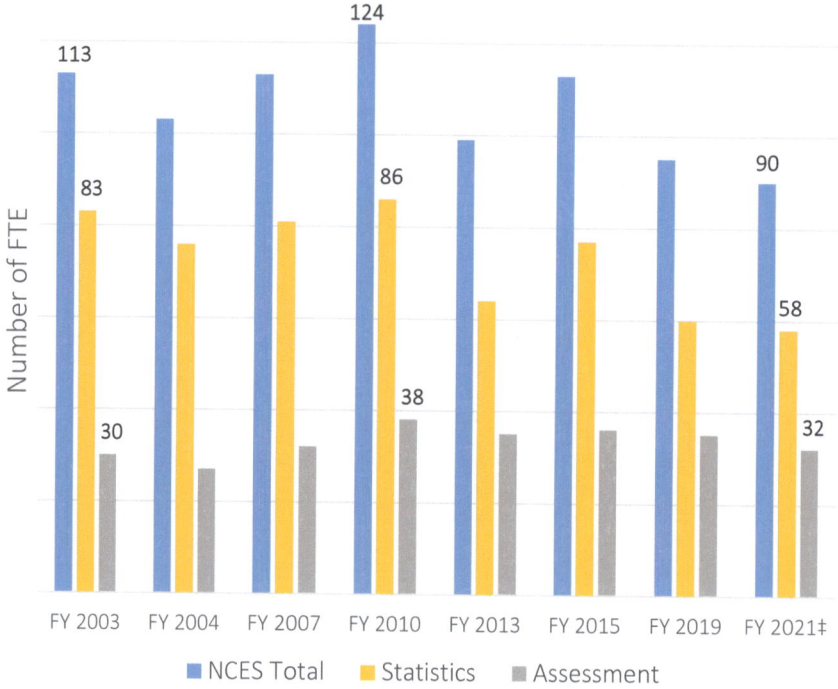

**FIGURE D-1** NCES organizational change in full-time equivalent employees (FTE) (select fiscal years).
SOURCE: IES document provided to the panel, "IES & NCES Historical FTE Data and IES Appropriations Historical"; NCES response to question from the panel, pp. 7–10.
LEGEND: NCES had a net loss of 23 FTEs (20%) from FY 2003 to FY 2021. Within NCES, the staff working in statistics units had a net loss of 25 FTEs (30%) in the same period. The decline since the FY 2010 peak is starker, at 34 FTEs (27%) for NCES as a whole and 28 FTEs (33%) for statistics units.
NOTES: These data represent how NCES staff are organized. All staff are paid indirectly through an allocation of the Department of Education's Salaries and Expenses appropriation. The organization of staff into statistics and assessment units does not align with program appropriations (Figure D-2). For example, staff who work primarily on international studies are organized in assessment units, while the program dollars for the international studies collections have always come from the statistics budget appropriation. The organization of FTEs does not fully reflect the functional roles of the staff. For example, staff located in a statistics unit may also support assessment work. Vacant positions are not represented.

The statistics count includes the Administrative Data Division, Sample Surveys Division and its predecessors, Statistical Standards and Data Confidentiality Staff, Annual Reports and Information Staff, and the Office of the Commissioner FTEs

*APPENDIX D*

working on statistics. The assessments count includes the Assessments Division plus one FTE from across multiple employees located in the Office of the Commissioner who work on assessments for some of their time. See Table D-2 for details.

‡The FY 2021 counts exclude two fellows who are not paid employees of the federal government.

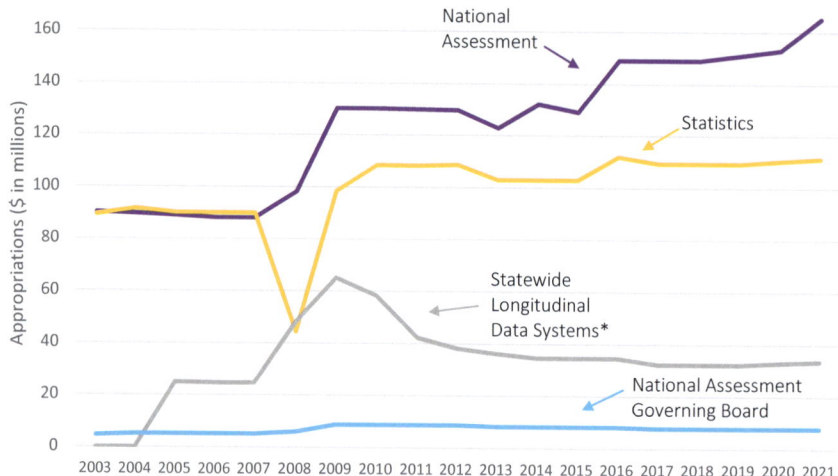

**FIGURE D-2** NCES Historical Program Appropriations Excluding Salaries and Expenses, FYs 2003–2021.
SOURCE: IES document provided to the panel, "IES & NCES Historical FTE Data and IES Appropriations Historical"; NCES response to question from the panel, pp. 3–6.
LEGEND: NCES's appropriations levels for FYs 2003–2021, excluding NCES's indirect appropriation from the Salaries and Expenses account. These figures reflect the program budgets only and do not cover FTE employee salaries, which are determined by the Department of Education and the Institute of Education Sciences. The statistics budget has been flatlined in recent years, which effectively results in a loss of purchasing power when adjusted for rises in cost of living. For instance, using the Consumer Price Index from the Bureau of Labor Statistics, the FY 2010 statistics program appropriation of $108,521,000 has the same buying power as $130,714,950 in FY 2021, or 17 percent less buying power.[1] NCES's actual statistics program appropriation for FY 2021 was $111,500,000, a difference of over $19 million.
NOTES: NCES's program appropriations typically support contracts and grants, do not fund NCES staff, and do not align with the organization of staff into statistics and assessment offices (Table D-2, Figure D-1). For example, the Statewide Longitudinal Data Systems Grant Program is administered by staff organized in a statistics unit; staff who work primarily on international studies are organized in assessment units, while the program dollars for the international studies collections have always come from the statistics budget appropriation. NCES receives an allocation from

---

[1] Calculated from the Bureau of Labor Statistics' Consumer Price Index calculator at https://www.bls.gov/data/inflation_calculator.htm [March 2022], comparing $108,521,000 in appropriations in October 2009 (the first month of FY 2010) to buying power in October 2020 (the first month of FY 2021).

the Department of Education's Salaries and Expenses (S&E) appropriation to pay employees (i.e., FTEs) indirectly. The S&E allocation amounts were not available and are not shown.

*Appropriations for the Statewide Longitudinal Data Systems did not begin until FY 2005.

**TABLE D-4** NCES Interagency Agreements (IAAs), Contracts, Contracting Officer's Representatives (CORs) and IAA Administrators, with Ratios

| | IAAs Outgoing | IAAs Incoming | Contracts | CORs | IAA Admin | Contract-to-COR Ratio | All IAAs + Contracts | IAAs + Contracts Ratio |
|---|---|---|---|---|---|---|---|---|
| Annual Reports | 0 | 0 | 3 | 1 | 0 | 3.0 | 3 | 3.0 |
| Statistical Standards | 2 | 1 | 10 | 4 | * | 2.5 | 13 | 3.3 |
| Sample Surveys | 11 | 1 | 27 | 12 | * | 2.3 | 39 | 3.3 |
| Administrative Data | 5 | 0 | 23 | 7 | 3 | 3.3 | 28 | 2.8 |
| Assessments | 7 | 2 | 69 | 16 | * | 4.3 | 78 | 4.9 |
| NCES Total | 25 | 4 | 132 | 40 | 3 | 3.3 | 161 | 3.7 |

SOURCE: NCES response to question from the panel, p. 15.
LEGEND: NCES has 43 staff (48%) who serve as CORs or administer IAAs in addition to other duties. On average, each COR or IAA administrator manages 3.7 IAAs or contracts, with the Assessments Division having the highest average contract/IAA management workload, at 4.9.
NOTES: *IAAs within the Sample Survey, Statistical Standards, and Assessment divisions are managed by staff who are also active CORs on contracts. Since these staff are already included in the count of CORs, they are not double counted in this column.

# Appendix E

# Institute of Education Sciences and NCES Product Review Processes

**TABLE E-1** NCES Products: Required Reviews

| Product: | Type of Review Required | | | | | | | |
|---|---|---|---|---|---|---|---|---|
| | Level 1 internal review | Level 1a rolling review | Level 2. statistical review | Level 3. AC/CS/OC | Level 4. AC | Level 5. NCES/RIMG/OMB | Level 7. IES external review | Level 7a. IES internal review |
| Compendium | X | | | | | | (X) | X |
| Directory | X | | | | | | | |
| NCES Handbook | X | | | | | | | |
| | | | | | | | | |
| Updated indicators | | X | | | | | | |
| Web Tables | | | X | | | | | |
| | | | | | | | | |
| Statistical Analysis Report | X | | | | | | X | X |
| R&D Report | X | | | | | | (X) | (X) |
| Technical/Methodological Report | X | | | | | | (X) | (X) |
| Statistics in Brief | X | | | | | | X | X |
| First Look/Highlights/Data Point | X | | | | | | | X |
| | | | | | | | | |
| Re-packaged Excerpts only | | | X | | | | | |
| Guide (e.g., Programs & Plans) | | | X | | | | | |
| Working Papers | | | | | X | | | |
| | | | | | | | | |
| Data File (including CD ROM/DAS/WEB) | | | X | | | | | |
| Data File Documentation /User's manuals (must accompany data file) | | | X | | | | | |
| Video/Data | | | X | | | | | |
| | | | | | | | | |
| Conference Report | | | | | X | | | |
| Non-data Videotape (e.g., conference, Commissioner's statements) | | | | | X | | | |
| Brochure/Pamphlet | | | | X | | | | |
| Newsletters | | | | X | | | | |
| Co-op Products (e.g., FORUM, NPEC) | | (X) | | | X | | | |
| Questionnaires | | | | | | X | | |
| Glossaries | | | | X | | | | |

(x) Review is at the discretion of the specified level

| | |
|---|---|
| Level 1. Internal Review | Requires BC/AC/CS/OC review and approval. |
| Level 1a. Rolling Review | Requires BC/AC/CS review and approval as parts of the whole are completed. Final product requires full Level 1 review. |
| Level 2. Statistical Review | Requires BC/AC/CS review and approval. |
| Level 3. AC/CS/OC | Requires BC/ AC/CS/OC review and approval. |
| Level 4. AC | Requires BC/AC review and approval. No official NCES distribution but made available via web or special request. |
| Level 5. NCES/RIMG/OMB | Requires BC/AC/OC approval within NCES plus review/approval by RIMG & OMB, and copy to Chief Statistician. |
| Level 7. IES External Review | Requires External comments and review/approval by IES Action Editor and IES DDS |
| Level 7a IES Internal Review | Requires review/approval by IES Action Editor and IES DDS |

SOURCE: Reproduction of Table 6-1-A from NCES's document, "Review Procedures: 6-1 Review of Reports and Data Products." Available: https://nces.ed.gov/statprog/2012/pdf/Chapter6.pdf [March 2022].

NOTES: This table shows NCES's standards for its report-review process. In practice, there is some flexibility as staff use their judgment on a case-by-case basis to determine which levels of review are needed.

## APPENDIX E

### TABLE E-2 NCES Web Products: Required Reviews

| Product: | Type of Review Required | | | | |
|---|---|---|---|---|---|
| | Level 1. internal review | Level 2. statistical review | Level 3. AC/CS/OC | Level 4. AC | Level 6. Author/web publisher |
| **Web Applications:** | | | | | |
| **NCES Products: (with #)** | | | | | |
| pdf file | X | | | | X |
| Html | X | | | | X |
| ASCII/ Excel/ data base file* | | X | | | X |
| Conference Reports/Co-op Products | | | | X | X |
| **Tools:** | | | | | |
| Locator | | | X | | X |
| Peer Tool: Public Access | | | X | | X |
| Data Tool./Table and model servers | | | X | | X |
| Questionnaire Tool | | | X | | X |
| Glossary Search - based on approved product with NCES #) | | | X | | X |
| Table/ Figure Search | | | X | | |
| **WEB sites; pages; information sources:** | | | | | |
| Survey /Program site | | | X | | X |
| Web Publications | X | | | | |
| Quick Facts | | | | | X |
| Video | | | | | |
|   Informational Videos | | | X | | X |
|   Data Videos | | | X | | X |
| PowerPoint Presentations | | | X | | X |
| Quick tables/figures | | X | | | X |
| Co-op Products | | | | X | X |
| Working Papers | | | | X | |

*Excludes pre-release data.
X All tools with micro data will be subjected to disclosure review, as well as technical review. A full review is required only for new products. Updates to current products only require review of the update information as appropriate.

| | |
|---|---|
| Level 1. Internal Review | Requires BC/AC/CS/OC review and approval. |
| Level 1a. Rolling Review | Requires BC/AC/CS review and approval as parts of the whole are completed. Final product requires full Level 1 review. |
| Level 2. Statistical Review | Requires BC/AC/CS review and approval. |
| Level 3. AC/CS /OC | Requires BC/AC/CS/OC review and approval. |
| Level 4. AC | Requires BC/AC review and approval. No official NCES distribution, but made available via web or special request. |
| Level 5. NCES/RIMG/OMB | Requires BC/AC approval within NCES plus review/approval by RIMG & OMB, and copy to Chief Statistician. |
| Level 6. Author/Web Publisher | Assumes full review as appropriate for the original NCES numbered product. |

SOURCE: Reproduction of Table 6-1-B from NCES's document, "Review Procedures: 6-1 Review of Reports and Data Products." Available: https://nces.ed.gov/statprog/2012/pdf/Chapter6.pdf [March 2022].

**TABLE E-3** Review Process Durations for NCES Reports: FYs 2019–2021

| IES Internal Review (n = 95) | | | |
|---|---|---|---|
| | Median | Minimum | Maximum |
| Time to Complete Review Between the NCES Chief Statistician and NCES Commissioner‡ | 25 d<br>5 w<br>1 m | N/A | 113 d<br>23 w<br>5 m |
| Time Between Receipt of Report by Office of Science and First Memo Sent to NCES | 5 d<br>1 w<br><1 m | 0 d<br>0 w<br>0 m | 39 d<br>8 w<br>2 m |
| Time Days Between Receipt of Report by Office of Science and Final Approval | 12 d<br>2 w<br><1 m | 0 d<br>0 w<br>0 m | 99 d<br>20 w<br>5 m |
| Time in Office of Science | 8 d<br>2 w<br><1 m | 0 d<br>0 w<br>0 m | 80 d<br>16 w<br>4 m |

| IES External Review (n = 25) | | | |
|---|---|---|---|
| | Median | Minimum | Maximum |
| Time to complete review between the NCES chief statistician and NCES commissioner‡ | 69 d<br>14 w<br>3 m | N/A | 214 d<br>43 w<br>10 m |
| Time between receipt of report by Office of Science and disposition memo sent to NCES | 30 d<br>6 w<br>1 m | 15 d<br>3 w<br><1 m | 83 d<br>17 w<br>4 m |
| Time between receipt of report by Office of Science and final approval | 67 d<br>13 w<br>3 m | 26 d<br>5 w<br>1 m | 234 d<br>47 w<br>11 m<br><br>*Without 2 outliers:*\*\*<br>126 d<br>25 w<br>6 m |
| Time in Office of Science *(includes time that reports are with external reviewers)* | 43 d<br>9 w<br>2 m | 23 d<br>5 w<br>1 m | 147 d<br>29 w<br>7 m<br><br>*Without 2 outliers:*\*\*<br>84 d<br>17 w<br>4 m |

## TABLE E-3 Continued

SOURCE: IES document provided to the panel, "Peer Review of IES Reports"; NCES response to question from the panel, pp. 35–36.

LEGEND: This table summarizes the duration of NCES product review at various stages, differentiated by whether the product must undergo IES internal or external review. For instance, NCES reports requiring an IES internal review took a median of 25 business days to complete the NCES internal review process, and then required a median of 12 additional business days between receipt of the report by the Office of Science and final approval.

NOTES: d means number of business days, w means number of calendar weeks (# days/5), and m means approximate number of calendar months (# days/22).

‡Timing information is only available for the chief statistician- and commissioner-review stage of NCES internal review since the iterative nature of the review process prior to this stage makes it challenging to measure timing. Duration information from NCES's Review Tracking System for FYs 2019–2021 includes 92 reports (instead of 95) undergoing IES internal review and 19 reports (instead of 25) undergoing IES external review. Thus, the summary of timing for the NCES internal review process is based on a significantly overlapping but not completely identical set of reports. These times are in addition to the times for IES internal or external reviews shown in the rows below.

The time in the Office of Science shows, of the total time between when the Office of Science receives a report and when the report is approved, how much of that time reports are in the hands of the Office of Science. For the balance of the total time, reports are with NCES for revision.

**The maximums shown for IES external reviews include two outliers, for which the maximum total days to approval was 234 and 190 days, and the maximum days in the Office of Science was 147 and 107 days. When excluding those outliers, the maximum total days to approval was 126 days and the maximum days in the Office of Science was 84 days. Both outliers were National Assessment of Educational Progress reports.

# Appendix F

# Open Meeting Agendas and Solicited Statements

**Agenda**
**First Virtual Open Panel Meeting**
**May 10, 2021, 2:30 pm EDT**
**Open Session**

2:30 pm EDT/11:30 am PDT
    **Welcome, Introduction of Panel Members**
    Brian Harris-Kojetin, Director, Committee on National Statistics

2:40 **Overview of National Academies of Sciences, Engineering, and Medicine Consensus Study Process**
    Mary Ellen O'Connell, Executive Director, Division of Behavioral and Social Sciences and Education

2:55 **Opening Remarks**
    Mark Schneider, Director, Institute of Education Sciences

3:25 **Background and Goals for the Study**
    James Lynn Woodworth, Commissioner, National Center for Education Statistics

3:35 **Discussion and Clarification of the Statement of Task with NCES**
    Larry Hedges, Northwestern University, Panel Chair

4:00 **Break**

4:15 **Brainstorm of Study and Workshop Agenda**
    Larry Hedges, Northwestern University, Panel Chair

5:15 **Summary and Final Words**
    Larry Hedges, Northwestern University, Panel Chair

5:30 **Adjourn**

**Agenda**
**Second Virtual Open Panel Meeting**
**May 26, 2021, 2:00 pm EDT**
**Open Session**

2:00 pm EDT/11:00 am PDT
    **Welcome**
    Brian Harris-Kojetin, Director, Committee on National Statistics

2:05 **Introduction of the National Center for Education Statistics**
    James Lynn Woodworth, Commissioner, National Center for Education Statistics

2:20 **Introduction of Panel**
    Larry Hedges, Northwestern University, Panel Chair

2:30 **How NCES Achieves Its Mission**
    James Lynn Woodworth, Commissioner, National Center for Education Statistics

2:45 **NCES Public and Restricted Data Products: Stakeholders, Uses, and Impacts**
    James Lynn Woodworth, Commissioner, National Center for Education Statistics

3:10 **Open Discussion with NCES**

3:30 **Break**

3:45 **NCES Data Programs**
    Chris Chapman, NCES Associate Commissioner
    Ross Santy, NCES Associate Commissioner

3:45 **NCES Survey Data Program and Stakeholders**

4:00 **NCES Administrative Data Program and Stakeholders**

4:15 **Open Discussion**

4:45 **Closing Statements**
    Larry Hedges, Northwestern University, Panel Chair

5:00 **Adjourn**


**Agenda**
**Third Virtual Open Panel Meeting**
**July 9, 2021, 3:00 pm EDT**
**Open Session**

3:00 pm EDT/12:00 pm PDT
    Welcome
    Melissa Chiu, Deputy Director, Committee on National Statistics
    **Models of Data Linkage Infrastructure for Analytics and Decision Making**

APPENDIX F 207

| | |
|---|---|
| 3:05 | **Speaker**<br>**Jack Buckley,** College Board (former), NCES Commissioner (former) – Data linkages at the College Board |
| 3:15 | **Q&A:** Panel and Jack Buckley |
| 3:20 | **Speakers**<br>**Peace Bransberger,** Western Interstate Commission for Higher Education (WICHE) – Regional Statewide Longitudinal Data Systems with wage data<br>**David Troutman,** The University of Texas System – Partnership with the U.S. Census Bureau to obtain postgraduation outcome data<br>**Carrie Conaway,** Harvard University – Massachusetts' cross-agency data linkage infrastructure and analysis/evaluation<br>**Doug Shapiro,** Research Center, National Student Clearinghouse – Data linkages for studying longitudinal student outcomes<br>**Mark Prell,** Economic Research Service, U.S. Department of Agriculture – Census-FNS-ERS Joint Project: the *Next Generation Data Platform* |
| 4:10 | **Q&A:** Panel and speakers |
| 4:55 | **Closing Statements**<br>Larry Hedges, Northwestern University, Panel Chair |
| 5:00 | **Adjourn Open Session** |

## Agenda
### Fourth Virtual Open Panel Meeting
### July 27, 2021, 12:00 pm EDT
### Open Session

| | |
|---|---|
| 12:00 pm EDT/9:00 am PDT | **Welcome**<br>Melissa Chiu, Deputy Director, Committee on National Statistics<br>**Session Topic: Models of Data Linkage Infrastructure for Analytics and Decision Making** |
| 12:05 | **Speaker**<br>**Gardner Carrick,** The Manufacturing Institute, National Association of Manufacturers – Credential data and data linkages to outcomes of manufacturing education programs |
| 12:15 | **Q&A:** Panel and speaker |
| 12:45 | **Closing Statements**<br>Larry Hedges, Northwestern University, Panel Chair |
| 12:50 | **Adjourn Open Session** |

## Agenda
## Fifth Virtual Open Panel Meeting
## July 30, 2021, 2:00 pm EDT
## Open Session

2:00 pm EDT/12:00 pm PDT
    **Welcome**
    Melissa Chiu, Deputy Director, Committee on National Statistics
    **Models of data linkage infrastructure for research**

2:05    **Speakers**
    **Barry Johnson**, Acting Chief, Research and Analytics Officer, Internal Revenue Service – IRS Statistics of Income's Joint Statistical Research Program
    **Shelley Bailey**, Director, Office of Data Development, Social Security Administration – Office of Research, Evaluation, and Statistics' extramural research program

2:30    **Q&A:** Panel and speakers
3:00    **Closing Statements**
    Larry Hedges, Northwestern University, Panel Chair
3:05    **Adjourn Open Session**

## Agenda
## Sixth Virtual Open Panel Meeting
## August 2, 2021, 2:00 pm EDT
## Open Session

2:00 pm EDT/12:00 pm PDT
    **Welcome**
    Melissa Chiu, Deputy Director, Committee on National Statistics
    **Speakers: Department of Education Initiatives, Innovations, Strategies**

2:05    **Matt Soldner**, Department of Education Evaluation Officer and Commissioner, National Center for Education Evaluation and Regional Assistance (NCEE), Institute of Education Sciences – NCEE initiatives and Evidence Act implementation

2:20    **Q&A**
2:45    **Peggy Carr**, Department of Education Statistical Official and Commissioner (Acting), National Center for Education Statistics (NCES), Institute of Education Sciences – NCES innovations, initiatives, and Evidence Act implementation

| | |
|---|---|
| 3:05 | **Q&A** |
| 3:55 | **Closing Statements** |
| | Larry Hedges, Northwestern University, Panel Chair |
| 4:00 | **Adjourn Open Session** |

## Agenda
## Seventh Virtual Open Panel Meeting
## August 6, 2021, 1:00 pm EDT
## Open Session

1:00 pm EDT/10:00 am PDT
**Welcome**
Melissa Chiu, Deputy Director, Committee on National Statistics
**Education Data Needs and Uses**

1:05 **Speakers**
**Carlise King**, Executive Director, Early Childhood Data Collaborative, Child Trends, Inc. – Early Childhood Data Collaborative, key questions, integrated data needs and uses

**Jennifer Bell-Ellwanger**, President and CEO, Data Quality Campaign – Integrated data needs and uses to inform education policy and decision making

**Gabriela Katz**, Director of Data Analytics, StriveTogether – Cradle to Career Network, high-priority topics, data needs and gaps

1:40 **Q&A** Panel and speakers

2:25 **Closing Statements**
Larry Hedges, Northwestern University, Panel Chair

2:30 **Adjourn Open Session**

## Agenda
## Eighth Virtual Open Panel Meeting
## August 23, 2021, 2:00 pm EDT
## Open Sessions

2:00 pm EDT/11:00 am PDT
**Welcome**
Melissa Chiu, Deputy Director, Committee on National Statistics
**Education Data Needs and Uses**

2:05 **Jo Boaler**, Professor, Graduate School of Education, Stanford University – Mathematics instruction, learning, equity
**Q&A**

2:35 **Erin Furtak,** Professor of STEM Education and Associate Dean of Faculty, University of Colorado at Boulder – Science education, curriculum, and instruction
Q&A
3:00 **Laura Justice,** Professor, Department of Educational Studies, and Executive Director, the Crane Center for Early Childhood, Ohio State University – Development, students with disabilities or disorders, and using experimental data
Q&A
3:25 **Daphne Greenberg,** Professor, Department of Learning Sciences, Georgia State University, and P.I., Center for the Study of Adult Literacy – Adult literacy education, instruction, equity, disabilities, and second-language learning
Q&A
3:50 **Liz King,** Senior Director, Education Equity Program, the Leadership Conference on Civil and Human Rights – Civil rights issues in education
Q&A
4:20 **Closing Statements**
Larry Hedges, Northwestern University, Panel Chair
4:25 **Adjourn Open Session**

## SOLICITED TESTIMONY

CARRIE CONAWAY, Harvard University. Topic: Ideas for a funded NCES liaison in each state.

GREG FORTELNY, Chief Data Officer, Department of Education. Topic: Implementation of the Evidence Act at the Department of Education.

DAPHNE GREENBERG, Georgia State University, with JUDY ALAMPRESE, Abt Associates. Topic: Innovative and successful adult education in state offices and local programs.

DARA SHIFRER, Portland State University. Topic: Issues and data needs for neurological learning disabilities.

KEVIN WELLNER, University of Colorado. Topic: Issues and data needs for educational equity.

# Appendix G

# Biographical Sketches of the Panel

**Larry Vernon Hedges**
Larry Vernon Hedges (he/him) is professor of psychology and medical social sciences at Northwestern University. He is also the Board of Trustees Professor of Statistics and Education and Social Policy. He has done research across many fields, including statistics, sociology, psychology, and education policy. He is widely published and has contributed to many journals and books in the field of meta-analysis and education research, such as *Statistical Methods for Meta-Analysis* (1985) and *The Handbook of Research Synthesis and Meta-Analysis* (2019). He received the 2019 Yidan Prize for Education Research for his work in education. He has made countless contributions to the development of statistical methods and meta-analysis. He is a member of the National Academy of Education, the American Academy of Arts and Sciences, and the Society for Research on Educational Effectiveness. He was nominated and confirmed to the Board of Directors of the National Board for Education Sciences. Hedges received his BA in mathematics from the University of California, San Diego, and his MA in statistics and PhD in mathematical methods in educational research, both from Stanford University.

**Matthew M. Chingos**
Matthew M. Chingos is vice president for education data and policy at the Urban Institute, Washington, DC. Chingos leads a team of scholars who undertake policy-relevant research on issues from prekindergarten through postsecondary education and create tools such as Urban's Education Data Portal. He is co-author of *Game of Loans: The Rhetoric and*

*Reality of Student Debt*, and *Crossing the Finish Line: Completing College at America's Public Universities*. Chingos has testified before Congress and his work has been featured in media outlets such as the *New York Times*, the *Washington Post*, and National Public Radio. Before joining Urban, Chingos was a senior fellow at the Brookings Institution. He received a BA in government and economics and a PhD in government from Harvard University.

**Donald Ray Easton-Brooks**
Donald Easton-Brooks is a professor and dean of the College of Education and Human Development at the University of Nevada, Reno. Easton-Brooks is internationally known as a critical quantitative, culturally responsive scholar and leader. He has over 100 presentations and manuscripts examining impacts/effects of systems, policies, and practices on the academic outcomes and success of students from marginalized communities. He received the 2019 Philip C. Chinn Book Award from the National Association of Multicultural Education for his book, *Ethnic Matching: Academic Success of Students of Color*. He also received the 2020 Neuner Award for Excellence in Professional-Scholarly Publication for a co-authored article in the *Journal of Higher Education Management*. He served as a board member of the American Association of Colleges for Teacher Education. He currently serves on the Board of Directors for WestEd; the executive board of the Council of Academic Deans from Research Education Institutions; and the editorial board of Urban Education. He is one of the founders of the Coalition of Black Education Deans and is a part of the AERA: Senior Scholars on Advancing Research and Professional Development Related to Black Education. He received his BA in sociology from Greenville University, his master's in early childhood special education and multicultural families, and his PhD in educational leadership, both from the University of Colorado Denver.

**Leilani Garcia**
Leilani Garcia is currently coordinator with the Stanislaus County Office of Education. She leads the Planning and Information Management Group for the Child & Family Services Division. Garcia manages strategic planning; ensures the integrity of the data-governance program; maintains oversight of the data-management system, analysis, and reporting processes; and identifies, plans for, and deploys new technology to meet business needs. Since 2014, She has served as the data manager for Stanislaus READS!, a local campaign for grade-level reading and, since 2018, the Stanislaus Cradle to Career Partnership. As data manager, She supports the ongoing data analysis and reporting needs of the Partnership while building the data infrastructure and governance program to support the long-term work. Garcia led the development of the Stanislaus Cradle to Career Data Trust and is working

on the deployment of a data warehouse that will support the future work of the Partnership. She is exploring privacy-preserving methods to study outcomes for students, including secure multiparty computing that could connect historical prekindergarten data with higher-education data. Garcia holds an MPA with a concentration in public management from California State University and a BA in child development from Mills College.

**Joshua Hawley**
Joshua Hawley (he/him) is professor in the John Glenn College of Public Affairs at Ohio State University (OSU). He also serves as director of the Ohio Education Research Center and associate director for the Center for Human Resource Research, both at OSU. Hawley has training in education policy and education economics. His primary fields of research are workforce development, including adult education, career and technical education, and human resource development. He and colleagues were responsible for the development of the Ohio Longitudinal Data Archive, a statewide longitudinal data system that provides researchers in government and academia with individual-level data on education and the labor force in Ohio. He is author of the 2020 Upjohn Institute book, *Data Science in the Public Interest: Improving Government Performance in the Workforce*. He completed his EdD from the Harvard Graduate School of Education and his MA and BA in history and Asian studies from the University of Wisconsin–Madison.

**Samuel R. Lucas**
Samuel R. Lucas is professor of sociology at the University of California, Berkeley. He co-authored *Inequality by Design: Cracking the Bell Curve Myth*, which received the Gustavus Meyers Award, and has authored three other books, including *Tracking Inequality: Stratification and Mobility in American High Schools*, which received the Willard Waller award as the best book in the sociology of education. His work has appeared in multiple journals, including *Social Forces, Sociology of Education, Sociological Methodology, American Journal of Sociology*, and others, and he has served on two National Academies of Sciences, Engineering, and Medicine panels, which produced *Minority Students in Special and Gifted Education and Measuring Racial Discrimination*. He received his BA in religion from Haverford College and his MS and PhD in sociology from the University of Wisconsin–Madison as a National Science Foundation Minority Graduate Fellow and Ford Foundation Dissertation Fellow, specializing in sociology of education, social stratification, research methods, and statistics.

**Josh McGee**
Josh B. McGee is associate director of the Office for Education Policy and a research assistant professor in the Department of Education Reform at the

University of Arkansas. McGee also serves as the chief data officer for the State of Arkansas. He is a director at the nonprofit research firm MDRC and at the retirement policy nonprofit Equable. McGee is an economist whose work focuses on evidence-based policy and public finance. His research investigates issues related to retirement policy, K–12 education, and economic development, and has been published in popular media outlets and scholarly journals. McGee is a former executive vice president at the Laura and John Arnold Foundation, chairman of the Texas State Pension Review Board, senior fellow at the Manhattan Institute, director at the education nonprofit EdBuild, and member of the Tax Policy Center's Leadership Council. He has also served as an adjunct faculty member at Rice University, where he taught in the Rice Education Entrepreneurship Program at the Jones Graduate School of Business. Josh holds a BS and MS in industrial engineering and a PhD in economics from the University of Arkansas.

**Amy O'Hara**
Amy O'Hara (she/her) is a research professor in the Massive Data Institute, and executive director of the Federal Statistical Research Data Center at Georgetown University. She is the lead of the Administrative Data Research Initiative and co-founder of the Civil Justice Data Commons. She explores ways to improve privacy and security while expanding access to data. Her research interests include population measurement, data quality, and record linkage. She has published articles on these issues in many journals during her time in the field. Prior to her positions at Georgetown, O'Hara worked as a senior executive at the U.S. Census Bureau. During her time at the U.S. Census Bureau, she founded their administrative data curation and research unit. She received her MA and PhD in economics from the University of Notre Dame.

**Patrick Perry**
Patrick Perry is the director of policy, research, and data for the California Student Aid Commission, where he oversees the research and financial aid–reform agenda for the Commission. Prior to this, Perry was the chief information officer of the California State University system, where he was responsible for the operation of all enterprise student, financial aid, finance, business intelligence, and human resources systems used by the 23-campus system. Patrick was previously the vice chancellor for technology, research, and information systems at the California Community Colleges Chancellor's Office, the largest 2-year higher education system in the nation. He is a national authority on the development and management of local, segmental, state, and national student longitudinal data systems, accountability reporting, metrics design, and institutional research. He received his BS in economics from the University of Nevada, Reno.

### Judith Singer

Judith D. Singer is the James Bryant Conant Professor of Education and the senior vice provost for faculty development and diversity at Harvard University. She has done extensive research in the fields of quantitative methods applied to social, educational, and behavioral issues. Her work has contributed to the development, improvement, and expansion of accessibility of statistical methods. She has been published in many journals and has co-authored three books, *By Design: Planning Better Research in Higher Education*, *Who Will Teach: Policies that Matter*, and *Applied Longitudinal Data Analysis: Modeling Change and Event Occurrence*. Singer is an elected member of the National Academy of Education and a fellow of the American Statistical Association. She received her BA in mathematics from the State University of New York at Albany and her PhD in statistics from Harvard University.

### Kathryn Stack

Kathryn Stack is the CEO of KB Stack Consulting, LLC. Prior to leaving federal service in 2015, Stack spent nearly three decades at the White House Office of Management and Budget. Under the G.W. Bush and Obama administrations, she was a deputy associate director overseeing budget, policy, legislation, regulations, and management issues for the Departments of Education and Labor, the Social Security Administration, the Corporation for National and Community Services, and major human services programs including Head Start, Temporary Assistance for Needy Families, child welfare, and food and nutrition assistance. In this role, she helped both republican and democratic administrations strengthen their focus on using data, evidence, and evaluation to improve program results. Recent publications include "The Office of Management and Budget: The Quarterback of Evidence-Based Policymaking in the Federal Government" in *Annals of the American Academy of Political and Social Science* (2018) and "Harnessing Data Analytics to Improve the Lives of Individuals and Families: A National Strategy," a 2020 working paper published by the Day One Project of the Federation of American Scientists. Stack holds a bachelor's degree in government from Cornell University and is a fellow of the National Academy of Public Administration.

### Lynne Stokes

Lynne Stokes (she/her) is professor of statistical science and director of the Data Science Institute at Southern Methodist University. She has extensive experience with surveys, polls, sampling, and nonsampling survey errors. Her research focuses on the fields of sampling, measurement error, and order statistics. Her research has contributed to the accuracy and improvement of statistical estimates of many organizations, including the National Oceanic and Atmospheric Administration. She is a fellow of the American

Statistical Association. She has served on a number of National Academies, panels, including panels on the Review of the Study Design of the National Children's Study, Alternative Census Methodologies, Assessment of the National Aviation Operational Monitoring Service, Integration of Data Sources to Improve Crop Estimates, and Recreational Fisheries Survey Methods. For the past 15 years, she has been a member of the Technical Advisory Committee for the U.S. Department of Education's National Assessment of Educational Progress. She received her PhD in mathematical statistics from the University of North Carolina at Chapel Hill.

**Katherine Wallman**
Katherine Wallman served from 1992 to 2017 as chief statistician of the United States, advancing long-term improvements and setting standards for the federal statistical establishment. During her tenure, Wallman increased collaboration among the agencies of the U.S. statistical system, fostered improvements in the scope and quality of the nation's official statistics, strengthened protections for confidential statistical information, and initiated changes that have made the products of the system more accessible. Currently retired, she continues to consult and contribute, particularly with respect to principles, policies, and priorities for activities of federal statistical agencies. Wallman has served as the president of the American Statistical Association (1992) and chair of the United Nations Statistical Commission (2004–2005). She is a fellow of the American Statistical Association and the American Association for the Advancement of Science and an elected member of the International Statistical Institute. She received her BA from Wellesley College.

**John Robert Warren**
John Robert ("Rob") Warren (he/him) is professor of sociology and director of the Minnesota Population Center at the University of Minnesota. His research focuses on the ways inequalities in educational, health, and cognitive outcomes emerge across the life course. With Chandra Muller, Eric Grodsky, and Jennifer Manly, he is co-leading midlife follow-up surveys of the High School & Beyond cohort—with a focus on the early life and educational factors that shape later-life disparities in health and cognition. Previous work has focused on the measurement of states' high school completion rates; the consequences of state high school exit examinations for educational and labor market outcomes; and the magnitude of "panel conditioning" (or time in survey) effects in (educational and other) longitudinal surveys. He received a bachelor's degree in sociology and anthropology from Carleton College and master's and doctorate degrees in sociology from the University of Wisconsin–Madison.

## COMMITTEE ON NATIONAL STATISTICS

The Committee on National Statistics was established in 1972 at the National Academies of Sciences, Engineering, and Medicine to improve the statistical methods and information on which public policy decisions are based. The committee carries out studies, workshops, and other activities to foster better measures and fuller understanding of the economy, the environment, public health, crime, education, immigration, poverty, welfare, and other public policy issues. It also evaluates ongoing statistical programs and tracks the statistical policy and coordinating activities of the federal government, serving a unique role at the intersection of statistics and public policy. The committee's work is supported by a consortium of federal agencies through a National Science Foundation grant, a National Agricultural Statistics Service cooperative agreement, and several individual contracts.